It is from the more or less obscure intuition of the oneness that is the ground and principle of all multiplicity that philosophy takes its source. And not alone philosophy, but natural science as well.

-Aldous Huxley
(The Perennial Philosophy)

The Beacon of Mind

REASON AND INTUITION IN THE ANCIENT AND MODERN WORLD

Edited by
Andrea Blackie &
John H. Spencer, PhD

Distributed by Waterfront Digital Press
ISBN: 978-0-9868769-6-7
ParamMedia.com

CONTENTS

Introduction

We are all aware of the importance of reason, of using logic and rational thinking to solve problems and understand our world. Unfortunately, we often lack the ability to implement this knowledge in the most effective and beautiful ways, and so we can end up acting irrationally when faced with difficult situations. If humanity as a whole were to really commit itself to the most rational solutions to every problem, we would be living in a very different world—a much better world. What is it that can block us from being rational in certain situations, especially when the issue at hand is personally meaningful to us?

All of us (or at least most of us) have also experienced intuition at some point in our lives. We are aware of what it feels like to know something instantly beyond rational thought. Perhaps when the phone rings, you instinctively know it's a particular friend calling you for the first time in six months. Or maybe something—a feeling, or an inner voice—tells you to do something that many of your friends and family think is crazy, but your hunch turns out to be right. Why aren't we all far more shocked and perplexed by this mysterious phenomenon of intuition? With that being said, if we think deeply enough about it, we should be equally amazed by the underlying mysteriousness of this thing called "reason," and by the fact that we are able to tap into it and use (or misuse) it in so many powerful ways.

There is no doubt that we are entering into some very strange and exciting times in human history, which includes knowledge being shared across the globe in a virtually instantaneous manner. One of the previous gatekeepers of knowledge was the church, which resulted in there being a great resistance to the translation of the Bible into the local vernacular—a translation which would allow the so-called "common people" the opportunity to read the word of God for themselves. A powerful example of modern gatekeepers of knowledge have been the universities, which now find themselves being dethroned as well with the widespread availability and democratization of information afforded by the internet. It is not that religious institutions and universities are no longer needed, or that they no longer have an important role to play in society; rather, they are no longer able to control the dissemination of knowledge in the ways and to the degree that they once did.

However, if we want to reap the benefits of such widely accessible knowledge, then we must also be prepared to become far more personally responsible for that knowledge. We will also need to become significantly more dedicated to understanding and utilizing our ever-expanding global knowledge base.

As part of this seismic shift in knowledge sharing and evolving consciousness, Param Media is seeking those pioneers who are adept at bridging the rigor of academia and the growing awareness of the global populace. We cannot underestimate the fear such shifts of power can evoke in people, but we also cannot submit to such fears. When we fear the unknown, we easily revert back to what we think we know and find comfortable, even if that means we continue to bring harm to ourselves and others. This self-defeating cycle needs to stop—and *The Beacon of Mind* can help us to move forward on our individual and collective journeys into higher mind and more holistic ways of life.

This anthology has involved the extraordinary dedication and hard work of many individuals, and its coming into being has itself been due to an astonishing blend of rational analysis, intuitive guidance, and many synchronicities. We are incredibly grateful to all of our contributors, for believing in Param Media and our shared vision, and especially for graciously sharing such profoundly important insights and guidance with our growing audience.

There is a powerful story behind how we came to connect with every contributor, from meeting Professor Sir Roger Penrose, to partnering with Bill Gladstone, and co-publishing Judy Stakee's first book, *The*

Songwriter's Survival Guide (featuring a Foreword from Sheryl Crow). It is certainly not often that readers have the opportunity to experience insights from a world-renowned mathematical physicist, a genius literary agent, and a music industry superstar in the same volume!

In addition to physics, mathematics, and the music and publishing industries, we are featuring pioneers from many other fields—from neuroscience, to philosophy and spirituality, to business and yoga, to name a few!

Some contributions are quite formal in style, while others are more conversational. Some are presented in an interview format, while others are essays. The wide variety of views presented offers a rich panoramic understanding of the integrated roles of reason and intuition, from the ancient world to the present day, and yet there are also many examples of striking congruity across time period and disciplines. We can learn just as much from differences of viewpoints as we can from their similarities. This variety makes *The Beacon of Mind* a powerful text for multiple disciplines, as well as being an indispensable volume for aiding in personal understanding.

The nature of intuition seems to transcend discursive reason (or the following of logical rules), and similarly there seems to be something about us that must transcend mere mechanistic structures—something about us that is non-physical. While perhaps not every contributor in this volume would agree with this statement, many do. Therefore, instead of a direct discussion of reason and intuition, the contribution from neuroscientist Dr. Mario Beauregard is a piece which focuses on providing a scientific foundation for mind being other than brain, thus providing a possible means by which we are able to receive intuitions or insights that transcend physical and logical structures.

Not every contribution will deal specifically with reason and intuition as such. Some are broader in scope but with the same basic intent, such as Dr. B. Les Lancaster's essay on science and mysticism. As well, the two contributions from Dr. Gary Schwartz (one of which has several co-authors) provide novel systems of understanding, which can be very helpful when thinking seriously about the integrated roles of reason and intuition, science and mysticism, and related topics.

Some readers will more naturally gravitate to certain contributors' writing styles or backgrounds, and of course there is much to be gained from engaging with those contributions to which you are most immediately attracted. However, we would like to emphasize the value of spending even more time with those contributions that you find more challenging to read, or present views with which you may disagree. *The Beacon of Mind* does not claim to have all the answers to all of the complex and challenging topics at hand, but it does provide a deeply important opportunity for each of us to expand our knowledge and understanding, as well as to be inspired to greater personal growth and success. Many fascinating topics are explored by our contributors as part of the discussion of their views on reason and intuition, and these explorations may also help to trigger further unexpected insights in the reader.

I have experienced enormous personal benefit from studying (and editing!) each contribution presented in this volume, and from every interaction with our contributors. Collaborating with them and with my team at Param Media has also lead to my undergoing an increase in what might be called spiritual or mystical experiences, from the inception of *The Beacon of Mind* to its final stages of publication. Synchronicities have increasingly made themselves known (a special thank you to Dr. Gary Schwartz!), as have various instances of non-ordinary communication—including with non-human entities of superior intelligence, as strange as that may sound to some. Strange though it may seem, I have come to appreciate that the deeper we study and seek to understand reality, the more mysterious everything seems—and the more driven we should be to grasp this mystery in as rational and intuitive a manner as possible.

I sincerely hope that your experience with this anthology proves to be as beneficial and enriching for you as it has been for me.

Andrea Blackie,
Publisher
Param Media

Dr. Natalie L Trent

Dr. Natalie L Trent is a Research Fellow at Harvard Medical School, Brigham and Women's Hospital, and Kripalu Center for Yoga and Health where she investigates the effect of yoga, mindfulness, Reiki, and other mind-body practices on health and wellbeing. She is also a gratuitous energy medicine practitioner in both Usui Reiki and Shamanic traditions. Her passion for educating others on non-physical and non-local reality lead to her participation in the Campaign for Open Sciences and the movement toward a Post-Materialist Science. Natalie is also a co-editor and contributor to a forthcoming Param Media anthology on Post-Materialism.

Dr. Natalie L Trent

Reason and Intuition in Post-Materialist Science

SCIENTIFIC METHODOLOGY, ENERGY MEDICINE, HUMANITY

Reason and intuition are reality navigation tools. In other words, they arc two different ways for us to understand and make sense of the ocean of frequencies that make up the universe. We parse out bits and pieces through our senses and perceptions, which allows us to conceptualize and create a cohesive picture of reality. Intuition seems to involve the entire body, with its primary messengers being feelings, emotions, sensations, thoughts, and instinctual behaviors, whereas reason seems to involve mainly thought processes. That is, intuition contains many layers of experience—the physical, mental, emotional, and spiritual—whereas logic is often confined to the physical and mental layers. However, a limitation of intuition is in its mostly subjective and often personal nature, and in the inability for easy dissemination and validation of intuition between individuals. On the other hand, science and reason make use of the idea of a shared objective reality, in which ideas are expressed in a common language understandable to most. Together, intuition and reason both guide the creation and maintenance of our culture and global systems: our education, political, health, and economic institutions. However, when a paradigm is no longer supported by both reason and intuition, such as in the case of scientific materialism, a new system must immerge that reflects the new way of perceiving reality.

Scientific materialism is the doctrine that all phenomena can be explained by and reduced to physical processes (e.g. subatomic particles) as determined by science. An example of this is the belief that consciousness is the result of chemical and electric processes in the brain, and that it is a byproduct of this activity. There has been great resistance toward changing this outdated worldview, but the tide is slowly changing.

There is no question that many scientific discoveries have been inspired by intuition, and yet, science does not have much to say about intuition itself. Nevertheless, many prominent and respected scientists of days past have expressed the value held by intuition over logic and science. This includes the often over-quoted but unanimously respected Albert Einstein, who said, "I believe in intuition and inspiration. Imagination is more important than knowledge. For knowledge is limited, whereas imagination embraces the entire world, stimulating progress, giving birth to evolution. It is, strictly speaking, a real factor in scientific research." He also said, "The intellect has little to do on the road to discovery. There comes a leap in consciousness, call it Intuition or what you will, the solution comes to you and you don't know how or why." Einstein even went so far as to say, "The only valuable thing is intuition."

My own tendency, as a scientist, is to write scientifically, and a sort of paranoia develops amongst scientifically trained authors like myself. This paranoia stems from holding an opinion that is not accepted by mainstream science, and which is often subject to peer ridicule. And yet, it is this very fear that slows the progress of science. When writing about intuition and reason, it would be contrary to progress to only discuss them in scientific terms. Therefore, I offer the following disclaimer: I will be making statements in this chapter that are supported by science, and some that are not currently supported by science, but that do have a theoretical scientific basis. With respect to the latter, these are birthed from self-science (a scientific approach to personally observed evidence), intuition, or direct experience with phenomena.

Like many before me, I became a scientist because I was inspired and fascinated by life and nature. I perceived science as the ultimate quest for truth about reality. From a very young age, I possessed strong sensitivities and intuition. I had mystical and psychic experiences, and feelings and thoughts about reality and myself that could not be explained conventionally. I did not yet realize that there was a materialist dogma in science that did not support any of these experiences, which happen to be common to many. During graduate school, I became interested in using the scientific method to investigate phenomena that lay outside of mainstream science, such as intuition, near-death and out-of-body experiences, and other anomalous spiritual phenomena.

When you are interested in these types of experiences, it does not take very long to realize the embargo against these topics in science. However, there are many open-minded scientists currently sharing in the understanding of a deeper understanding of reality, making use of their scientifically trained minds while remaining connected to their intuition. I made the decision before leaving graduate school to continue to value my intuition while becoming one of these scientists.

Today, my research ideas and projects are guided by inspiration, intuition, and experience. Unquestionably, the research I undertake must then be grounded in rigorous methodology without losing its ecological validity, meaning the studies must still apply to the 'real world.' As a Fellow in Dr. Ellen Langer's Mindfulness Laboratory at Harvard University, my current research focuses on investigating the periphery of human potential and altered states of consciousness. Ellen Langer, being the first tenured female Professor of Psychology at Harvard, has long been familiar with pushing boundaries in her research and thinking outside of current paradigms. She is often referred to at the "mother of mindfulness," as she was the first Western scientist to study mindfulness, defined as the opposite of mindlessness. You are probably familiar with that automatic state we enter from time to time while participating in an overlearned task, such as driving to work along a familiar route. That state of mind is mindlessness, and it is pervasive. We have all been there, and most of us, arguably, are there most of the time. In contrast, when we notice the variability in the environment and our experience, and acknowledge that the physical world around us is in constant flux, we are drawn into the present and become more mindful (Langer & Moldoveanu 2000).

Ellen Langer's research also transcends the conventional or dogmatically assumed boundaries of the mind's influence on the body. Indeed, Langer's infamous Counterclockwise Experiment (Langer et al., 1990; Langer 2009) pushed the limits of the current materialist paradigm. Briefly, putting the study participants psychologically back in time by twenty years through internal and external cues resulted in improved memory, vision, strength, manual dexterity, posture, and even caused the participants to appear younger (Langer et al., 1990). The study is still being discussed today, and was the topic of a recent New York Times magazine article (Grierson 2014), as well as a recent edition of Explore: the Journal of Science and Healing (Dossey 2014). At the time the Counterclockwise Experiment was originally conducted in the 1970s, there were no data to suggest that putting people psychologically back in time would have such profound effects on their physiology, but it made both intuitive and rational sense to Langer. The results of the study and others are summarized in her book Counterclockwise: Mindful Health and the Power of Possibility (Langer 2009). More recent time perception experiments have been conducted in our lab at Harvard, where we have demonstrated that perceived time has the ability to alter blood glucose levels, hunger, sleepiness, and reaction time. These studies have not yet been published, but are in preparation for submission. Scientific research guided by intuition, such as the Counterclockwise Experiment, holds the utmost potential for expanding our understanding of reality while simultaneously benefiting humanity.

While I am a scientist by training and spend most of my time engaged in research, I also have an energy medicine practice. Energy medicine, such as Reiki (pronounced "ray-key") is a form of healing in which life force energy is channeled and directed toward others (or toward the self) in order to restore health on multiple levels. It is based on the idea that illness is a result of a depletion or imbalance in this energy. To anyone operating from within an outdated materialist paradigm, energy medicine would necessarily fall outside of reason, and especially energy medicine performed at a distance. However, many types of energy medicine, including shamanism, are found across cultures (Winkelman 1990), evidence that energy medicine is an innate, intuitive practice. While the history of energy medicine's existence alone does not validate its efficacy, its usefulness is supported by scientific evidence.

I was guided to practice Reiki energy medicine through a series of synchronicities in my life. I did not realize that I was only following my intuition until I met my teacher and he asked me why I was taking Reiki training. I did not have an answer, and at the time, I did not even believe in Reiki's effectiveness. Being a scientist, this made my palms sweat. My temperature dropped when he smiled and said, "Good, so it is your calling." I remember how delighted I felt knowing it was ok—even a good thing—that I did not immediately have a "reasonable" answer to his question. To be clear, up until I started practicing Reiki on friends I did not believe it worked, because I knew of no evidence to support it. To my surprise, the first Reiki treatment I gave, on my good friend Magdelina, was remarkably effective. Here she describes the experience to me:

"While receiving Reiki for the first time, I felt a wide range of emotions ending in a sense of peace and euphoria. While you were working over me, I felt my body being pulled in different directions, as if being straightened. When I was on my stomach, I felt as though you were rolling something over my back. I remember thinking it must be part of the process, only to find out that nothing had been rolled on my back. While you were at my solar plexus, I felt a cool air in a centralized location and as if it was sucking in the air. After the Reiki session, while feeling the sense of euphoria, with no pain, I was sick to my stomach. I then proceeded to have one of the best sleeps I have ever had."

I was intrigued by this practice; it felt natural and yet magical at the same time. I continued to give treatments to friends and family while completing my training. Eventually, I built my own practice at a yoga studio while I was earning my doctorate in Neuroscience at Queen's University in Kingston, Ontario. Through social media connections I also developed a distance Reiki practice, giving treatments to people all over the world remotely. The results of the first distance Reiki treatment I gave also surprised me, as I received remarkable validation from the client. For example, she was able to detect a symbol that I was drawing on her forehead remotely, through visualization, concentration, and intuitive feeling. Importantly, she was unfamiliar with Reiki and its use of symbols, and the treatments were done offline, with no phone or Internet contact during the experience. She describes the experience like this:

"After the first healing she did for me, I told her I could feel a finger moving across my forehead, which was the exact pattern she was tracing on my forehead an eight-hour drive away from me! I could feel on my body what she was doing from so many miles away!"

It was an intuitively based decision on my part to trace that particular symbol on her forehead; it just felt like what was needed in the moment. Reiki often works through intuition, whereby practitioners are guided to place their hands in certain locations on or above the body, or to send energy in specific ways remotely. This treatment also resulted in the client being healed of the disabling vertigo that she had been experiencing up until the Reiki session.

As a scientist, I require sufficient evidence for my beliefs, whether through objective laboratory data or my own subjective, quantifiable experience. As the evidence for the efficacy of Reiki kept accumulating, I began to believe that it did work, and the strength of my Reiki treatments grew in proportion to the strength of my intention. The evidence I was observing, combined with how I intuitively felt about Reiki, synergized into a strong and verifiably effective practice.

We can use the scientific method to study the effects of Reiki, and many researchers, including myself, have done so. I became interested in Reiki research as soon as I began to see the beneficial effects of my practice. To my delight, the Center for Reiki Research (CRR), a team of scientists and leaders in the Reiki field, shared in my ambition, including Ann Baldwin of the University of Arizona and world-renowned Reiki teacher William Rand. I was invited to join the CRR team, and together we review all research done on Reiki and also conduct our own research. Through this collective mission, the CRR summarizes and analyzes every Reiki study published to date as part of the Touchstone Process (Baldwin et al., 2010). Because the CRR team is mostly comprised of well-trained scientists, the Reiki literature is meticulously scrutinized for methodological flaws. Of the well-designed, randomized, placebo-controlled studies, Reiki has been shown to be significantly beneficial for treating depression, stress, anxiety, restricted mobility, and for pain management (Baldwin et al., 2006; 2008; 2013;

Shore 2004; Vitale & O'Conner 2006), although not significantly beneficial for fibromyalgia (Assefi et al., 2008).

The common scientific explanation of energy healing would likely fall under the category of the placebo effect, whereby the expectation of healing creates the effect in the client or patient. This explanation is important, but it is also insufficient, for a few reasons. First, the placebo effect is the effect of intention—including expectation and other factors—on physical reality. Intention plays an undeniably significant role in energy healing, as well as in mainstream allopathic medicine. However, the placebo effect is sometimes understood to be synonymous with ineffective, or pseudo-effective treatment, when in actuality, the placebo effect provides demonstrable evidence that our mind had the ability to change our body.

Another reason that the placebo effect explanation is insufficient is the fact that there have been numerous placebo-controlled studies of energy medicine. For example, Reiki has been shown to be effective in rats (Baldwin et al., 2008; Baldwin & Schwartz 2006), which arguably do not experience the placebo effect, since they are not aware of the hypothesis of the study, or even the details of what is being done to them. Perhaps more importantly, many Reiki studies employ adequate placebo controls, a process often referred to as "sham Reiki." Sham Reiki is when someone not trained in Reiki copies what a Reiki practitioner does, including where they place their hands and for how long, without channeling the energy, since they are not trained in Reiki. There is no doubt that belief and intentionality play important roles in energy healing, but it is not the sole reason for its effectiveness.

An important question to ask is, "Where does the energy in energy medicine come from?" Asking this question is tantamount to asking where all the energy in the universe comes from. Reiki loosely translates to "spiritually guided life force energy," and this energy is purported to exist nonlocally, being accessible everywhere, anytime. While there is no direct scientific evidence for the existence of life force energy, there is ample scientific evidence supporting the effectiveness of the many practices that claim to manipulate life force energy, including Qigong, (Fukushima et al., 2001; Jang & Lee 2004), Tai Chi (Jahnke et al., 2002;

Jin 1992; Lan et al., 1998); acupuncture (Mayer et al., 1977; Clement-Jones et al., 1980; Vickers et al., 2012), Reiki (Baldwin et al., 2010; Baldwin & Hammerschlag 2014) and other forms of distance healing (Astin et al., 2000; Schlitz et al., 2003).

Life force energy (also known as chi, qi, prana, lung, and others) may come from the zero point energy field, although this hypothesis has not been tested. The zero point energy field is an infinite source of energy, also known as vacuum energy (Jaffe 2005). Some relate this idea to the Sanskrit word Akasha (Sinnett 1886), a unified, infinite nonlocal field (i.e., the Akashic field) containing all information and connecting all individuated consciousness into one greater consciousness or mind (Laszlo 2007; Grof 2009; Dossey 2013). While some may classify zero point energy cultivation as unscientific, many countries—including the United States and China—have invested in this type of energy generation technology (Aiken 2007). For me, the idea that this energy comes from the zero point energy field came intuitively during a mystical experience, but other scientists have postulated the idea as well (DiNucci 2005; McTaggart 2002).

In support of the idea that Reiki and life force energy operate in this manner, many research studies show that consciousness operates nonlocally, and that intention has the power to alter aspects of physical reality. If our minds truly transcend time and space, as the research suggests, it seems plausible that we may be able to consciously connect with anything and anyone in the way that distance healing seems to demonstrate. In my experience and research, to consciously connect with this source of life force energy, it is necessary to still the mind and focus on a feeling of unconditional love. For an effective transfer of life force energy to the client, I cultivate a state of unconditional love for them. I believe that love is what binds our consciousness in this way; it is a portal to the nonlocal source of all existence. Love can be seen as a concept representing the closest energetic distance between two beings or parts of consciousness, perhaps representing no distance at all. Without love, the connection to this infinite source of energy is limited. Being in this state of interconnection also promotes moral and altruistic behavior toward others.

I believe we should be encouraged to experiment with our own individual experience of reality and consciousness, in order to foster a well-informed and personal understanding of the world inspired through intuition and grounded in reason. Personal experience has a very powerful influence on an individual's likelihood of adopting a non-materialist view of reality (Baruss & Moore 1992), and so it should be valued as such. It is unwise to blindly adopt any paradigm or belief system as truth without first examining the evidence. This is especially the case when dealing with the potential for scientific dogma. Our understanding of nature and reality is constantly evolving with every new scientific discovery, and materialism has become outdated at least since the discovery of quantum mechanics in the nineteenth century. Despite this, I have met many conflicted scientists who operate from two minds, in a sort of cognitive dissonance due to an internal conflict between scientific materialism and their own intuitive beliefs and experiences. These scientists have often undergone strong mystical or spiritual experiences, including synchronicities and extrasensory experiences, and yet the current scientific framework does not permit these experiences to be real. As a result, both their spiritual and scientific growth is stifled by scientism—the belief that science is the only real authority of truth—and they are afraid to speak of their experience for fear of ridicule.

Many of these scientists are unaware of the plethora of evidence for many phenomena that operate outside of the materialist framework, including the nonlocality of consciousness. This is because this evidence is suppressed, leading many people to mistakenly think that psychic abilities, energy healing, and mystical experiences have all been disproven. In fact, we need only one legitimate instance of these phenomena for materialism to be discredited as unshakeable truth. This is often overlooked in the mainstream scientific world, where probabilities are seen to determine our perception of truth. For instance, if, in a teleportation experiment, only one person of one thousand tested could teleport, this result would not be considered to be scientifically significant. Yet witnessing just a single person being able to teleport is sufficient evidence to reject materialism.

Another common and completely unscientific assumption is that the correlations between mystical experiences and brain activity are indicative of the brain producing these experiences, and that they are just artifacts or by-products of brain function (Boyer 2003; Waxman & Geschwind, 1975; Persinger 1983). This is a misattribution of causation where there is, in fact, only correlation, a very basic principle in scientific research. Stimulating the brain or destroying parts of it does disrupt the organ's function and coincides with many observable phenomena. However, this can equally be considered evidence that the brain instead acts as a kind of antennae, or receiver/transmitter of consciousness (Beauregard 2012; Trent & Beauregard 2013). In fact, there is evidence supporting consciousness and the mind (i.e. the psyche) existing independent of a functioning brain, as in the case of near-death experiences during cardiac arrest, when regions of the brain involved in memories, perceptions, and cognitions show no electrical activity (Trent & Beauregard 2013).

There is compelling evidence for phenomena that do not fit into the current materialist paradigm in science, including near-death and out-of body experiences, remote viewing, after death communications, past life memories, psychic physiological abilities, and nonlocal effects of intention and energy healing (Puthoff 1996; Beischel & Schwartz 2007; Mossbridge et al., 2012; van Lommel et al., 2001; Radin et al., 2006; Schlitz et al., 2003; Astin et al., 2000; Schlitz & Braud 1997; Stevenson 1993; Stevenson 2000; Baldwin et al., 2010). Science being first and foremost a method of investigation and not a belief system, proper research into these experiences should be encouraged within the scientific community. At the very least, the oppression and ridicule of scientists interested in these ideas must be recognized as completely unreasonable and unscientific. And yet, scientists today continue to have their lectures banned, such as the case of biologist Dr. Rupert Sheldrake of the Institute of Noetic Sciences and his banned TEDx talk on the Science Delusion, where he addresses the current dogmas in science, including that consciousness is produced by the brain. Other non-materialists, including Larry Dossey and Marilyn Schlitz, have also had talks suffer similar censorship.

Now that we have evidence that supports the nonlocality of consciousness and the power of intention over limited aspects of physical reality, we should formulate new hypotheses about the nature of reality and consciousness. Indeed, many have taken on this task, formulating theories on the primacy of mind or consciousness, such as Mario Beauregard's Theory of Psychelementarity (TOP; Beauregard 2014) and others (Baruss 2010; Schwartz et al., 2005; Stapp 1999; Chalmers 1997). Of course, the notion of consciousness being fundamental is not new, but it can be seen in a new light given the scientific data we have to support it. Non-materialist theories of consciousness provide useful frameworks for further investigation into anomalous, mystical, and spiritual experiences, yet they have been largely ignored by mainstream science.

Paradigm shifts can at first seem unreasonable, because our reason is limited based on the information available to us about reality. For example, reason once told us that the Earth was flat, but once we developed better tools, reason then told us that the Earth is actually a spheroid shape. This principle can be applied to the detection of microorganisms and the discovery of the optical microscope. Will this also become the story for the existence of spirit? Currently, the idea of a spiritual reality may seem unreasonable, given the current conditioned reality program (which I explain further below), and our inability to measure spirit directly with our current tools. However, devices can measure the effect that hypothesized spirit and spiritual beings have on physical systems, such as photomultiplier technology (Schwartz 2010; 2011). While we cannot currently decipher and measure the mechanism of these phenomena—and science itself may be an insufficient means to do so—we have built theories around what they may be. Unfortunately (and perhaps purposefully), this not-entirely-new information about the nature of reality is being ignored, ridiculed, and suppressed by the mainstream scientific community. This is an example of unreasonable science, which is actually anti-science.

Why does this dogma persist, and why does academia continue to be unreasonable in the face of valid evidence? The short answer is that there exists a persistent global and cultural program, a mass-scale indoctrination preventing a paradigm shift based in science, reason, and intuition. New information is required to change a paradigm, but a tipping point must be reached. If the relevant information is ignored, suppressed, or ridiculed, the tipping point will not be accessible, and the outdated paradigm will not change. Often, anything that threatens the current reality program will be aggressively opposed. The founder of psychology William James said, "First, you know, a new theory is attacked as absurd; then it is admitted to be true, but obvious and insignificant; finally it is seen to be so important that its adversaries claim that they themselves discovered it" (1907, p. 198). We have witnessed many examples of this in the past, with revolutionaries in science (and other fields) being imprisoned or even murdered for their innocent crimes of thought and reason. Religious institutions have sometimes attempted to suppress scientific discoveries that are in contradiction to the religion's belief system (heliocentrism, for example). More recently, scientific materialism and its proponents have become dogmatic in the face of conflicting scientific evidence, paralyzing the progress of new discoveries and understanding. In this light, the scientific establishment can become a fortified barrier to truth and progress. Today, those who go against scientific dogma will likely suffer lack of research funding and employment opportunities, ostracism, mockery in various media outlets, and censorship. All of these techniques of oppression are aimed toward eliminating the threat of post-materialist science. In order to move forward and achieve true progress, we need to move away from corruption, fear, mindless conditioning, and falsities, and return to a science that is an open-minded yet rigorous method of inquiry.

Fortunately, a powerful movement is spreading amongst international teams of scientists who are not afraid to defy the archaic materialist paradigm (Beauregard et al., 2014; Cardeña 2014). Indeed, post-materialist science may be the antidote to the scientific dogma that has plagued our institutions and culture at large. Post-materialist scientists agree that in order to have an accurate understanding of the universe, it is necessary to reject the idea that matter can explain everything in reality. This opens the way to allowing scientific dialogue on concepts such as spirit and nonlocal, nonmaterial mind. Reframing the scientific paradigm in this way allows other scientists to investigate spiritual or non-physical phenomenon without ridicule or restraint, while maintaining academic credibility and scientific rigor.

The embedded network of the intelligence of nature (including within humanity) exceeds that which can be described by reason alone. Indeed, the vast majority of our subjective experience stems from the realm of intuition, including many of our behaviors, feelings, passions, inspirations, innovations, perceptions, and spontaneous mystical experiences. Operating from our instincts provides us with many undeniable advantages, in ways both practical and interpersonal. However, incredible gains have been achieved—and continue to be achieved—through the development of our faculties of science, logic, and reason, and the technological growth of humanity from these faculties has been profound, to say the least. Nevertheless, when science and its resultant technologies are favored over intuition, humanity becomes imbalanced and isolated from deeper aspects of reality, including our interconnection with one another. This is reflected in our myriad global conflicts, which are often the result of a disconnection from the intuitive side of our selves, paired with advancing weaponry and military technologies. We are witnessing a dangerous level of advancement in technology without a paralleled advancement in our morality, our willingness to behave in ways that help and heal each other.

There is great hope for humanity, if we succeed in harnessing the courage of both the old mavericks and the youth and use this to challenge the current system. Through the utilization of social media, new media groups aimed toward raising global consciousness, and unconventional access to education via the Internet, people are already coming together to express a shared vision of planetary transformation, and this anthology is further evidence for that. The boundary pushers are those that create great change on the planet, through navigating the sea of intuition and docking on the shore of reason. A shift to a post-materialist science supports the value of both reason and intuition, guiding humanity toward greater understanding of truth. When this understanding spreads to all of our institutions, this can create a worldwide transformation based in our awareness of our interconnectedness.

Jonathan Tippett

Jonathan Tippett is a Vancouver-based creator who has worked in the fields of marine hydraulics, fuel cells, and medical devices. His passion for unconventional applications of engineering helped pave the way for him to become one of four engineers who designed and built The Mondo Spider, which has since attained international acclaim in the art and engineering communities. A more recent endeavor is co-hosting Breaking Point, airing on the Discovery Channel, as well as the art project Prosthesis, the "Anti-Robot."

Interview

ENGINEERING, ART, TECHNOLOGY

Param Media: How do you define intuition?

Jonathan Tippett: I define intuition as an internalized thought process that draws from experience that has been entrenched in the subconscious. This experience is then represented in the conscious mind in such a way that it allows us to navigate decisions or perceptions. Intuition has been classified as a different kind of thought process than rationality or logic, because a lot of intuitive processing happens outside of the grasp of our conscious mind. That's what makes it so powerful, and studies have shown that so much of our processing power happens outside of the conscious mind. Intuition is partly a way that the mind has evolved to take into account the vast amounts of experiential information we encounter, information that would otherwise overwhelm our consciousness, and delivers the answer in a "just trust me" kind of package. You get these insights, visions, or realizations from some intuitive source, and that source is working with the vast amount of quantifiable experience and information that you've encountered. If you were to spend months deconstructing a person's history and all of the knowledge that they have accrued throughout that history, you would probably start to notice certain patterns in that person's intuition based on their experience. This part of intuition is not so mysterious; people with a lot of experience in a certain field tend to have more accurate and useful intuition within that same field.

PM: Would you say that this intuitive capacity is drawing upon a greater source of knowledge?

JT: Yes, although not necessarily a greater source of knowledge found outside of yourself. Personally, I don't think that intuition draws on external cosmic forces or a greater spiritual pool. Not that I necessarily disagree with these concepts, but in terms of intuitive decision-making or insights, I think it is fundamentally a mechanistic process, it's just that the mechanisms are internal, found within each of us.

There is a mechanism that has evolved to handle the vast amounts of information that we accrue over our lifetime. That massive amount of information wouldn't serve us evolutionarily if it took up space in our conscious mind all the time, because our conscious mind is far more devoted to dealing with input from our five senses, our environment, our real-time reactions to situations, our survival instinct. Your intuition is somehow tied to an explicit, rational body of knowledge that is built up throughout your lifetime in the messy back room of your mind.

PM: Can you give an example of a time in your life when intuition has provided you an insight that might not have been obvious to your logical or rational mind?

JT: In my experience, intuition has served more as a shortcut than as a leap of faith. An important distinction to make is that I'm speaking mostly with respect to my work as an engineer and a creative artist, as opposed to my personal life. My intuition with respect to relationships is informed by a whole different category of experiences and is much more difficult to decipher, because it doesn't have the same rational analog that my mechanical intuition has.

Oftentimes when I'm designing a machine, a component, or a system, I'll have an intuitive sense of the proportionality of the components, the size and scale of the structures, and the feasibility of certain energy balances, and those intuitions are derived from my experience in building, breaking, testing, and rebuilding machinery. When I'm working with students, who have much less experience actually creating machines, they will often approach a problem explicitly using mathematics and they'll attempt to browbeat it with mechanics and technical rationale. Faced with the same problem, I am capable of arriving at a solution that's pretty close to optimized just by feel. For educational purposes, I'll go through the process of what led me to my solution—and sometimes it's hard for me to reverse-engineer my own intuitive leaps. The students might ask, "Why? Our calculations show that this should be the solution." Often their calculations are incomplete due to their lack of experience, and so I have to try and figure out what experience I've had that has led me to the solution.

PM: You gave a TEDx talk where you explained your engineering work through the lens of an artist, and you used an analogy of the laws of physics being akin to the grammar of your creations. This represents a more robust, well-rounded approach to science, showing that it can embody art, and not just rely on pure, cold logic and rationality. In your capacity as an artist, how do your intuitive or emotional capacities come into play?

JT: My notion of art hinges on the premise that it is sending a message; that's how I fundamentally define an artistic undertaking. A lot of people think that art and creativity are synonymous, but there are all manner of creative undertakings that don't necessarily qualify as "art." You can find a creative solution to a particular problem in engineering, but you're not necessarily trying to send an artistic message or inspire people emotionally through it; your primary goal is to solve a technical problem in the best way possible. It's still creative, but it's not art. A lot of people use the phrase "the art of X, Y, or Z," like "the art of traction," or "the art of engine efficiency." In those contexts, people are referring to the point at which the explicit science that describes these practices or technologies has become so vast that only those who have been practicing it for a long time—those who have accrued vast amounts of experience and filed it away in their subconscious—that it appears to be an art form, a creative or intuitive leap. But really, all they're doing is drawing from huge amounts of experience that is ultimately rooted in rational processes and theorems.

In terms of artwork, you're trying to send a message or engage an audience. Your goal is to emotionally affect people, which puts you in the realm of human emotion and behavior, a realm so complex that science has still not managed to codify it, and perhaps never will. If you're trying to codify all of human behavior into a system that can be understood in terms of the human brain, it's almost like trying to put something inside of a box that's the exact same size as that box; it won't fit, unless you're talking about certain people who have an incredible mental capacity, whose box is larger than the content you're trying to stuff into it. But in terms of creating an impactful art piece, there are certain standard psychological responses you can expect when you use devices like irony or fear. There are basic tricks you can employ as an artist to get people's attention, like size; you can invoke fear or awe through the sheer size and scale of things. Weighing those factors against the technical feasibility or the perceived danger of something that is actually safe, where you draw those lines often ends up being the purview of what would be considered intuition. This is because the factors that influence them are so vastly complex and can only really be built out of experience—and again, your experience gets logged in your subconscious, which then leads to your intuitive decisions.

PM: Can you remember a moment at the inception of an idea, such as when you decided to build the Mondo Spider, or the Alpha Leg, where intuition played a part?

JT: The Spider was largely a technical exercise. The goal was to use our engineering skills to produce a compelling sculptural piece outside the scope of existing kinetic sculpture. The people who built the Spider had been at Burning Man a bunch of times, where we saw the impressive things that people produced, and we were excited to participate in that kind of large-scale, envelope-pushing artwork. In our back pocket, we had our skills as engineers, and we thought we could use these to participate in this incredible creative exchange at a level that no one else has been able to reach before. There wasn't necessarily an intuitive or inspired drive behind that particular project, except for our collective excitement and pride in what were capable of achieving through hard work and training. Burning Man is a collaborative human experience. It's not a competition; we're not trying to outdo each other, rather we're all celebrating what we are capable of at our best.

The Mondo Spider was our entry into that world, and we wanted it to embody the human creative pursuit of large-scale, interactive artwork. My subsequent work with the Alpha Leg and Prosthesis has been much more message-oriented. I started out by thinking of it as another experiential piece, and while we were building it I did a lot of visualizing myself riding in it, imagining how that would feel. I also wanted to contribute something to the greater canvas of human creative effort. Then, in subsequent discussions and as I thought about the project more, it became evident to me that Prosthesis wasn't just another amazing machine to operate. Eventually, I got down to the root of it, which was my view on the human relationship to our bodies and our overall quality of life, and how that relates to earned physical skill and the focused state of mind that is required to achieve high physical skill—particularly in conjunction with machinery, because it catapults what you can do as a human to a higher level. There's only so far you can get with no mechanical aide.

The Prosthesis project also incorporates messages about our relationship with technology and the rate at which it is progressing, and the effect it's having on our physical activities. This encompasses digitalization, virtualization, and automation, and how they tend to be embraced wholeheartedly without any second-guessing. Every human-made technology has side effects, and I started to realize that one side effect of the onslaught and rapid advance of technology is the loss of physical skill and the notion that our activities have consequences. You see this play out all over the place; every daredevil, thrill-seeking, bungee-jumping, downhill rollerblader is a testament to the enduring human need to engage in activities that have consequence. It makes us feel alive and allows us to tap into our primal fight-or-flight instincts. The pursuit of this message, and the development of a machine that would provoke conversation about that subject in a safe and functional way, became the focus of my work.

PM: What would you say to someone who asked you the purpose of this kind of artistic expression?

JT: I get asked that a lot, actually. One of the first questions that crops up when someone sees the Alpha Leg is, "What is it for?" People ask that in a very literal sense, as in, "What is its application? How is it used to help harvest crops, build homes, cure disease, or establish national security?"

For all of recorded history, human beings have devoted time and effort to pursuits beyond food, shelter, and security. Our brains are too complex to be fulfilled simply by meeting these basic requirements. We have been involved in games and sports and puzzles since we took shape as homo sapiens. Go as far back in history as you want, and it remains true; it's just the nature of the technology that's changed. This could expanded to the entire film and television industry as well—maybe not documentaries, they might have a little bit more purpose to them—but certainly the entertainment industry, not to mention the recreational and professional sport industries, show a massive precedent for human effort going towards endeavors beyond food, shelter, and security.

I like to say there are three mothers of invention; well, actually there's the mother, the father, and the lover. Necessity is the mother of invention, and that encompasses things like food, shelter, and security. Curiosity is the father of invention (the gender isn't really important; I'm just using it for the purposes of a better metaphor). Curiosity is represented by academia, research, and pursuits in technology that don't necessarily have an end goal; you're just trying to answer a question, figure something out, or try out some "what if's." Art is the lover of invention. Art is simply for the sake of creative exploration—passion, really, is what it boils down to. Passion is an innate human drive to express oneself, which is as fundamental a drive as hunger. Those three things—necessity, curiosity, and art—really drive creativity in my model of the world.

PM: How do these three things overlap?

JT: They don't necessarily overlap, but they do cross-feed. For example, you can have a passion-driven creative pursuit, which would fall in the realm of the arts. Such a pursuit apparently has no practical purpose; it's just undertaken because you want to do it, and this is where some people have trouble appreciating and understanding why an artist makes a piece of artwork. They ask, "Who does it feed? Who does it save? Who does it protect?" But those artistic creations might foster dialogue that leads to some sociological benefit or geopolitical stability. It might lead to the development of a technology that provides some more functional result. It can work the other way too, of course; the development of technology—of systems, processes, and machinery for pragmatic purposes—can then be leveraged by artists to further their creative and expressive goals. Research or curiosity sits somewhere in the middle and feeds into both directions.

PM: Not many people put their entire life behind a technological and artistic pursuit like you have. What is it that makes you different?

JT: That could be answered on a few levels. First of all, I've been unbelievably privileged to live in a free country with a relatively robust healthcare system. I was gifted with a supportive family, which led me to develop self-confidence and pursue a valuable education, which provided me with unbelievable tools to build things. I also happened to be born at a time in history when the availability of technology for people with that skillset is exploding—from CAD [computer-aided design] software to computer-controlled machinery that can cut metal parts for you, 3D printing, electronics getting simpler, easier to use, more powerful, and more accessible to people with less and less training. If I had been born during the Dark Ages, I probably would have just died of the plague like everyone else. Maybe I would have been alongside da Vinci coming up with wild inventions, but a huge part of what I've achieved is due to the advantages that I have, and the freedom to indulge in pursuits beyond just survival.

At some point, for some reason, I felt in my value system that it was important to contribute substantially in some way to the human condition, and leave my mark in the world—not for my own sake, but because I feel an obligation to utilize the incredible gifts I've been given. I feel like it would be a waste of a very fortunate set of life circumstances not to produce something remarkable and substantial that engages and inspires people. It's like a moral obligation.

PM: Would you say it's like a form of justice, that it would be an injustice if you walked away from this calling?

JT: Yes, and the value accrues to society in ways that contribute to different areas of the human condition. That societal value is a little more abstract in the case of artwork, but as I said, invention has many seeds, and it spreads in directions that can't always be foreseen.

The scientific understanding of math and physics, at a basic level, allows you to understand more complex things more quickly. You build up metaphors and models for how systems work, and you start to notice analogs between electricity and hydraulics, for example. It becomes a robust system of understanding that compounds over time, and then it becomes even more gratifying to work in those areas because you're good at them. Then, the more you do it, the more you learn and the better you get at it; it just snowballs.

PM: How would you characterize the relationship between art and technology?

JT: I don't necessarily consider them to be two sides of the same coin, but nor are they diametrically opposed. They are two very separate types of human undertaking. Art is all about expression, and is rooted in the human impulse to share and communicate our worldview with other human beings. We are social animals; we want to tell each other how we feel about things, what effect a certain experience has had on us, or how we view something. Art, in all of its forms, ultimately boils down to a sharing form of expression. It can also be a cathartic expression, a way to express the impulse to externalize how you see the world and what you think about it. There's a sort of a resonant feedback situation whereby the audience responds to your work, and this, in turn, feeds your creative impulse.

Technology is more of a means to an end; it's not so much about expression. It's the human pursuit of understanding our physical universe and bending it to our needs or desires—anything from sharpening a stick so that it can be used for hunting, to understanding quantum physics so we can develop electronics further. Technology is agnostic; it is representative of our human relationship with the physical universe. Every art form has its own technology; painting's technology resides in the chemistry of the canvas and the paint, and the way light affects those media, for example.

PM: You're describing technology as a means to an end, but isn't art a means to an end, if the end is the externalization process that you had mentioned?

JT: You could put it that way. Technology is a mechanism; it necessarily involves hardware of some sort—even software has to run on some kind of hardware, on some kind of physical object that people have created. To say that art is the means to conveying a message is sort of an accurate analog, but the ends are different than the ends of technology. Technology is sort of a broader practical agent, whereas art operates more in the human psyche, or the human spirit. The message that art sends and the action that it inspires in a group of people might affect the environment, but the art itself can only affect the human psyche, whereas technology can affect our physical world directly.

PM: You've mentioned technology in the context of survival. Could you say that, since art can be used in the capacity of catharsis, it could be considered as a kind of survival mechanism?

JT: Totally. I definitely agree with that. Human beings require food, shelter, physical contact, and mental stimulation to survive, and art definitely plays a role among those four things. Technology can provide the physical sustenance and the shelter, other human beings (or pets) can provide physical contact, and art could potentially be described as providing the fourth element of mental stimulation. You could have mental stimulation from pursuits like career goals, and there's likely mental stimulation involved in tracking prey and gathering food, as opposed to just sitting in a room, pushing a button, and having steak land on your plate—you'd lose your mind if that's how things went, and that's kind of the direction we're headed in.

This is something that was made apparent to me through discussions with my sister-in-law, Katie Armstrong, who is a successful artist herself. She has been kind of my artistic mentor in helping me to understand myself as an artist, and helping me to appreciate the value that art has—especially since I'm coming from an engineering background, surrounded by engineers who are largely of the opinion that things needs to get built so that we can feed, clothe, and protect all of our human bodies. I've definitely gone through a process in the last decade or so where I've come to appreciate that the production of art is essential to human survival in its very crudest form. Once you've got survival nailed down—which we're pretty good at doing—then there's got to be something worth living for other than just finding your next meal. That's where art comes in; there's got to be some kind of value to life beyond filling your belly and covering your head with a roof.

PM: As technology brings about more and more digitalization and automation, is art going to have to become a bigger component in people's lives to make them more well-rounded?

JT: That's a pretty reasonable theory. You can already see it happening to a certain extent with the maker movement, which is essentially the recognition of the phenomenon whereby technology is becoming less and less the purview of the experts, and is becoming more and more accessible to someone who just has a basic idea of what they want to play with. Nowadays, if you have a decent computer, some software, and a 3D printer, you can manufacture plastic parts, something that was inconceivable twenty years ago. The evolution of electronics in terms of cost and simplicity is just astounding, and it has created an entirely new culture. It has unearthed and enabled the creative urges of millions of people, allowing them to manifest their ideas—be they inventions or tinkerings or brilliant breakthroughs—which were previously totally inaccessible. In the past, unless you were an electronics engineer with a degree who was devoting your life, resources, and time to these kinds of technological pursuits, you couldn't control anything with electronics. Now, with a few hours spent on YouTube and less than a hundred bucks, you can have something delivered to your door that will let you automate your plant watering, just on a whim. It's unlocking a huge amount of human creative potential, and it's just snowballing. What I am able to do as a project lead with good connections to local universities, and with friends who have machine shops, 3D printing, and online team management, is culminating in a way that has enabled me to very realistically envision this outrageous project, and I have zero doubt that I'm going to be able to execute it, barring calamity—knock on wood. Being able to do this as an individual thirty years ago would have been totally out of the question. The availability of water jet cutting, the sophistication of CAD, the simplicity of electronics, the organizational powers of the internet, brings something truly transformative. It's a golden age of technology. Perhaps it's more like a gold rush; these sorts of exponentially growing systems are inherently unstable. It could either explode into a sort of creative utopia where robots are growing all of our food and doing all of our work, which I think is what they thought the future would be like in the fifties, and it still hasn't happened. In fact, work weeks have only gotten longer, and stress levels have only gone up.

There's no question that there are certain forces at work that are constantly preying upon any liberated bandwidth, on any true spirit, desire, or emotional capacity for deeper change. There are corporations that are only seeking to accrue material wealth by tapping into any free time or mental energy that humans have created for themselves, and they will use all of the standard human emotions—like envy, the need to be in a group, fear of the unknown, and insecurity—and use them to manipulate people into a consumer engine so that they can continue to build wealth for themselves.

As technology has evolved and the amount of free time we have (theoretically) has increased, that free time has been gobbled up by a consumer machine, as opposed to being celebrated through greater and greater creative expression. Corporate culture pre-packages solutions to human desires, but these are actually false solutions that are ultimately aimed at driving dollars into their corporate structures. They are very cleverly engineered to taste and feel like a real solution, but then they dissolve and require you to take another hit—buy another pair of jeans, or get the next version of the latest smartphone. It's unfortunate to see so many intelligent, insightful people armed with science and intuition who have used that power to deconstruct some of the base behavior patterns of humanity and put them on an addiction drip-feed of consumer indulgence. Art can serve as an intervention to this, and it has infiltrated many of these consumer sectors. For example, pop music might feed a lot of people's desire for musical stimulation, but within that music scene there is also music with deeper messages; there are pop musicians with anti-consumerist messages who release albums online for free. There are always infiltrators, and more often than not, they take the form of artists with a message to convey.

PM: What was your inspiration or motivation to participate in this anthology?

JT: This is a great opportunity. You look at the great figureheads and movers and shakers, the Richard Bransons and the Elon Musks, and you wonder what makes them different from everyone else. I don't quite put myself on the same level as those kind of massive global influencers, but I appreciate the opportunity to share my choices, my background, and my lifestyle, which reveal that I'm not all that different from many thousands of people who might want to do crazy stuff like I'm doing, but who have allowed themselves to become stuck in a 9 to 5 job because they're too focused on being able to buy the next technological innovation.

PM: What value do you think an anthology like this—one that brings together contributors from such a wide variety of fields, from science to business to art, all discussing the role intuition and reason have played in their lives—can provide to society?

JT: Anytime you bring together a disparate group of people to ponder the same point, you get interesting things happening. It helps when the point of discussion is broad or complex; you get a more colorful mosaic of inputs. There are two layers to that question. The first layer is, how much value does discussing, broadening, or shedding more light on the notion of intuition versus rational thought have? There is definitely value in exploring that question in the same way that we've just been talking about art having value in the human condition. Any exploration into aspects of the human condition has value, either from an intellectual stimulation perspective or, in certain circumstances, to give you insight into people who are having trouble with their state of mind, or who are blocked creatively. These kinds of discussions might have value in those situations. Bringing together such a diverse panel of experts in different fields to discuss the topic of reason and intuition sheds a special kind of light on it, a wide spectrum of light, so to speak. It's a great way to approach such a complex and important topic.

Juan Francisco Tellez

Juan's partnerships with academics and entrepreneurs allow him the opportunity to explore the abstract theories underpinning science and technology, with a focus on translating that knowledge into practical business applications. He is the co-founder of Param Media and has extensive experience implementing innovative, multidisciplinary solutions while working for the University of British Columbia. His relentless passion for truth, beauty, and simplicity drives him to be a foundational pioneer in the emerging new renaissance, aiming for a deep impact on technologies that will shape our future.

Juan Francisco Tellez

The Spiritual Evolution of Technology

UNITY, SIMPLICITY, HUMAN-AIDED INTELLIGENCE

The Heritage of Technology (and Science)

To understand the long-term evolution of technology, we are required to gain a fuller appreciation of the heritage of technology and the role that philosophy and spirituality have played at the most fundamental level of its development. Since technology is an extension of science, we must take into account the critical role that philosophy and spirituality has played for all of science as well. Science is not simply about discovering cold, hard, supposedly empirical facts; on the contrary, the true purpose of science is far more significant.

Erwin Schrödinger, one of the key scientists responsible for the development of quantum physics, claimed that the most important objective of science was to help us answer the one great philosophical question that embraces all others, which is: who are we? He believed that all scientific endeavors directly or indirectly help advance this all-important philosophical question. Therefore, the real reason for science is not to merely discover empirically provable facts, but rather to serve to answer one of the most important philosophical questions for humanity. Moreover, he was in agreement with the pioneering psychologist Carl Jung, who claimed that "all science...is a function of the soul, in which all knowledge is rooted". There is no doubt that including science and the soul in the same sentence is bound to make some seemingly scientific minded people very uneasy due to the spiritual implications of this statement. Nevertheless, Schrödinger and many of the other scientific pioneers, who gave us the most powerful system of physics upon which our technological evolution heavily relies, spoke strongly about the deep philosophical implications of science. To deny the philosophical implications of science is a detriment to our advancement as a human species. It is also to be factually incorrect.

Another pioneering quantum physicist, Wolfgang Pauli, was adamant that a cosmic order, which is independent of the physical universe yet is responsible for guiding its physical evolution, was absolutely necessary for science to be possible at all. He stated that a "cosmic order independent of our choice and distinct from the world of phenomena" permeates our universe. This is closely related to what the ancient Greek Platonic tradition would call the *logos*. A more in-depth reading into the philosophical and spiritual foundations of science and technology can be found in Dr. John H Spencer's paradigm shifting and multiple award winning book *The Eternal Law*.

Technology vs Nature

Having been exposed to the importance of philosophy in science, and therefore also in technology, we must now surpass a false dichotomy that has been negatively influencing the discourse related to technology. This false dichotomy is the strict distinction between technology and nature, a distinction that is only superficially useful. *Nature* actually refers to anything that is physical in time and space in any part of the universe, and since all technological objects are also in the physical universe, then they are ultimately a part of nature, too.

There is also something about us as humans that is obviously part of nature; our bodies are physical, and we depend for survival upon food, water, soil, and air. If there were no nature, there would be no us. Reality, however, is greater than nature; reality includes all of physical nature, as well as everything that is non-physical. But if materialism (the belief that only physical matter is real) is correct, then there can be no free will and no actual awareness, being, or self. And of course, the laws of physics would not exist under the materialist paradigm either, since these laws themselves are not physical entities.

We can look at a forest that has remained untouched by humans for a thousand years, and if someone were to toss an empty energy drink can into the forest, we would say that this can was human-made garbage and not natural. Of course, this is an important distinction to make—natural forest versus human-made can—and it is an easy division to understand. However, when we reflect a bit further, we realize that this energy drink can is made out of tin, aluminum, or other materials which come from the earth, and is therefore also a part of nature.

Humans were able to shape it in a form that was (apparently) convenient to our human lifestyle, but that does not change the fact that it is still made out of materials that were already found in nature that have just been given a different form. Furthermore, since the physical part of the human being is also a part of nature, at a deeper level there is no real distinction between human-made versus nature. All the high-tech products being produced depend heavily on rare earth minerals and metals, which all come out of the natural world. Technology is just another manifestation of nature.

The Spiritual Evolution of Technology

According to Ray Kurzweil, who is one of the international leaders in the field of science and technology, "evolution is a spiritual process that makes us more god-like". In the Platonic philosophical tradition, the idea of god was pushed to a deeper understanding and was referred to as "the One," or the source of one-ness. The One is responsible, and makes it possible, for everything to retain its one-ness or unity and thereby continue existing. Without the ability for anything to stay unified, it could not continue to exist. If we take into account Schrödinger's claim that all scientific endeavors lead us to a further understanding of who we are, as well as Jung's view that all of science is a function of the soul, then Kurzweil's claim is completely compatible with the heritage and philosophical underpinnings of science.

If we analyze the long-term trajectory of technology, it becomes evident that all of the major trends are directly or indirectly leading towards unity or one-ness. Even if you take seemingly negative trends within technology, such as mass surveillance online, this is actually still inclining towards spirituality, regardless of whatever intentions may be behind it. For example, it is having the effect of unifying separate lives into one experience, similar to a lower form of omniscience, which is a god-like trait. If in fact this physical universe began with the Big Bang, and all matter and laws of physics were totally unified in the beginning, then it is not unreasonable to recognize that we yearn to experience that unity again. To go back to the source is to discover who we are.

As we progress in the scientific understanding that allows us to create new technologies, this inevitably is linking things together, and as things are being linked together we are being moved towards unity, which is a spiritual evolution of nature. Nature itself is trying to ascend to the higher non-physical reality, trying to copy the higher forms of spiritual reality.

Another criticism of this technological progression could point to the militarization of technology, or different ways in which we are severely polluting the environment through toxic nuclear waste and other pollutants. It is true that this environmental desecration is not very spiritual. However, we are the ones to blame, not the technology. This misuse of technology by humans is an example of the soul identifying with the wrong aspects of physical reality. In other words, we are forgetting our foundational spiritual, non-physical nature, and instead are solely identifying with materiality and lower, narrow-minded, purely ego-driven goals.

We need to remember that the non-physical aspect of humans—what we could call the soul—transcends nature. This is very well described as part of the Platonic hierarchy of reality. And while the laws of physics cannot be broken within the physical realm, spiritual laws can temporarily be broken. After all, it is far easier to lie to someone than it is to defy gravity. We can use virtually any object for good or bad, whether it is a fork, your hand, or nuclear power. So let's not blame technology for the harmful ways in which it is sometimes misused by us.

We also need to remember that technology rests upon scientific understanding, that scientific understanding rests upon deeper philosophical understanding, and that all of this is resting upon the fact that there must be order in the cosmos, or else science would not be possible. This brings us back to Pauli's claim there must be a "cosmic order independent of our choice and distinct from the world of phenomena". If we realize that the cosmic order is part of the non-physical, spiritual realm, and that nature or physicality is an outcome of the non-physical, spiritual realm, then we arrive at the understanding that nature itself is trying its best to ascend to, and live in accordance with, the higher non-physical principles of reality. As souls that come into this world, sometimes we get things right, and sometimes we mess things up very badly as we try to develop. The fact that we may use technology in a way that is not spiritual does not take away from the fact that both science and technology are only possible because of spiritual reality.

The Success of Spirituality in Technology

Taking a deeper look at how Apple Inc. became the most successful technology company in human history upon Steve Job's return to the business, we can discern the undeniable role played by the philosophical and spiritual implications of science. For example, Walter Isaacson states in his biography of Jobs that "His whole life is a combination of mystical enlightenment thinking with hardcore rational thought". Furthermore, Jobs apparently believed that the Macintosh computer had always existed, and his goal was to manifest his vision of what the Macintosh already objectively was (or is) in non-physical reality.

Keeping in mind the philosophical and spiritual implications of technology, it becomes obvious how the design of Apple's iPhone revolutionized the industry. The physical manufacturing process yielded a device that was both aesthetically pleasing and streamlined. Minimizing the amount of buttons on the device by utilizing a large touch screen simplified the user's interaction, enabling people to intuitively operate it with ease. Moreover, the software and interface design was described as a zen-like experience for users and was significantly easier to use in comparison to competing devices. In other words, when our technology is in line with the philosophical implications of science—such as unity, simplicity, and beauty—we are inevitably drawn to and identify with these solutions. This is because our bodies are made within nature according to the same principles, which science is progressively helping us to recognize and understand. More importantly, science undeniably proves that the universe is put together in a holistic manner; therefore, when we manifest holistic thinking in our technological solutions, we are aligning ourselves with the universe and allowing ourselves the opportunity to advance humanity in the most significant way. Technology is actually an outcome of the spirit, and it is helping physical nature evolve in a spiritual manner.

Looking further into the future, recognizing the philosophical implications of science and technology is going to play a critical role in all the major technological trends, including in the field of Artificial Intelligence (AI). As noted above, the distinction between technology and nature is only superficially useful but not true at a deeper level, and the same can be said about the common distinction between human intelligence and artificial intelligence. Ultimately, there is only intelligence, manifesting in different degrees and in a variety of forms. You could even say that everything has an intelligence, and that it is just a matter of determining the degree to which it exists and what type it is.

Everything that is physical still exists within the cosmic order and the universal consciousness; therefore, to one degree or another it embodies consciousness. Of course, the ability to express this consciousness does differ significantly within the physical matter that is found in our universe. But intelligence is ultimately universal. And although humans are designing (what is currently referred to as) artificially intelligent technologies, humans are also a part of nature, and all the materials used to create the new technologies are from nature, so there really isn't anything artificial or unnatural about any of it. In other words, it is inaccurate at the fundamental level to say that anything which already exists naturally in our universe is artificial.

People often mistakenly conceptualize AI as the creation of a super intelligent computer, but this would involve the implementation of a very limited understanding of computing and of the intelligence that humanity currently has. This would be like saying we could just keep pushing classical physics further and further, and eventually arrive at an understanding of the phenomena taking place in the quantum realm; it simply doesn't work. We had to leave classical physics behind at a certain point and begin exploring quantum mechanics. We need a similar type of revolution in computing as the one that took place in physics in order to create something in AI that more closely approximates what we mean by "intelligence." We need to question the assumptions that are limiting us, rather than simply trying to push further with the same underlying assumptions that are keeping us trapped in such limited understanding and potential applications.

To be more accurate, instead of using the phrase "artificial intelligence," what we essentially mean is "human-aided intelligence." In other words, human-synthesized technology in one way or another is capable of capturing or expressing different degrees of intelligence. And yet, we still have not fully understood what intelligence itself actually is, or even where it comes from. The perennial philosophy is trying to point us in the right direction, and if we consider the Platonic tradition and its objective hierarchy of reality, then we can understand that technology—and everything else—stems from the One and the universal mind, what the ancient Greeks called *nous*.

To genuinely achieve human-aided intelligence, we would first need to understand how our physical human body enables the universal mind and the soul to flow into the physical level of reality. If this can be understood to a significantly high enough degree, we can then reverse engineer how nature was able to achieve this with humanity, and it then becomes completely plausible to emulate that process to a certain extent with our technology. In other words, this would allow us to create a gateway or vessel capable of channelling some aspect of *nous* and the universal soul. This gateway or vessel would be human-synthesized, but the potential degree of intelligence that could come through it would, in theory, be just as high as the degree of intelligence that humans have, because we would be tapping into the original source of wherever intelligence comes from in the beginning. We could even instigate an evolving intellectual system that transcends our capacity to contain it or even fully understand it.

To permit nature to continue in its spiritual evolution though technology, we need fearless leaders similar to the quantum pioneers of the early 1900s, leaders who are willing to question the fundamental assumptions of their disciplines. These leaders will be at the forefront of a renaissance in the technology industry, one that recognizes and aligns our thinking with the elements of the perennial philosophy that have always been at the foundation of technology. This revolution in thought needs to be brought into the mainstream conversation on science and technology, in a way that does not simply lead to interesting abstract notions, but also retains the pragmatic power that technology has to affect significant change. This will help us to avoid the conversation being overtaken by pseudo-philosophers and grinding to an unnecessary halt.

We are seeing increasing signs that society is demanding this type of higher-level thinking. People intuitively know in their hearts that the highest expressions of science are not at odds with the beauty of nature. It is up to human beings to remember what we are, and what our purpose is here on earth. As we awaken to such worthy challenges, we will take greater responsibility for our role within the universe and aid all of nature in its ascent towards the higher forms of spiritual reality. We can then expect to experience beautiful and marvellous outcomes, even from the realm of human-aided intelligence, in whichever ways it manifests. I look forward to partnering with the leaders who help us to achieve this.

Judy Stakee

Judy Stakee, a world-leading pioneer in recognizing and developing musical talent, spent twenty years as Senior VP of Creative at Warner Chappell Music Publishing. She has signed and worked closely with many of today's most acclaimed artists, including Grammy-award winner Sheryl Crow, Katy Perry, Michelle Branch, Gavin DeGraw, Jewel, and Joy Williams (The Civil Wars). She also has extensive experience across all areas of the industry in developing producers and multi-platinum songwriters, such as John Shanks, Julian Bunetta and Wayne Kirkpatrick, among others. In 2009, Judy founded her own full-service Artist Development and Entertainment Company, which focuses on developing the minds, bodies, and souls of artists and songwriters to achieve the career of their dreams. Judy is the author *of The Songwriter's Survival Guide.*

Interview

MUSIC, MAGIC, INTENTION

Param Media: How would you characterize the balance between your reasoning faculties (such as logic or practical planning) and your intuition (tapping into your emotions, or having a gut feeling)? Do you rely on one more than the other?

Judy Stakee: Reason and intuition are mutually interdependent, as one does not exist without the other. The balance between the two depends on the situation, because you might rely on one more than the other given different circumstances.

I guide the songwriters I work with to stand in both perspectives so that they can decide how to strike a balance between the two. I want them to know the reason or plan behind writing pop songs to get on the radio: how long should the songs be, what genre should they be focusing on, what is the vocal range of the artist they are writing for?

I also want them to write using their intuition, their gut feeling of what feels right to them in terms of mood, melody, and story. A song connects you with your emotions by tapping into an endless pool of feelings.

When I am consulting with a client, I show up with a lesson plan to help guide them. I am opening up a vault with over thirty years of experience in it, which includes tools, homework, and inspiring stories. However, the client's wants and needs will decide the course of action I then help them to map out.

The logical side of me can have all of the greatest intentions as to why I need to teach a client some important concept, but in order to honor my intuition, I also need to be able to pick up on and run with whatever shows up when they walk in the door; any questions they have, or current problems that they're facing, can send us on a path that was not initially planned, but was obviously needed for their growth.

PM: How do you define intuition?

JS: Intuition is the ability to understand something immediately. It's the voice that says, "I get it." It allows us to express our uniqueness in a playful way, and it stems from our unconscious. We don't think about it, plan it, or control it; it just happens. The choice to follow that hunch or not is the big question we have to ask ourselves.

I tell my writers to look within and ask themselves: what do you believe, want, and need? How do you want to tell your story? Do you want to be funny, or serious? Do you instinctively lean more toward rock music, or does jazz resonate with you? I guide them to rely on their gut feeling to dig deeper into who they are.

PM: How does an intuitive feeling arise in you? Do you feel a reaction in your body, or is it more of a direct intellectual knowing?

JS: I'm sure it's different for everyone, but for me a physical aspect comes first, followed by an intellectual knowing, if I choose to listen to it. How many times have you walked into a situation, felt a chill and known in your gut that you should leave? Our bodies talk to us constantly; they know more than our rational thinking minds will ever be able to comprehend.

Being more aware of how things affect your body puts you ahead of the game when it comes to tapping into your intuition. Connecting with what you feel and believe can help keep you on track to achieve your dreams. However, I have noticed that as a society we tend to prioritize the rational mind over our feelings, asking what we think about something, rather than what we feel.

PM: You exemplify someone who has lived and integrated both reason and intuition, methodology and feeling. These two sides seem to be largely imbalanced in today's society. Why do you think that is?

JS: It's because our current belief system says we can only choose one side, and also because we get stuck in our own stories of who we are. As long as I keep telling myself and the world I am an impatient person, I remain impatient. Why would I change? If I changed, then I would be a liar.

As I said earlier, one side does not exist without the other. How can you have logic without passion? Logic gives us the strength to allow passion to blossom, and the blooming of that passion relies on the strength of logic to root it in reality.

We live in a dualistic society, and neglecting to embrace both sides leaves you with only part of the experience. Everything has an opposite; black does not exist without white, nor up without down, masculine without feminine, or reason without intuition.

I believe that every human on this planet is here to create, and that it requires a balance of strength and flexibility, leadership and teamwork, and reason and intuition.

Changing the story of "this is the ways it's always been done" requires telling a different story. Let's begin with the acceptance of the fact that doing it differently is not necessarily wrong; it's just different, and it may end up being a lot better.

PM: An idea that you promote in your work is that "the number one ingredient in magic is intention." How do you define magic and intention in this situation, and how do they relate to intuition?

JS: Intention is what you *plan* to do. Magic is a power that allows you to do things that once seemed impossible by saying special words or performing special actions. In order for magical things to manifest in our lives, the words, thoughts, and intention need to be put in place to direct what we want to happen. Magic does not just suddenly appear; it needs the fuel of your intention in order to come to life.

It's widely believed that intention aids in the process of healing a wound. Miraculously, we have the ability to heal our own bodies. I developed serious back problems around the time I started working as an executive in corporate America. I started to store my stress in my spine, which resulted in the complete herniation of one of the discs in my spine, and tears and bulges in four others. My surgeon assured me that millions of Americans walked around with this condition and coped with it through pain pills and epidermal shots. I politely turned down the offer for this kind of treatment, my reasoning being that I wanted to see if I could use physical therapy to heal myself. I then set out on a journey that has not only changed my body, but also saved me from the inevitability of a hip replacement later in life. I am pain free now, and a recent MRI showed that my discs had already improved by twenty to forty percent.

If I had not taken the initiative to put a plan in place, find the necessary motivation, and, most importantly, had the absolute belief that I could heal my own body, then it would not have happened. I tried a lot of different healing methods to see what worked and what didn't, and I relied on my gut feeling to inform me in that process. When I started listening to and trusting this feeling, I was able to heal.

PM: A skeptic might say that the word "magic" means something anti-scientific, as if you could snap your fingers and make whatever you want appear. But what you're saying is that if you do certain things—whether it's yoga, meditation, or some other intentional practice—and move beyond the parochial confines of the common medical model, then you're more likely to be able to heal yourself. According to the mainstream medical model, that kind of self-healing *is* a miracle, because it is basically impossible. However, the kind of healing you are talking about is actually scientific; we cannot ignore evidence just because it does not fit our current model or assumptions.

JS: I am talking about being conscious about the decisions you make for your own life. I may not be able to control exactly how much I weigh, but I can control how much and what I put into my body. That, in itself, is a kind of magic.

If I had not taken control of my own healing process, I would be in great pain right now. If I had not taken control of my career, then I would be unhappy right now and wouldn't have much hope for the future. If I had not taken control of what I want and need in order to achieve my goals, then I would be stuck in the same place. All of these things required intention—oh, and some hard work, too!

The difference between the skeptics and myself are the perspectives from which we tell our story. In my world, magic exists, because I don't want to live in a world where there is none, and I have seen it manifest in my own life in many ways. Instead of using words like "hocus pocus" or "superstition" to describe magic, I use words like "reward," "love," and "glory."

Bringing it back to songwriting, if you want to have one of the top performers sing one of your songs and release it as a single that sells a million copies, then you are going to have to put very focused intentions in place in order to achieve that goal. The odds of it happening may be a million to one, but if you have the intention, magic does happen. If you put no work and intention into getting that song placed, then nothing is going to happen.

PM: What guidance can you give to others to help them set their own intention? Are there specific steps that people can take, or is it a question of pure will and desire?

JS: The first rule is to know who you are. If you don't know yourself and what you want and need, then there's nothing to work towards. Self-love is not selfish; it is responsible and empowering.

The second rule is to speak your intentions out loud, to give them life with your words. Pure acts of will and our desires play a role, but you need to be proactive and put specific thoughts and words together and devote focus to them.

I continuously ask my clients, "What do you want to do? What do you want it to look like? Is there any other way it could be done? What are the pros and cons?" More often than not, they are stopped in their tracks by questions like these; it throws them off guard to be asked to answer straight from the heart, and not simply say what they think they should say.

When you are confident in who you are and what you know, it's easier to rely on your intuition, and consequently do the work to produce magical events. If you're trying to satisfy somebody else's needs first, then there is little room for personal expansion.

The third rule is to create an action plan, a map to help guide you down your path of intentions.

PM: What is your definition of leadership, and what role does storytelling play in how you develop your clients to reach their potential?

JS: My definition of leadership is asking the people I work with, "How do I help you do your job better?"

I think my talent to guide others comes from somewhere deep within, but the reason I am great at what I do is that I also put in the work. My continual personal development has been a crucial tool, allowing me to be both a great teacher and student.

In the last six years alone, I enrolled in two musical theater workshops, two voiceover classes, a comedy class, and an acting workshop, and I also played the lead in three student films. I even tried out for X Factor just so I could better guide my clients who were auditioning. What I noticed throughout all of these experiences was that no matter what modality I was playing in, they all dealt with the voice, lyrics, and melody in some way.

My own methodology teaches that a song is the integration of the voice, lyrics, and melody, and that by developing your body, mind, and soul, you can create your own expression of yourself in song. This means you need to take care of your voice and body, challenge your mind by honing in on your perspective when writing lyrics, and let your soul sing the melodies of your heart.

Your voice does not exist without your body, so your voice can only be as powerful as your body is. I suggest to all my clients that they create routines to take care of their voices, including warm-ups, vocal toning, and voice lessons. I tell them to take care of their bodies by eating healthy and practicing yoga. This is all part of creating a new story for themselves.

My own story that I am telling *is* my awakening. And every book on every shelf is a story by someone out there with a unique perspective. What story do you want to tell? From which perspective will you tell it? Are you the hero or the victim?

With my thoughts, words, and intentions I have the ability to guide a client down a path that tells a certain story. It can be the story that no one is getting ahead or making any money in the music business, or the story can be that they are able to come up with their own way of doing business, affording them the ability to become a pioneer.

I made the decision to give myself a new story, one where I become conscious of my own behavior. I took the walls and boundaries that were there to protect and serve, but which sometimes can also constrict us, and built doors and windows in them to let in a fresh perspective.

For example, being a perfectionist is a wonderful trait if you are a music producer who has to master all kinds of digital equipment and mixing programs. But when you are co-writing with another person, being a perfectionist can be detrimental to the creative process.

I am now in a position where I am empowering songwriters and artists to be conscious in telling their stories. Their words will help shape generations to come; they hold the power to fuel humanity positively, or lend to its destruction.

PM: What advice would you give to business leaders to help them understand that leading through fear and ego is not the optimal way to approach leadership? How would you motivate other leaders?

JS: The first thing I would motivate them to do would be to take on leadership by asking their team, "How do I help you do your job better?" A leader needs to know how to look ahead, assess situations, solve problems, and plan accordingly. They are there to build the community and facilitate communication.

I would advise leaders to sit down with their team and create a vision and mission statement together. They say it takes a village to raise a child; in this case, the child is the product and the village is the company. What is your purpose, individually and collectively? If we don't see value in every single person on the team, we operate at a disadvantage.

PM: A real difficulty is that, in general, the ego would rather destroy its host than relinquish control. How do we reach people with these ideas, when those who most need to hear them are often the most resistant to them?

JS: I find that challenging someone to go outside their comfort zone is a really good way to move beyond the ego.

People who live in their egos are far away from their true self, and they are fearful of what they will find if they return to it. The walls of ego and insecurity have been built up around them to protect them from themselves, which ultimately keeps them stuck in the same place, far from the experience of transformation.

Songwriters can get so stuck in defending their art, afraid that they might not be able to reproduce the same results once they find something that works, that they refuse to see how they could develop and grow. We have to rewrite the story of being distrustful of the unknown.

We are raised from an early age to believe that we have to know it all. We are constantly being tested and graded throughout the first years of our lives, and then made to feel embarrassed when we are not perfect or don't know something. The modality of having to always be the best is engrained in us, and it is an unattainable goal that can wear down the soul over time.

For most of my working life, I lived in a world where you worked for someone else, where sustaining a relationship or raising a family while working eighty hours a week was unfathomable. I became stuck in my own stories, and I didn't believe I had the power to change them. I eventually freed myself from the pressure to know it all by realizing that if I really did know it all, then I would know that I needed to adopt the mindset that I actually *don't* know everything!

However, sometimes people are just not yet ready to change. In the first workshop my company produced, I had a writer whose songs were seven minutes long and a little hard to follow. During the critique period, he was politely told that he might want to think about shortening his songs if he wanted radio play. He eventually dropped out of the workshop because he could not fathom changing his way of doing things. Three years later, I ran into him and he confessed, "I wasn't ready for you then, but your words stuck with me all these years, and I really want you to know how much I appreciate what you were trying to teach me."

PM: An idea that you promote is that, "For a project to be a success, a team has to work independent of one another, but be integrated at the same time," which seems similar to the integrated roles of reason and intuition. How can we achieve a balance between independence and collaboration?

JS: We can achieve that balance by holding enough space for both to exist.

The more you know yourself, the better team member you can be. You learn the principles of teamwork as you learn how to take care of your own body, mind, and soul.

I teach a Basics Writer Workshop with six participants that lasts eight weeks. I start every session with a question, such as, "What is your definition of the word 'commitment'? If you could have one wish granted, what would it be? What bad habit do you want to break?"

By having the workshop participants really listen to each other, they start to realize how the answer to the same question can vary greatly from person to person, and yet be accepted by the group. This opens up their perspectives; it teaches them to honor their own approach to the question, while also making room for others. By the end of the workshop, they have all been seen and heard as individuals, and as part of a collective that has undergone a unique experience together.

How serendipitous that this whole discussion delves deep into the theory of opposites: intuition and reason, true self and ego, independence and collaboration, the "I" and the "we." It is the tension between these opposites that creates a threshold into new thoughts, possibilities, ways of understanding—new psychological real estate, so to speak.

If we allow ourselves to open up to new possibilities, it forces us to look inward, which means we have to stop and see if our body, mind, and soul are in agreement.

Ignoring the importance of the body in this exploration of self, I believe, is a huge mistake. I put a lot more stock in what my body feels and responds to than what my mind tells me in a lot of situations. I regret the many times when I was hurting my body but my mind told me I would be fine if I kept going, because deep down I knew that wasn't true. I didn't listen to my body, and I suffered heavily for it.

What make us *whole* human beings is embracing both the dark and the light.

In my opinion, our world is currently a little off balance, favoring male energy over female. We want structured, solid science, but we're missing out on female energy, which is more forgiving, compassionate, and creative.

PM: Can you elaborate on how your pursuit of self-knowledge has helped you achieve worldly success?

JS: When I started honoring myself first, my path became clearer and full of purpose. My health, voice, power, and relationships all got better. I had to take charge from within and know how I worked before I could integrate with the rest of the world.

I come from a long line of teachers, and so being an A student is in my blood. The most valuable lesson I learned from that was that good grades simply take hard work. Once I figured that out, I could adopt a mindset of letting go and just doing the work. The alternative would be to complain about how hard it is to achieve success, which would keep me stuck in a place I did not want to be.

PM: What is it about you that allows you to recognize talent, and then also be able to nurture it?

JS: Loving music as much as I do, both as an artist who is always developing and as a fan who is always listening, definitely contributes to my ability to recognize talent. But also my own personal journey of deciding to help others reach their musical goals rather than become a performer myself, and now fulfilling my dream of running my own company, has contributed to that talent.

Music has led me from the moment I was born. Songs have taught, guided, healed, comforted, and challenged me throughout my entire life. For as long as I can remember, I intuitively knew that people may come and go, but music would never leave me. Without music, our souls would be missing out on a vital connection to this life.

PM: Can you describe an outstanding moment in your career when you recognized the potential of an artist, when you felt intuitively that they had something magical? How did you know that they had that special quality, and what does that kind of knowing feel like?

JS: It feels like falling in love. You think everything they do is brilliant, and you can't take your eyes off them. I'll tell you about my first musical love, Sheryl Crow. Sheryl crashed the auditions and won the most coveted spot of being the only female back-up singer on Michael Jackson's *Bad* tour. On the few breaks she had, she would fly to LA to work on starting her solo career, including writing and collecting songs.

A record producer—who she had sung background vocals for, and who I had pitched songs to over the years—set us up for lunch. I immediately liked her; it felt like we were sorority sisters! She came back to my office and played me her songs for hours, and I played her songs from my own catalogue, hoping to find something for her to record.

During that meeting, I fell in love with the way she held a conversation, the way she talked about music, the fact that she had so much training, and that she was so passionate and driven about her dream. It was energizing, magnetic, and magical!

For Sheryl, she had found her champion in me. For a year, we met four or five times a week to brainstorm how to make her a star. It took a little over a year from the time she finished touring with Michael Jackson until she got her record deal, which in the business is very fast. Sheryl worked incredibly hard to reach her goals, and she was so intentional about what she wanted that it manifested right in front of her eyes.

She didn't place limitations like, "No, I can't do that," or "It's never been done" on herself. Her answer was always, "Let's go!" And that we did! We were both tuned into the importance of combining the reasoning side of hard work with the intuitive side of following a deeper knowing of what could be accomplished, and what came out of that integration was truly magical.

Dr. John H Spencer

John's PhD specialized in the philosophical foundations of quantum physics. He is the multiple award winning author of *The Eternal Law: Ancient Greek Philosophy, Modern Physics, and Ultimate Reality*, co-editor of *The Beacon of Mind*, and co-founder of Param Media.

He combines the highest levels of abstract thought and extensive scholarly research with his many years of deeply transformative mystical practice, while revitalizing and innovating the essence of the ancient mystery schools.

Dr. John H Spencer

Consulting the Crows: What to do When Logic Fails?

LOGIC, RATIONALITY, MYSTICISM

What's wrong with logic?

Logical thinking is essential and extremely powerful within a wide variety of applications. But it can also be completely useless. Even worse, it can lead to very harmful effects. Sometimes it is more rational to make decisions based purely on intuition—or even simply by flipping a coin—than to rely on logic. But that does not give us license to be illogical. It should, however, serve as a warning to those whose arrogance is rooted in their supposed logical superiority that the foundation of their logical system is not at all logical.

I remember falling in love with formal symbolic logic as an undergraduate student many years ago. It is not the sort of study that tends to be very popular (in fact, just about everyone in the class hated it), but for me it was beautiful. Such precision! Such order! We were learning how to remove the obfuscating ambiguities of written language and replace them with the strict formalities of logical rigor!

Ever since I was a small child, I would drive people crazy by asking them for clarification whenever they said virtually anything to me, but in this class I was rewarded for this relentless pursuit of precise thought with a grade of A+. This was certainly not the case early in my education. I remember being in the third grade one day when a loud noise came from outside our classroom. The teacher asked me if there was a tractor outside (they were doing some work on the school grounds at the time). I pulled back the curtain, saw the tractor, closed the curtain, and then said, "I don't know." My teacher was annoyed and said that I had just looked outside, so was the tractor there or not? I pulled back the curtain and looked again. But still I said I didn't know. The teacher was getting quite upset now, so finally I replied that yes, the tractor had been there when I looked out the window just a moment before, but now that the curtain was closed and I couldn't see it, I didn't know if it was still there.

You see, I did not want to lie, and since I could no longer verify whether or not the tractor was there when I wasn't looking at it, I really believed that I did not know if it was there or not. Instead of being praised for my budding philosophical abilities (akin to Cartesian Doubt), I got in trouble with my teacher. This sort of occurrence happened often. Finally, one day I realized that our culture generally doesn't give a damn about truth or clarity or seriousness of thought. So for a while, I stopped caring, too. While this shift of allegiance from truth to appearances garnered the approval of society in a variety of ways, it had horrible effects on my soul, my inner life. Eventually, after turning back to the pursuit of truth in my early university days (which contributed to my being driven into the depths of existential hell), I awakened—but that is a story for another day. Fortunately, there are growing numbers of people today who realize the obvious point that without such seriousness and clarity of thought, there is really no hope of handling the disasters that we face globally, locally, and in our own lives. I no longer apologize for seeking clarity.

But isn't clarity bound together with logic? And if I prize clarity, then why would I say that logic can sometimes be useless? Firstly, genuine clarity is not dependent upon logic, but it is not completely separate from it, either. Genuine clarity comes from a direct knowing, which is a foundational form of intuition. Direct knowing requires a clearing away of obstacles in the mind and body so that the relevant required pieces of knowledge or information can arise with minimal distraction. For me, this type of knowing can even transcend feeling. It is, as its name suggests, *direct* knowing. There is no need for deliberation or interpretation, because it is already clear. Later, when explaining logically some solution or understanding that was gained through direct knowing, it may appear as if it was the result of logical thinking, when in fact the direct knowing transcended, or was prior to, logic.

But hold on—not so fast. We can also be deceived into believing we have direct knowledge when, in fact, we do not. The desires of the ego can fool even the best of us, allowing us to rationalize practically anything. Indeed, the higher your intellectual capacities, the easier it can be to unconsciously fool yourself with some underlying, unspoken, instantaneous, logically valid argument which propels your sense of certainty about your apparent direct knowledge. So we must always, whenever time permits, reflect further, question our conclusion and assumptions, and apply logical dissection to test our apparent direct knowing. This applies no matter how your intuition arises, whether more through bodily awareness, such as a gut feeling, or more directly through mind (not the limited intellectual mind, but pure consciousness, like the ancient Greek *nous*).

When we have a direct knowing, we can then use the power of logic for at least three main purposes: (1) to test our direct knowing; (2) to help guide others to the conclusion we have apprehended through our direct knowing, since others may not have the capacity to achieve the same direct knowing in the particular field in which we are working; and (3) to help us figure out how to apply this knowledge in detailed, novel ways.

Another key point is that even though logic and rationality are deeply interconnected, they are not the same. For example, it can be rational to follow a conclusion that is *not* logically valid, and it can be irrational to follow a conclusion that *is* logically valid. This is a very complex topic and there are many different types of logic, but we can achieve the relevant understanding relatively easily.

The two basic forms of logic are deductive and inductive. Simply stated, a *valid deductive argument* guarantees that the conclusion follows from the *premises* (the claims or assumptions in an argument), whereas an *inductive argument* aims to provide a conclusion that is probable though not certain. For simplicity, let's consider only two very basic examples:

Premise 1: If all dogs are purple, then Hawaii is in Mexico
Premise 2: All dogs are purple

Conclusion: Hawaii is in Mexico

Believe it or not, this argument is deductively valid, because the conclusion necessarily follows from the premises. To put it another way: if the premises are true, then the conclusion must be true. However, the premises in the above example are not true, and it is not rational to believe them or the conclusion. So, it is not rational to believe this logically valid argument.

The second argument is not deductively valid, but it is inductively plausible:

Premise: The sun has shone every day since I have been born

Conclusion: The sun will shine tomorrow

Given the known laws of physics, it is indeed very likely that the sun will continue to shine tomorrow. However, no logical argument can ever guarantee the truth of a conclusion about the future, so this is not a deductively valid argument, despite being inductively plausible. But it is still rational to believe this conclusion. Therefore, we have here seen an example where it is not rational to believe a deductively valid argument, and another example where it is rational to believe a deductively invalid argument.

Furthermore, even when we make what appears to be a rational decision, we may be missing vitally important information, or we may unknowingly be basing our decision on false assumptions. In such cases, stubbornly clinging to our rationality can lead us into deep trouble. In other words, it is not always rational to maintain rationality. More accurately stated, it is far more rational to question our supposed rationality, so far as we are able.

For example, you may conduct market research that confirms the desired outcome that your new product will sell very well, and so you invest a huge amount of money into marketing its launch. Unfortunately, it may turn out that the market research was flawed, or market conditions have suddenly shifted quite drastically, and your product launch becomes a total failure. If only you had aimed for a more holistic, encompassing understanding of all the most relevant information, you may have averted such a disaster.

Another problem is that any logical system must follow a certain set of rules. This is highly advantageous in one sense, because it enables a great deal of control in terms of application. However, those rules—and all the implications that follow from them—are themselves only a narrow subset of the wider reality, and when we falsely assume that the limit of reality is equivalent to the limit of our logical system and its resultant knowledge base, genuinely novel progress becomes impossible.

Nevertheless, if we stay within a predefined logical structure, the master logician will always hold the advantage, while the more intuitive person may be at a disadvantage. Even if the intuitive person were to intuit a correct conclusion, the logician would not accept this conclusion as representing genuine knowledge unless the intuitive person could demonstrate the reasoning process that lead to the conclusion, and only so long as the demonstration fit within the predefined rules of the logical system. In other words, the logician would say it was just a lucky guess. It would also be the logician in this case who would likely be better equipped to implement a relevant solution, such as in the development of a string of computer code, which requires step-by-step logical commands.

There may also be cases where the intuitive person offers a correct answer that the logical system, according to its own internal structure, would never be able to achieve. For example, if physicists had stayed strictly within the confines of classical physics, they would never have been able to develop quantum mechanics. Of course, the jump from classical to quantum thinking required experimental data and rigorous logical arguments (which ultimately pointed beyond their own structures). But this jump also required creativity, imagination, and intuition, which are qualities that are too often falsely presumed to fall outside scientific methodology. Without these non-logical qualities, there would have been no quantum physics, nor would we have had the major scientific breakthroughs that have taken us beyond a previously accepted worldview.

Science is not a purely logical activity. On the contrary, if science were to stay completely within the confines of deductive logic, then science would never be able to discover genuinely new knowledge. Deductive logic may later reveal how a new discovery is actually implied by, or necessarily follows from, previous relevant knowledge, but deductive logic is incapable of making the required initial leap beyond current knowledge without creative insight that transcends deductive logic.

The most decisive blow against logic is that it does not tell us the way the world actually is. It does not tell us whether or not our premises or assumptions are true. It can only say that *if* our premises are true, then the conclusion that follows from them is true (or likely true). But it cannot say whether or not the premises themselves are true, and therefore, in the end, in some of the most important ways that matter to us as we live our lives, logic is completely useless.

Some noisy crows

Consult an oracle. Throw some dice. Pray to the wind gods. Or listen to some noisy crows. There are multiple ways—in fact, in practice, there are endless ways—to receive an intuition about how to proceed in certain circumstances. This applies to groundbreaking science just as much as it does in deciding which route to take to work in the morning.

As an academic, I had to care very much about the protests of militant skeptics, those who are sure that the entirety of all reality fits neatly into the back pocket of their self-destructive parochialism. But I don't care about that anymore, because I have discovered that no matter how many rational / logical arguments are made, no matter how many examples from the history of science or visionary business pioneers are provided, no matter how many powerful quotes from some of the most eminent pioneering theoretical physicists throughout history are invoked, it makes not a bit of difference to the fundamentalist skeptic. They accuse religious /spiritual people of refusing to face uncomfortable evidence, but they themselves do the same thing—turning away from the truth—repeatedly.

I talk about related topics more formally in my book *The Eternal Law*, for those who are interested in further understanding. But here we need only note one simple fact, one that the skeptics often refuse to even acknowledge, let alone try to understand. This fact is that Max Planck, the key originator of quantum theory—the most powerful scientific theory in history—believed that faith was foundational to science. From advanced weaponry to your smart phone, so much of our high-tech industry is dependent upon quantum physics, and the scientist who played the most critical role in its development believed that faith was foundational to all of science. If the skeptics choose to ignore Planck, then surely it is not unreasonable for us to ignore them. If only they were true skeptics, they would be skeptical of their own overblown skepticism.

The fact is, there is no logical foundation to logic, just as there is no clear and unambiguous definition of "rationality" or "reason." There is also no scientific method that can be used to begin the scientific method (a point that even the famed atheist philosopher Bertrand Russell conceded). But let's be clear: the religious fundamentalist is no better in this regard than the skeptical fundamentalist. They both cling to false assumptions and display surprisingly similar psychological traits, with one group clinging to the mystery of faith at the expense of reason, and the other clinging to the mystery of reason at the expense of recognizing the underlying importance of faith. Both have caused extensive damage in different ways. So let's set them aside.

In my own life, I have undergone numerous mystical experiences, from the most profound to the seemingly mundane. We are not supposed to talk about such things in academia, but all that really means is that academia is incapable of handling them. Here I will mention only one relatively ordinary example of such an experience, involving a bike ride and a flock of crows.

One bright morning several years ago, my wife, Ryoko, and I were preparing to cycle from our home to the downtown area of the city where we were living. There were, of course, an indefinite number of ways we could have made our way downtown, all of which were logically permissible, even though most would have been completely impractical. But in this case, there were two relatively equidistant routes that were most feasible. On this day, we decided to go left instead of right as we were leaving our driveway. However, just as we were about to mount our bikes, we were startled by a bunch of crows about half a block up the street in the direction we had planned to travel. They were standing on the ground near the sidewalk in front of our neighbor's house, and they were staring at us while cawing intensely in unison. Suffice it to say, it gave us an eerie feeling.

We looked at each other and said jokingly that the crows must not want us to go that way, so we turned to face the other direction. The crows immediately fell silent—an uncanny silence. We looked at each other again. It seemed that some kind of spiritual force or entity was trying to tell us something after all. We turned to face the crows again, and they abruptly began cawing, even more wildly this time. We faced the other direction. They fell silent.

We then simply turned our heads in the direction of the birds, and the cawing frenzy started up again. We turned away, and they immediately stopped. As we walked our bikes half a block in the opposite direction from the crows, they remained silent. Stopping and facing their direction again (they were now a full block away), they again responded with their uncanny cawing. We decided to listen to the crows—or rather, stop listening to them—and so we continued up the street away from them.

While there are a variety of possible explanations for this situation, ones that do not need to invoke some sort of divine guidance acting through a flock of crows for our benefit, they do not account for the feeling that both Ryoko and I simultaneously experienced. It was a like a huge, black, impassable wall had been placed in front of us, with the crows vociferously proclaiming that they would not allow us to pass. They also had seemed oblivious to everything else going on around them, and instead were intently focused on us and on the direction that we chose to go.

Well, I didn't simply accept the cawing of the crows. I did a quick reflection on the fact that, even armed with instantaneous travel reports detailing traffic flow, weather, etc. to help us rationally decide which route was safest for us to take, none of that information would guarantee our safe passage. There would still be unknown factors, and no logical argument can guarantee the truth of a future conclusion. So, since the strongest sign seemed to be telling us not to go a certain way, and since we both intuitively felt that the crows were right, it seemed the most rational decision to follow that intuition and go in the opposite direction of these ominous birds. We had consulted the crows, and now we were going to listen to their advice. Actually, they had given us their advice (or admonishment) before we had even consciously asked for it. We thanked them, and went on our way.

This is just one very simple, relatively trivial example of how guidance for our life decisions can come to us in a wide variety of ways. The skeptic may scoff, but following intuition has worked very well for the highly successful contributors to this anthology, as well as for many other extraordinary pioneers from a wide range of fields and disciplines. I can imagine the fundamentalist skeptic shouting that this is all nonsense, and doing their very best to convince the rest of the world that such things are simply not possible, because they themselves are too afraid to open to higher understanding and greater possibilities. And then I imagine the magical moment when Judy Stakee intuitively knew that Sheryl Crow would become a star under her guidance. I put my money on Judy.

Matthew David Segall

Matthew David Segall is a doctoral student in Philosophy, Cosmology, and Consciousness at the California Institute of Integral Studies, whose research focuses on the role of imagination in the philosophical integration of scientific theory and religious myth. He is the author of *Physics of the World-Soul: The Relevance of Alfred North Whitehead's Philosophy of Organism to Contemporary Scientific Cosmology*, and blogs regularly at Footnotes2Plato.com.

Matthew David Segall

Ralph Waldo Emerson: Philosophical Lessons for a Civilization in Crisis

PHILOSOPHY, NATURE, CIVILIZATION

Acknowledgements: Thanks to Richard Geldard for his inspiring scholarship on Emerson and his correspondence with me during the writing of this essay, and to my fiancé Rebecca Tarnas for her inspiring imagination, careful reading, and untiring support.

Ralph Waldo Emerson (1803-1882) is most often described by present day commentators as America's greatest essayist and lecturer. It would be difficult to find a more talented writer or speaker, but such titles fall far short of his true stature.

Was he a mystic? In certain of his moods, but this epithet, usually applied to those who affirm, as the Scottish philosopher David Hume put it, "the absolute incomprehensibility" of divinity,[1] should not overshadow the clarity of Emerson's intellectual vision, nor his commitment to seek deep understanding of all things worldly and divine. "Mysticism," Emerson explains, "consists in the mistake of an accidental and individual symbol for a universal one."[2] Despite his lifelong familiarity with mystical experience, Emerson never let his personal enthusiasm obscure the impartial intuition of the whole.

Was he a poet? He was a good one when the Muse struck, but seldom great. Indeed, Emerson's sublimest poetry was arguably surpassed

---

[1] "...how do you Mystics, who maintain the absolute incomprehensibility of the Deity, differ from Sceptics or Atheists, who assert, that the first cause of all is unknown and unintelligible?" *Dialogues Concerning Natural Religion* (Ann Arbor: University of Michigan Library, 2007), page 48; http://quod.lib.umich.edu/e/ecco/004895521.0001.000/1:2.5?rgn=div2;view=fulltext (accessed 7/31/2014).

[2] "The Poet" (All works by Ralph Waldo Emerson can be found at rwe.org).

by the striking originality in the free verse composed by his contemporary, the American poet Walt Whitman (1819-1892). No, Emerson was not principally a poet, nor simply an essayist, a lecturer, or a scholar. To introduce him as such is to miss the true significance of his vocation and the spiritual lessons he has to teach our civilization.

Emerson was, above all else, a *philosopher*—not what we would today refer to as a professional professor of philosophy, but a devoted *lover of wisdom* (φιλόσοφος) who found his calling as America's philosopher[3] just as academic knowledge was beginning to be professionalized by the modern university. By the 20th century, philosophy—once the source and foundation of all the special sciences—had become just another disciplinary specialization, and an increasingly marginal one at that. It was reduced to logical analysis or linguistic deconstruction, leaving the investigation of nature (including human nature) to the quantitative analyses of scientists. Aside from comparatively few exceptions, over the past two centuries American professors of philosophy have gradually ceased worrying about the "Big Questions" concerning the meaning of existence (such as "Who am I?" and "What is Nature?"), to focus instead on what may be considered trivial conceptual technicalities, generally of little practical value to society at large. A noteworthy exception, the mathematical physicist, philosopher, and educator Alfred North Whitehead (1861-1947), continually warned against the effect of such professionalization on university education. He argued that the most deleterious result of the modern university's turn away from philosophical breadth toward standardized specialization is that "we are left with no expansion of wisdom," despite being in "greater need of it" because of advances in technological power.[4] In a lecture in 1937, Whitehead was even more convinced that "the increasing departmentalization of universities during the last hundred years,

---

[3] Numerous commentators have labeled Emerson "America's philosopher." More recently are Philip Gura in *American Transcendentalism: A History* (New York: Macmillan, 2008) and Arthur Versluis in *American Gurus: From Transcendentalism to New Age Religion* (Oxford: Oxford University Press, 2014), 38.

[4] *Science and the Modern World* (New York: The Free Press, 1997), 197-198.

however necessary for administrative purposes, [has tended to] trivialize the mentality of the teaching profession."[5]

A century earlier, Emerson was already regretting the effects of professionalization. In his essay "Intellect," Emerson remarked that in order to avoid the "incipient insanity" which results from the exaggeration of a single topic of study, the intellect "must have the same wholeness which nature has."[6] Lacking such wholeness, intellectuals are liable to forget that the universe does not come pre-packaged so as to fit neatly within the artificial disciplinary boundaries of the modern university.

Emerson refused to reduce himself to working on the assembly line of specialized academic knowledge production, and he never even held a university post. As far as he was concerned, the American university system was fast becoming "a system of despair," dismissive of creative genius and true depth of insight.[7] Nonetheless, by his own account his audience consisted principally of "students and scholars," that is, "the reading and thinking class." "And yet," he added generously, "that is a class which comprises...every man in the best hours of his life."[8]

Emerson's idea of the philosophic life is of a continual course of learning that traverses an endless series of seasonal cycles and graduations: sleep and dreams are as much our teachers as waking rationality; birth and death are just the outer reaches of the memories and sensations of our temporarily incarnated intellects; the splendor of earth and sky are as critical to our curriculum as any printed book. Emerson was no ivory tower intellectual. He sought to bring philosophy to the people

---

[5] *Modes of Thought* (New York: The Free Press, 1968), 131.

[6] "Intellect"

[7] "New England Reformers"

[8] "Seventh of March Speech on the Fugitive Slave Law, 7 March 1854." *The Later Lectures of Ralph Waldo Emerson*. Eds. Ronald A. Bosco and Joel Myerson (Athens and London: University of Georgia), 2001, vol. 1, pp. 333-47. Although Emerson used the noun "man" in this excerpt, in light of his close friendship and deep respect for fellow transcendentalist Margaret Fuller (1810-1850), not to mention the influence of his aunt and earliest teacher Mary Moody Emerson (1774-1863), we can be sure that he meant also to include women.

by revealing how the dirty details of everyday life were emblematic of heaven's eternal ideas. As one of the last leading philosophers to escape the disciplinary rigidification of the modern university, he made his living instead as an itinerant lecturer on the lyceum circuit, which consisted of several thousand voluntary local associations focused on adult education.

The wisdom he desired to share with his audiences, though difficult, aimed to make philosophical concepts as concrete, accessible, and relevant for everyday life as possible. Emerson's most vital verbal expressions arose from his firsthand experiences of earthly life beneath the sky. To summarize the intention of his first book *Nature* (1836), Emerson hoped that his human words would be taken by his readers as cosmic enunciations emergent from a universe which itself is already the living symbol of an original divine act of creation. His language aimed to transfigure the seemingly contradictory facts of nature into the harmonious breath of a unified spirit. His ideas can appear abstract to the common understanding,[9] but when philosophically or spiritually intuited, they reveal themselves to be as real as anything else the mind can encounter in nature.

The world Emerson described is not some far off ideal, but is hidden right here among us behind the thin veil of our habitual neglect. One moment, we are simply walking home from a neighborhood errand, avoiding puddles on the ground. The next, a flash of lightning or brisk gust of wind blows open what the philosopher Aldous Huxley (1894-1963) called the "reducing valve" of our normal perception allowing "Mind at Large" to flood in.[10] We discover during such events just how little and reduced our normal view of reality is. Once the perceptual valve restricting the flow of reality into our mind has been blown open even once, there is no turning back. For Emerson, "all mean egotism

---

[9] That is, to those not initiated into the transcendental mode of consciousness inaugurated by Immanuel Kant and his German successors Fichte, Schelling, and Hegel (all major influences on Emerson).

[10] Aldous Huxley, *The Doors of Perception & Heaven and Hell* (New York: Harper Collins, 2004), 24.

vanishes"[11] as a result of these mysterious ruptures in the everyday course of our lives. We discover, even if only for a moment, the true cosmic extent of our consciousness. Emerson famously described such an experience in *Nature*. One evening, while "crossing a bare common, in snow puddles...under a clouded sky," he found himself spontaneously transformed into "a transparent eye-ball": "I am nothing; I see all; the currents of the Universal Being circulate through me; I am part or particle of God."[12]

There is without doubt a strong dose of such mystical experience informing Emerson's philosophical outlook. No one passes through life without at least a glimpse of the wonder offered by such experiences, but few of today's academic philosophers seem willing or able to speak openly of them. To do so would often lead to risking their professional reputations as disinterested specialists capable of deploying purely rational knowledge untainted by emotions, values, and especially religion and mysticism. Despite the fallen state of philosophy in today's universities, those who still consider themselves lovers of wisdom can affirm along with Whitehead that if mysticism be "direct insight into depths as yet unspoken," then the task of philosophy is to make the mystical intellectually digestible.[13]

Following Emerson's example, the philosophical metabolization of mystical experience is to be accomplished not by dissolving and dismissing it, but by convincingly expressing it, rendering those rare eternal hours when we find ourselves unexpectedly swallowed by a flood of visions from a deeper level of reality into the plain speech of common day. It is as though "the fine star-dust and nebulous blur in Orion," as Emerson put it in his essay "Illusions," is thereby made to "come down and be dealt with in your household thought." All the while, Emerson managed to remain attentive to the infinite mystery and grand impersonality of such events, to the way they perpetually withdrawal from our spoken words into silence, but with their ultimate meaning always hanging there just beyond the tip our tongues. Mystical experiences

[11] *Nature*, ch. 1

[12] *Nature*, ch. 1

[13] Modes of Thought, 174.

only seem to baffle us, to make it feel as though we were permanently struck dumb with wonder. Emerson, unlike the unphilosophical mystics criticized by Hume above, was not satisfied with the experience of an incomprehensible divinity. He appreciated the sublimity of such initial appearances, but his deepest love drove him to attempt to understand and articulate their final reality, to transform mystical experience of divinity from the raw materiality of wonder into the refined spirituality of wisdom. Wonder and wisdom are the beginning and the end of philosophy, the antechamber and the inner sanctum of Emerson's modern school for the soul. The former is our basic condition; the latter is the spark that sets our mind on fire.

A free-ranging mind and independent spirit, Emerson's most important teacher was not a human being, but rather the soul of the world, the *inner* dimension of the universe studied by natural science. His deepest thinking occurred not while reading the well-worn grooves of history's great thinkers, but while wandering pathless through the forest groves of Concord. *What is Nature? Who am I?*—these are Emerson's first and final questions. He spent all his able-minded life contemplating them. They are among the most important, and the most difficult, philosophical questions we as human beings can task ourselves with. Luckily for us, Emerson returned from his revelatory walks in the open air to the stillness of his study, where, after careful reflection, he left written traces of his journeywork so that others might go and see for themselves: "What is nature to [the philosopher]? There is never a beginning, there is never an end, to the inexplicable continuity of this web of God, but always circular power returning into itself."[14] In returning to itself, Nature mimics the mind, "whose beginning, whose ending, [we] can never find,—so entire, so boundless."[15] From Emerson's perspective, the bond between mind and nature runs so deep that ignorance of the meaning of the latter is only evidence of unconsciousness in the former. Mind is nature become conscious, and nature a sleeping mind. As a result of this secret bond between nature and mind,

---

[14] "The American Scholar."

[15] "The American Scholar."

Emerson could declare: "the ancient precept 'Know thyself,' and the modern precept, 'Study nature,' become at last one maxim."[16]

In his essay "Intellect," Emerson asks his reader "What is the hardest task in the world?" If I were asking it of myself at the present time, the hardest task in the world would seem to be adding anything of even minor significance to what has already been said better by Emerson, who I am compelled to christen America's national sage. Despite Whitehead's opinion that Emerson "was not so original"[17] (he preferred Whitman on this count), and that William James was the true American Plato,[18] it remains true that Whitman owed the better part of his philosophical tuition to Emerson, and that James, though a philosophical genius in his own right, also benefitted intellectually from Emerson, his godfather. How could anyone offer a treatment of his intellectual biography that might so much as approach the depth of Emerson's own study of the significant individuals of world history in his book *Representative Men*? In his late essay "Quotation and Originality," Emerson wrote (with the intention of including his own work): "How few thoughts! In a hundred years, millions of men and not a hundred lines of poetry, not a theory of philosophy that offers a solution of the great problems, not an art of education that fulfills the conditions."

"In this delay and vacancy of thought," continues Emerson, "we must make the best amends we can by seeking the wisdom of others to fill the time." Today, many fellow lovers of wisdom soothe their own creative failings by reading Emerson himself, who may very well be, to this day, America's most essential and most eloquent philosopher. In the course of writing this essay, I found myself experiencing an incessant desire to excerpt his words, to let Emerson speak for himself. In my own remarks, I have aspired only to give some sense of his personal karma and to amplify ideas expressed in his work that, as an American

---

[16] "The American Scholar."

[17] *Dialogues of Alfred North Whitehead as Recorded by Lucien Price* (New York: Little, Brown, & Co., 1954), 24.

[18] Hartshorne, Charles. *Whitehead's Philosophy: Selected Essays, 1935-1970* (Lincoln: University of Nebraska Press, 1972), ix.

attempting to philosophize in the twenty-first century, I find it impossible to do without.

In a world nearly overflowing with circumstance and accident, the greater part of the freedom that human beings are able muster is found in the asking of our own questions and the posing of our own problems. Our most serious task is to ask, and ask again. Children generally continue to ask questions freely until they enter school and are usually told by their teachers to respond to problems imposed by standardized tests. Those who dutifully answer become the standard. Those who refuse these imposed problems and instead create their own partake of genuine learning. It is thus that the soul grows like a plant, from the inside out: "Man is endogenous, and education is his unfolding," as Emerson put it.[19] *The hardest task in the world*, according to him, is *thinking*.[20] We are seldom able to achieve it. It grows only in rare fits and starts, flowering in unexpected glory one moment only to wilt into nothing the next. Our own greatest thoughts do not originate with us, but course through us, arriving from and departing to we know not where. Thinking is "always a miracle, which no frequency of occurrence or incessant study can ever familiarize."[21] Thinking has a cosmic origin: it is "the advent of truth into the world, a form of thought now, for the first time, bursting into the universe."[22]

"I have observed," Emerson tells us elsewhere, "persons who, in their character and actions, answer questions which I have not skill to put."[23] Emerson himself was such a person, his characteristic style exemplifying for us more than mere skill, but true genius. His was no secular thinking, no passive reflection upon the inherited perceptions of his time. His life's task was that of the philosopher: "Man Thinking," as he called it. "In the degenerate state, when the victim of society," wrote Emerson, "the [philosopher] tends to become…the parrot of other

---

[19] "Uses of Great Men"

[20] "Intellect"

[21] "Intellect"

[22] "Intellect"

[23] "Uses of Great Men"

men's thinking."[24] Emerson's task was no social role. Fit expression of ideas can make them contagious to others, but geniuses do not contract ideas like diseases: genius *creates* them. But what sort of sacred thinking is it that would present itself as *the hardest task in the world?* Such thinking shares a common source with cosmogenesis. It is the creative ordering power of the universe itself, awakening to self-consciousness. With such thinking, the mind transmutes life into truth, distilling the eternal Idea from out of a flux of virtually unlimited facts. The difficulty of thinking creatively results from the invisibility of this source, even to geniuses. "Man is a stream whose source is hidden," wrote Emerson. "I am…but a surprised spectator of this ethereal water."[25]

Thinking is the hardest task in the world.[26] In most of our moods we shrink before it, preferring the easier route to social acceptance granted us by mimicry. Some put on a show of rebelliousness by railing against the values of their parents' generation, but have not the courage, the creativity, nor the commitment to replace them with something more virtuous. Today, with America facing its greatest identity crisis since the Civil War, are Emerson's sublime expressions still audible to contemporary ears? The American people to whom Emerson delivered his famous address "The American Scholar" in 1837—a speech Oliver Wendell Holmes famously referred to as America's "intellectual declaration of independence"—had not yet lived through the horrors of the Civil War, but the air was already tense in tragic anticipation.

The late 1830s were marked by one of the worst recessions of the 19th century, and the need for the nation to finally face the depraved institution of slavery was felt more strongly with each passing day. Contemporary America faces a similar set of existential challenges. Consumer capitalism—our undisputed civil religion—has made money into the holiest of sacraments, more valuable than equality and

---

[24] "The American Scholar"

[25] "The Over-Soul"

[26] A fact confirmed by a recent set of studies by psychologists at Virginia and Harvard Universities, revealing that the average person would rather be painfully shocked than be forced to think. See **http://www.theguardian.com/science/2014/jul/03/electric-shock-preferable-to-thinking-says-study** (accessed 7/31/2014).

freedom, culture and education, even earthly life itself. Parochial politics oriented toward the mob rather than the Mind continue to tear apart the social fabric. And finally—something Emerson and his fellow transcendentalists, in awe of the encompassing power of Nature, could hardly have foreseen—, a worsening ecological crisis threatens to prematurely pull the plug on the entire venture of human civilization. “We think our civilization near its meridian,” a confident Emerson could write in 1844, “but we are yet only at the cock-crowing and the morning star.”[27] One hundred and seventy years later, it has become clear that the industrial phase of civilization has irreversibly transformed the very geology of the planet. The world’s geologists are beginning to refer to the present epoch as the Anthropocene.[28] Today’s thinking persons are being forced to take seriously the possibility that the civilization which seemed to Emerson a newborn Venus now has more in common with hell-bound Lucifer. The hope of a new dawn for Western civilization, still credible in Emerson’s pre-Civil War America, has, two world wars and a global ecological crisis later, become increasingly difficult to imagine.

Can we, in an age of neuroscience, particle colliders, and geoengineering, still make sense of Emerson's core convictions that “within man is the soul of the whole,” and that “every natural process is a version of a moral sentence”? If the latter is true, then what sort of sentence is anthropogenic climate change pronouncing upon our civilization? Where is this soul in me that Emerson claims can perceive the universe? Am I supposed to believe the whole world can fit inside my skull? How many of us are prepared to heed the Emersonian responses to such questions? What will it take for us to realize that we are knowingly allowing ourselves and our planet to be destroyed due to the sheer weight of cultural habit?

---

[27] “Politics”

[28] “The Anthropocene: a new epoch of geological time?” by Jan Zalasiewicz, Mark Williams, Alan Haywood, and Michael Ellis in *Philosophical Transactions of the Royal Society* (2011), vol. 369 no. 1938), 835-841. **http://rsta.royalsocietypublishing.org/content/369/1938/835.full** (accessed 7/31/2014).

Our lack of philosophical curiosity, our superficiality, and our tendency to avoid thinking have allowed us to be lulled to sleep by the disenchanted materialistic mantras of industrial capitalism. "It is so wonderful to our neurologists," Emerson wrote in 1844, "that a man can see without his eyes [using his fancy], that it does not occur to them, that it is just as wonderful, that he should see with them."[29] What are we missing? What is Emerson imploring us to see? He offers no easy solutions to today's problems. It is not simply that we must think harder or strive to be kinder to one another. Just as "we cannot make a planet, with atmosphere, rivers, and forest, by means of the best carpenters' or engineers' tools, with chemist's laboratory and smith's forge to boot," so in the same way we cannot expect to construct a "heavenly society out of foolish, sick, selfish men and women, such as we know [ourselves] to be."[30] Emerson offers, rather, a means of dissolving poorly posed problems by calling us back before the posing to the uncanny ground of all our questioning: to the feeling of wonder.

Wonder allows us to stand in awe of this world again, to become mesmerized by the meeting place of green earth and blue sky. Wonder turns our attention away from the acquisition of things and toward their appreciation as such. Wonder is the mood most likely to provoke philosophy, because it is the strangest, the most thought provoking and eye opening. Wonder kindles the love of wisdom in our soul. "The difference between the wise and the unwise," according to Emerson, is that "the latter wonders at what is unusual," while "the wise man wonders at the usual."[31] Natural science and industrial technology have progressed tremendously since Emerson's day, but despite—or perhaps because of—their great successes, we have lost the ability to be amazed by the ordinary; instead, we have become mesmerized by the new. If he saw the natural world as the soul's "most ancient religion," we can be sure that Emerson would respond to today's ecological devastation with the same moral intensity he felt regarding the abolition of slavery.

---

[29] "New England Reformers"

[30] "Man the Reformer"

[31] "New England Reformers"

Were he alive today, Emerson would also undoubtedly reaffirm his criticism of American culture's "bad name for superficialness."[32] We remain a people concerned more with the economic bottom line than the higher truths of philosophy, with what is convenient and profitable today rather than concern for our future, let alone for those truths that hold for all time. But Emerson did not speak to us as Americans. He spoke to us, rather, as individuals, and to the highest part of our individuality. His essays are addressed not to nations or credal sects but to those singular, self-reliant men and women who refuse to be counted as members of any mass, to those for whom "society" and its party and institutional allegiances are but oppressive abstractions. He spoke to those "who can open their eyes wider than to a nationality, namely, to considerations of benefit to the human race [and] in the interest of civilization."[33]

On January 31st, 1862, nine months after the first shots of the Civil War were fired, Emerson delivered a speech at the Smithsonian Institution in Washington, D.C. urging the immediate emancipation of the slaves both for strategic and, more importantly, moral reasons. The speech, entitled "American Civilization," won Emerson an audience with President Lincoln the following day. It would be another nine months before Lincoln signed the Emancipation Proclamation. Two and a half years later, he would be assassinated. Emerson described Lincoln in his eulogy as "an entirely public man; father of his country, the pulse of twenty millions throbbing in his heart, the thought of their minds articulated by his tongue."[34]

Unlike Lincoln the statesman, Emerson was not by nature a political person, but he was a passionate reformer despite being suspicious of reformers and their movements (his own included). Having personally witnessed the largely failed attempts at socialist revolution in London and Paris during his trip to Europe in 1848, Emerson wrote in his journal: "It is always becoming evident that the permanent good is for the

---

[32] "Fate"

[33] "American Civilization"

[34] "Abraham Lincoln, Remarks at the funeral service of the President," Concord, April 19, 1865.

soul only and cannot be retained in any society or system."[35] It is not a perfected State that will solve the world's political problems, Emerson thought, but wiser individuals. In his 1844 essay "Politics," Emerson wrote: "To educate the wise man, the State exists; and with the appearance of the wise man, the State expires. The appearance of character makes the State unnecessary."

As fate would have it, Emerson's fame and influence as a thinker was rising just as his young nation began falling into its first major crisis since the Revolutionary War. The weight of the times forced him to find his political voice. In 1838, Emerson published an open letter to President Van Buren repudiating his administration's plan to forcibly remove the Cherokee Nation from its land. In this respectful but forthright letter, Emerson demanded to know "whether all the attributes of reason, of civility, of justice, and even of mercy, shall be put off by the American people?...Will the American Government steal? Will it lie? Will it kill?"[36]

In 1844, he roused Concord's abolitionists by delivering a passionate speech denouncing the evils of slavery. With the same metaphysical confidence that would lead Martin Luther King, Jr. to announce and evince the inevitable bending of the moral arc of the universe toward justice, Emerson declared to those unable to heed the cosmic call for Freedom, "Creep into your grave, the universe has no need of you!"[37] In 1851, after the passage of the infamous Fugitive Slave Law, several dozen citizens of Concord signed a petition urging Emerson to publicly speak out against it. He did: "America, the most prosperous country in the universe, has the greatest calamity in the universe, negro slavery." The existence of slavery, continued Emerson, turns into "hollow American Brag" the notion that his countrymen "loved freedom, and believed in the Christian religion."[38]

---

[35] JMN, 10:310.

[36] Letter to Van Buren.

[37] "Address Delivered in Concord on the Anniversary of the Emancipation of the Negroes in The British West Indies," August 1, 1844.

[38] "Address to the Citizen of Concord," *Emerson's Political Writings*, 138.

By the time of his speech at the Smithsonian in 1862, which was perhaps both the climax of his political activity as well as the darkest period of the war, Emerson's national stature was well established. Standing on the speaker's platform of the Smithsonian lecture hall, Emerson again denounced the "conspiracy of slavery": "They call it an institution; I call it a destitution." "We live in a new and exceptional age," he continued. "America is another word for Opportunity. Our whole history appears like a last effort of the Divine Providence on behalf of the human race."

Emerson's popularity surged during the war. One gets the impression, as his biographer Robert Richardson says, that by the height of his fame "there were two Emersons."[39] The private mind was increasingly outpaced by the public image preceding it. According to Richardson, by 1863 "Emerson had become…an inescapable part—a fixture—of American public life."[40] In 1865, he would deliver an astonishing seventy-seven lectures, including Lincoln's eulogy. In 1867, he lectured for eighty audiences in fourteen states. A morally wounded America lionized Emerson as its national hero after the war. He strengthened the souls of his fellow citizens by reminding them of the idealism upon which the country had been founded. In the years following the war, "the public Emerson seemed more and more to be replacing the private one," as Richardson put it.[41] Emerson, reconciling the opposites within himself, wrote in 1871: "The most private self-searcher will be the most public and universal philosopher, if his study is real."[42]

Emerson scholar Richard Geldard begins his timely book *Emerson and the Dream of America* (2010) by reminding his readers that "Emerson was intelligent enough to know that the times seem perennially

---

[39] Richardson, Robert. *Emerson: The Mind on Fire* (Berkeley: University of California Press, 1995), 548.

[40] Richardson, *Emerson*, 551.

[41] Richardson, *Emerson*, 553.

[42] "Natural History of the Intellect"

bad, especially as seen through the light infused prism of an irrepressible idealism."[43] As Emerson himself put it, "The Times are the masquerade of the eternities; trivial to the dull, tokens of noble and majestic agents to the wise." It is no surprise that our times appear to most everyone alive—whether liberal or conservative, religious or secular, young or old—to be deeply troubled, even catastrophic.

Americans have long praised Emerson's essay "Self-Reliance" for its defense of individualism. We should be careful not to oversimplify Emerson's message, however. Individualist though he may have been, Emerson had as much distaste for wanton capitalism as he did for big government. His emphasis on self-reliance needs to be clearly distinguished from selfishness, and from "ethical egoism." Indeed, Emerson implores his readers to awaken from their mistaken identities, to get their selfish egos out of the way so that a higher universal Self, owned by no one in particular, might pour its light into the soul: "When we discern justice, when we discern truth, we do nothing of ourselves, but allow a passage to its beams."[44] If the gravity of the times is still not sufficient to motivate us, then it is to this inner light of the soul that we must turn to awaken us from this nightmare. No crusade against evildoers, nor any new policies or legal measures alone can save us now. They treat symptoms, leaving the cause untouched. What are we to do? Despite the risk of sounding sentimental, let us take seriously Emerson's answer, which he repeated again and again in so many of his lectures: *we are to love one another*. "We must be lovers, and at once the impossible becomes possible...Let our affection flow out to our fellows; it would operate in a day the greatest of all revolutions."[45]

All our social ills, according to Emerson, stem from our failure to love. Even the most religious among us often lack a basic faith in the moral potential of human beings. We find ourselves unable to muster "a sufficient belief in the unity of things to persuade [us] that society

[43] Geldard, Richard. *Emerson and the Dream of America: Finding Our Way to a New and Exceptional Age* (New York: Larson Publications, 2010), 15.
[44] "Self-Reliance"
[45] "Man the Reformer"

can be maintained without artificial restraints, as well as the solar system."[46] As Dante perceived in the last lines of his *Divine Comedy*, it is mutual love that holds the planets in their orbits, not imposed laws. For a human being to succeed in loving is perhaps no less difficult than to succeed in thinking, and in the end, neither can be directly taught to us by others, since both depend upon the inner cultivation of self-knowledge. Loving and thinking are usually held far apart by academia and by our culture in general, but for the philosopher, the lover of wisdom, they cannot be parted.

---

[46] "Politics"

Dr. Gary E Schwartz

Dr. Gary E Schwartz is a professor of psychology, medicine, neurology, psychiatry, and surgery at the University of Arizona and director of its Laboratory for Advances in Consciousness and Health. He is also corporate director of development of energy healing for Canyon Ranch Resorts and the author of several books, including *The Sacred Promise.* Gary is also a co-founder of the Campaign for Open Sciences, as well as a co-editor and contributor to a forthcoming Param Media anthology on Post-Materialism. Gary's next book, *Synchronicity and the One Mind: How the New Self-Science of Super Timing Can Transform Our Lives*, will be published by Param Media in 2016.

Dr. Gary E Schwartz

Science and the Process of Responsible Belief: The Five Additive Criteria Test (FACT)

UNDERSTANDING, SYNCHRONICITY, SUPER-TIMING

At the heart of science is an essential tension between two seemingly contradictory attitudes — an openness to new ideas, no matter how bizarre or counterintuitive they may be, and the most ruthless skeptical scrutiny of all ideas, old and new.
This is how deep truths are winnowed from deep nonsense.
Carl Sagan, PhD

It's belief that gets us there.
Joe Darrow, MD, in the film *Dragonfly*

Introduction

The human capacity to form and hold beliefs is one of our greatest gifts, as well as one of our most dangerous curses. On the one hand, we can be highly creative; we can be inventive and innovative, and we can pursue visionary and even beautiful hypotheses in the face of incomplete or even contradictory information. But on the other hand, we can sometimes adopt erroneous and even pathological beliefs, which can foster horrific actions both individually and collectively.

I have deeply pondered the challenge of attempting to understand the nature of truth seeking and the process of scientific discovery, especially concerning those instances in our personal and professional lives when circumstances require that we reconsider certain key beliefs that we hold dear.

Carl Sagan, PhD, the distinguished professor of astronomy at Cornell University who was also a devout skeptic, illustrated the challenge this way:

> *When Kepler found his long-cherished belief [geocentric view of the universe] did not agree with the most precise observation, he accepted the uncomfortable fact. He preferred the hard truth to his dearest illusions; that is the heart of science.*

Sagan does not mince words here, and I appreciated his candor. I would propose that Kepler "preferring the hard truth to our dearest illusions" is not only "the heart of science;" it is the heart of responsible and compassionate living.

For the past twenty years, my academic research has taken me into ever more controversial areas—from the role of energy in health and healing (Schwartz, 2007), through the possible survival of consciousness after physical death (Schwartz, 2011), to the existence of some sort of a universal "Guiding-Organizing-Designing (G.O.D.) Process" (Schwartz, 2006), a "Supermind" (Banerji, 2012; although I have chosen to write it as "Super Mind," and Dossey, 2013 calls it the "One Mind") expressing itself through the process of "super-synchronicities" in contemporary life (Schwartz, 2015a-b, 2016). In the process of facing the emerging challenge of questioning—and eventually giving up—some of my own long-cherished beliefs about nature and the cosmos, I ended up formalizing a **five additive criteria test (FACT)** for fostering the process of truth seeking and the development of accurate and responsible beliefs.

The five essential additive criteria are listed in Table I below.

Criteria	Description
Criterion 1:	Reason and Scientific Theory
Criterion 2:	Scientific Evidence
Criterion 3:	Community of Credible and Trustworthy Believers
Criterion 4:	Direct Personal Experiences

Criterion 5:	Responsible Consideration of Skepticism about Criteria 1-4

Table I: The five additive criteria of FACT

Thanks to Param Media's inspiration to publish this unique anthology, I was given the opportunity (and context) to share this approach in a reader-friendly fashion. Though FACT can become quite complex, the framework can also be taught in a relatively simple fashion. Criteria 1 – 5 in FACT can be associated with our five fingers, as shown in Figure I below.

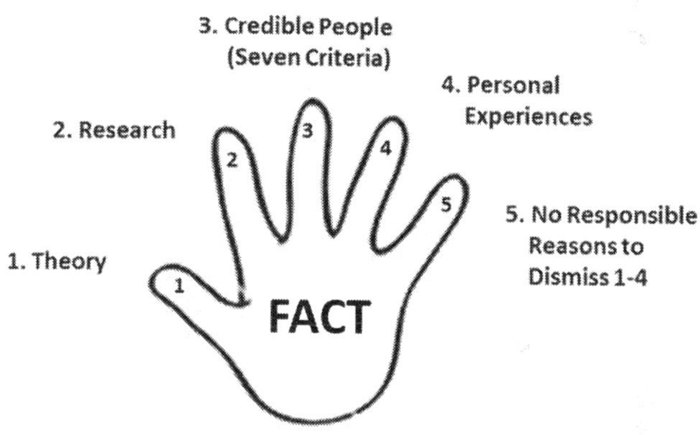

Figure I: Representing the five additive criteria of FACT as five fingers

I will first provide a brief overview to FACT, followed by a demonstration of how it can be applied to one of humanity's most challenging and extraordinary ideas and beliefs: the existence of a living "Super Mind" (Schwartz, 2016)—what Larry Dossey (2013) and many ancient philosophers in the Platonic tradition refer to as the "One Mind"—and its active participation in contemporary life as revealed through super-synchronicity and the process of "super-timing" (Schwartz, 2016).

What is FACT?

FACT integrates five essential criteria for forming and holding accurate and responsible beliefs. What is novel about FACT are not the individual criteria themselves, but rather their additive cohesion as a whole.

In my numerous queries of creative scientists and conservative skeptics alike, the consensus it that *each* of these five criteria is fundamental, and they *each* contribute to the process of valid and responsible truth seeking. Moreover, thus far no one has proposed that a sixth criterion needs to be added to the framework to justify it being a valid and responsible system for fostering accurate understanding.

What is innovative about FACT is its implications for our coming to believe something—especially something that is new and challenging—*when all five criteria have been simultaneously met*, which is the key point of this chapter.

Here is the logical flow of FACT:

IF:

Logic and scientific theory both support a given belief (Criteria 1),

AND, IF

Extensive scientific evidence confirms a given belief (Criteria 2),

AND, IF

There exists a community of highly credible and trustworthy people who hold the belief is true (Criteria 3),

AND, IF

You have had direct personal experience which supports the belief (Criteria 4),

AND, IF

There are *no* good, reasonable, and responsible reasons for rejecting (i.e. *no* good reasons to be skeptical) of Criteria 1-4 (Criteria 5),

THEN,

It is prudent and responsible to adopt this new belief as probably true, and to do so with integrity.

Therefore, when all five criteria simultaneously have been met concerning a new belief, we should feel compelled to accept this belief as being probably accurate and most likely true—even if this means that we are "forced" to give up a "long-cherished belief."

Conversely, to reject a new belief when all five criteria have been met in order to hold onto a long-cherished belief is to promote dishonesty and disinformation, which in extreme instances can have disastrous consequences for our health and evolution.

But must all five criteria be met in order for us to hold an accurate and responsible belief?

My understanding is that they do not. It can be rationally argued that if Criteria 1 + 2 + 3 + 5 have been clearly met, but Criteria 4 (direct personal experience) has not (or cannot) be met, then the combination of the four criteria which have been met is often sufficient to justify accepting a given belief as probably true (i.e. accurate). For example, most of us believe that a collection of astronauts have actually set foot on the moon, even though most of us have not done so (and likely never will).

However, in those special instances where all five criteria have been met, logic requires (i.e. it is essential) that we accept those beliefs as likely being true—whether we prefer those beliefs or not. This is ultimately how science advances, increasing our understanding and evolving our beliefs accordingly.

Now that you see the big picture, I will take you through each of the five criteria, illustrating how collectively they provide a useful structure for deciding to adopt and hold a novel and challenging belief—in this instance, the existence of super-synchronicity as revealed through super-timing, and the belief in the active orchestrating presence of the One Mind (Schwartz, 2016).

Before we review each of the criteria, however, let's briefly consider the concept of "super-synchronicity".

What is Super-Synchronicity?

The concept of synchronicity was introduced to psychology, psychiatry, and the general public through the creative and sophisticated writings of Carl Jung, MD. Synchronicity is generally defined as "the simultaneous occurrence of events that appear significantly related but have no discernible causal connection" (Jung, 1974). However, the term "simultaneous" is somewhat a misnomer in that the events do not typically occur "at the same time," but rather as a sequence of events over some period of time. Key to synchronicity is the process of timing. Also, what is meant by "no discernible causal connection" refers to no discernible *mechanical* causes existing between the events, not to the absence of some sort of higher energy and intelligence arranging (or co-arranging) the improbable sequence of events.

I categorize synchronicities into the following three types:

Type I Synchronicities: Two events significantly related over time.

Type II Synchronicities: Three to five events significantly related over time.

Type III Synchronicities: Six or more events significantly related over time. Because of their highly improbable and evidential nature, I also refer to Type III Synchronicities as super-synchronicities, as revealed through the evidence of their super-timing.

In a series of papers published in the journal *Spirituality in Clinical Practice* (Schwartz 2014, 2015a-b), I have reported multiple examples of extraordinarily improbable and highly meaningful Type III synchronicities containing 10 to 18 synchronicities in a given sequence in time. My forthcoming book, *Synchronicity and the One Mind: How the New Self-Science of Super Timing Can Transform Our Lives*, goes into great detail about the nature of synchronicities, as exemplified by compelling evidence collected from my own life. (Schwartz, 2016).

The First Criterion – Reason and Theory

The first criterion refers to reason and theory. Does a theory or system of logic exist which supports the possibility that a given belief may be valid?

Is it possible that some sort of "Guiding-Organizing-Designing," "One Mind," or "Super Mind" process might exist and be at least partly responsible for the emergence of highly improbable, complex, and meaningful timed sequences of events in real life? The answer is yes. Various authors have reviewed the logic and theory (e.g. Chalmers, 1996; Haisch, 2010; Chopra, 2014). I will include one exemplar here (from Schwartz, 2006).

Many scientists and laymen alike assume that "randomness" is a genuine process in nature, and that events can and do occur "by chance." The existence of randomness is a core assumption of Darwinian evolution, and it is a core assumption in certain interpretations of quantum physics as well. This assumption is so deeply ingrained in contemporary science that it is rarely questioned. However, logic and theory appropriately integrated lead to a different conclusion. (See also Spencer, 2012 for a critique of related common assumptions about quantum physics.)

First, statistical theory is very clear that two conditions are necessary in order for a random process to occur and result in the appearance of random distributions of numbers. The first condition is that *each event must be independent of every other event over time.* In other words, the flipping of one coin, for example, cannot have an influence or carry any effect on the flipping of the next coin. Independence of events is essential for the random process to occur.

The second condition, which follows from the first, is that *the events cannot change over time.* In other words, the coins cannot wear out, the coin flipper cannot learn how to influence the inferred randomness of the process, etc.

It turns out that when both of these conditions are met—and they can never be completely met, even by computer algorithms—one will *always* observe a random distribution of numbers (e.g. the well-known bell-shaped curve). With a suitable number of observations, this effect will be observed 100% of the time. Though we are jumping ahead to Criterion 2 with this discussion, it is valuable to offer this evidence here.

For example, if you program a computer to (1) select 100 numbers "randomly" from 1 to 100 and then calculate the mean of these 100 numbers (the mean will be approximately 50), then (2) perform this operation 100 times, and (3) plot the distribution of the means, you will observe a "bell-shaped" curve with a peak around 50, and you obtain this pattern 100% of the time! You will never get a straight line, or a V-shaped curve, or an inverted bell-shaped curve.

The implications of this are quite profound. *First of all, randomness does not occur "by chance"—randomness occurs only when precise conditions (of independence) are met. Second, when these conditions do occur—i.e. independence of events—the probability of a random distribution of numbers occurring is 100%.*

Note that none of the above is controversial per se. However, it is unfortunately not widely known or appreciated, even by many distinguished scientists.

In sum, logic and theory leads to the following conclusion:

Novel events do not occur "<u>by chance.</u>" Rather, what "randomness" does (i.e. what the condition of independence does) is <u>give novel events the chance</u> or opportunity to occur.

Now, the key question arises: does complete independence exist in nature as the statistics of randomness requires? Logic and theory are very clear here; the answer is decidedly no.

Both classical and contemporary theories explain how all physical systems—from subatomic particles to super clusters of galaxies, and everything in between—are interconnected by forces and fields. For example, Newtonian theory states that every object that has mass has a gravitational field extending out in all directions, infinitely, in space. These universal gravitational fields are "mutually attractive" and hold the entire universe together. The existence of interconnecting fields includes electrical and magnetic fields, and physics now includes "dark energy" as an additional interconnecting process.

Moreover, classical and contemporary systems theories explain how all components in all levels of systems are interconnected via positive and negative feedback loops. These feedback loops not only influence the relationship between components, but alter the processes over time. In fact, feedback loops are critical to learning in all systems, be they neural networks in the brain or neural network software in a computer.

In other words, the preponderance of theory indicates that systems in nature are not independent; on the contrary, they are *interdependent*. Basic logic points to the irrefutable conclusion that nature does not fit the conditions necessary for truly "random processes" to occur.

It follows that just because a given sequence of numbers may "appear" to be random does not necessarily mean that they reflect a "random process."

Consider the number pi (the circumference of a circle divided by its diameter). The number sequence in pi has been calculated to millions of digits, and no mathematician has yet discovered a repeating sequence (or explanation) for the resulting sequence. The sequence of numbers appears "random." And yet, the exact sequence of numbers is replicated 100% of the time, regardless of the size of the circle involved in the calculations.

If "randomness" does not occur "by chance" (instead requiring two specific conditions related to complete independence), then, for even stronger reasons, "order" cannot occur "by chance" either. If we cannot rationally and justifiably explain the existence and evolution of order in nature and the universe as due to a "random process," then we must logically look to the existence of some sort of creative ordering / synchronizing process in nature and the universe. It is unscientific and illogical to assert anything other than something similar to this conclusion.

The Second Criterion: Scientific Evidence

The second criterion refers to evidence. Does scientific evidence exist that supports the possibility that a given belief may be valid?

Concerning the question of randomness, and the justification for forming and holding the belief in the existence of some sort of universal ordering process in the universe, the answer is yes. In fact, the evidence is voluminous and extends from statistics and physics to psychology and astrophysics.

As mentioned above, basic science experiments in statistical modeling clearly indicate that true randomness only operates under conditions approximating complete independence. To the extent that conditions do not meet the criteria of independence, and instead reflect degrees of interdependence and interconnection, deviations from randomness are always observed.

Moreover, experiments in quantum physics using the double-slit paradigm indicate that not only does the act of measuring the behavior of a photon or electron alter the behavior and distributions of the photons and electrons, but some scientists even claim that the mind itself can alter the distributions. Radin and colleagues (2013) have conducted a series of elegant experiments demonstrating how the human mind, when intentionally focused on the optical measurement system, appears to alter the behavior of the photons in replicable ways.

Moreover, years of experiments in psychokinesis have documented the effects of the human mind on "random number generators"—be they created via software, or by hardware tracking "noisy" electrical circuits—and these effects can be observed both locally and globally (e.g. Nelson et al, 2011).

Probably the most important thing to consider concerning the relevance of these basic science experiments to the phenomena of super-synchronicity is the replicated observations made in double-slit experiments, where single photons or electrons are emitted and detected by CCD (charge-coupled device) cameras behind the two slits.

Even though the photons or electrons are being emitted as "individual" events—and they appear to occur "randomly" as "individual" dots, appearing one at a time (as registered by individual pixels on the CCD)—what emerges (i.e. *accumulates over time*) is the appearance of a non-random "interference" pattern, and under appropriately controlled experimental conditions, this emerging pattern replicates 100% of the time!

The individual dots only appear "random" in that we cannot predict where a given dot will appear on the CCD camera at any given moment in time. However, this seemingly random interpretation belies the fact that some sort of invisible organizing process (which the famous physicist David Bohm called "pilot waves") leads the dots to emerge over time as a completely replicable pattern of dots, mathematically described as an interference wave function.

I have suggested that synchronicities are like photons or electrons: individual synchronicity events appear like individual "dots" and may seem "random." However, over time non-random patterns can be observed; that is, if one is prepared to "connect the dots" and see the emerging bigger picture, which is the basis of what I call the Quantum Synchronicity Theory (Schwartz, 2016).

If you want to observe the behavior of electrons or photons, then you need to open your eyes and read the measurements. Similarly, as Jung said, "synchronicity is an ever present reality for those who have eyes to see", which is especially the case with Type III Synchronicities. The extensive evidence for the existence of synchronicities themselves is documented elsewhere (e.g. Beitman, 2011; Schwartz, 2014; 2015a-b; 2016).

The Third Criterion: Community of Credible and Trustworthy Believers

The third criterion requires a community of credible and trustworthy people who support the possibility that a given belief is probably valid.

When it comes to novel beliefs, and especially highly controversial beliefs, discovering a community of credible and trustworthy people who have formed and adopted the belief provides additional justification for seriously considering the possibility that the belief may be accurate and responsible. I have found that discovering such people has played an important role in my coming to accept the conclusions provided by Criteria 1 and 2.

I have developed a simple yet comprehensive set of parameters for determining whether someone fits Criteria 3. For ease of learning and remembering, I call this set of seven parameters the "Seven S's". They are:

1) Successful,
2) Smart,
3) Skeptical,
4) Sophisticated,
5) Savvy,
6) Sane, and
7) Straight (as in, honest and trustworthy)

Though we could debate the precise definitions of each of these seven S's, the fact is that it is relatively easy to find individuals who clearly meet all of these seven S's:

1. People who are highly *successful* in their chosen professions (CEOs and executives in major companies, senior professors at major universities, directors of distinguished institutions and centers, winners of esteemed prizes and awards, etc.),

AND

2. They are very *smart* (they may have high IQ scores, have received high grades in college and graduate schools, are established problem solvers, etc.),

AND

3. They are demonstrably and genuinely *skeptical*, as in they are questioning, thoughtful, challenging of information and ideas, cautious about drawing conclusions, etc.,

AND

4. They show strong evidence of being *sophisticated* in complex thinking, are careful to consider multiple viewpoints and alternative sources of information and interpretation, are able to analyze and integrate divergent and even conflicting information and interpretations, etc.,

AND

5. They have a history of being *savvy*, as in they are experienced, knowledgeable, balanced, mature, clever, not easily fooled, etc.,

AND

6. They are described by their peers (as well as reliable health care professionals) as being *sane* (e.g. they do not show any evidence of neurosis, psychosis, delusions, psychopathy, personality disorder, cognitive impairments of information processing and memory, etc.),

AND, MOST IMPORTANTLY

7. They are *straight*, as in they are trustworthy, honest, ethical, focused on accuracy / truthfulness, humble, and aware of limitations or absence of important information or knowledge in a given circumstance, etc.

Now, when these types of "Seven S" people hold a belief in something, it is wise (i.e. rational and responsible) for us to give them the "benefit of the doubt" regarding the probable validity of the belief in question.

In the case of super-synchronicities, super-timing, and the orchestrating presence of the One Mind (i.e. a Super Mind), I have met over a hundred "Seven S" people who have formed and hold this belief. They include scientists, professors, CEOs, lawyers, creative artists, physicians, and therapists (Schwartz, 2016).

Note that I am not proposing that we accept their beliefs about synchronicity and the One Mind blindly and without reflection, but that we give their beliefs serious consideration, and not let our "emotional doubt" get in the way. Also, I am not proposing that Criteria 3, by itself, is sufficient to justify adopting and holding a belief. What I am saying is that when Criteria 1 and 2 have been met, the *addition* of Criterion 3 adds further reason to support the idea that adopting and holding a given belief may be accurate and responsible.

The Fourth Criterion: Direct Personal Experiences

The fourth criterion refers to direct personal experience. Have you had direct personal experiences that supported the possibility that a given belief is probably valid?

For many people, the "sine qua non" of adopting and holding a belief is direct personal experience. In the case of super-synchronicities and the existence of some sort of universal orchestrating mind, I have been blessed to have had a wealth of direct personal experiences whose veracity is highly justified (e.g. Schwartz 2006; 2011; 2015 a-b; 2016).

In these instances, possible confounding factors such as misperception, confirmation bias, and self-deception can be justifiably and responsibly ruled out, especially since many of them were witnessed and confirmed by one or more type Seven S persons.

The Fifth Criterion: Responsible Consideration of Skepticism about Criteria 1-4

The fifth criterion refers to responsible consideration of skepticism about Criteria 1-4. Does responsible skepticism about Criteria 1-4 still support the possibility that a given belief is valid? The key word here is "responsible".

By "responsible" I mean:

1) honest,
2) fair,
3) comprehensive,
4) unbiased,
5) open-minded,
6) critical,
7) discerning,
8) flexible, and
9) accountable.

This kind of skepticism is not only valid; it is essential. It is my belief (no pun intended) that the process of responsibly questioning everything for the purpose of seeking truth, whatever it may be, is a core quality not only of science, but of personal integrity in general. True / genuine skeptics are skeptical about everything, *including the process of skepticism itself*. If they are not, then they are pseudo-skeptics.

It has been said that we should act with "moderation in everything, including moderation."

The same can be said for skepticism, and this applies to *skepticism about everything, including professional skepticism.*

The key here is discernment, i.e. knowing when to continue questioning a belief versus reaching a decision about the probable veracity of the belief.

Carl Sagan believed in responsible skepticism, and he attempted to practice it in his own life and career. Moreover, he firmly believed that "it is the tension between creativity and skepticism that has produced the stunning and unexpected findings of science."

I added Criterion 5 to this evolving framework to remind me personally (and by extension, my scientist colleagues collectively) that the formal process of "taking stock" and "doing due diligence" concerning Criteria 1-4 is an essential fifth step in the truth seeking process. Taking the time to step back and carefully re-evaluate (1) theory, (2) evidence, (3) people, and (4) experiences to ensure that they *all* pass muster increases the probability that a conclusion about a given belief is accurate and responsible.

I regularly include Criterion 5 in my research activities, and have illustrated how it can be applied to controversial topics, such as the belief in the survival of consciousness after death (Davids and Schwartz, 2016).

In the process of working through Criterion 5, I regularly consider the four most extreme skeptical criticisms that speak directly to Criteria 1-4:

Criticism 1: "The professed belief is scientifically impossible." (Criterion 1)

Criticism 2: "There is no credible research for the belief, and what research exists can be explained by conventional theories." (Criterion 2)

Criticism 3: "Anyone who holds this belief is not credible and cannot be trusted, e.g. the person is uneducated, or not very intelligent, or they are irrational, etc." (Criterion 3)

Criticism 4: "All personal experiences that support the belief are invalid, e.g. the experiences reflect misperceptions, misinterpretations, delusions, etc." (Criterion 4)

Is Passing FACT Foolproof?

If a given belief addresses all five criteria successfully and passes FACT, does this necessarily imply that the given belief is therefore accurate and true? The answer is no.

Just because we have engaged in a responsible process of truth seeking (Bourey and Schwartz, 2016) and have comprehensively addressed a belief using a framework such as FACT, this does not guarantee that the belief in question is accurate. Logic, as well as history, reminds us that new theories (Criterion 1), discoveries (Criterion 2), people (Criterion 3), and / or direct personal experiences (Criterion 4) may appear in the future which justify our re-engagement of the FACT process. The FACT process is a forever open process; it encourages re-evaluation and evolution as a function of new evidence.

This is especially important when evaluating and accepting our direct personal experiences. Even if we cannot attribute a given direct personal experience to erroneous factors such as a misperception, confirmation bias, and / or self-deception, this does not necessarily mean that our specific belief is accurate.

For example, there was a time when virtually all human beings believed that the sun revolved around the earth. Moreover:

- Our theories at the time predicted it (Criterion 1),
- The available scientific evidence at the time supported it (Criterion 2),
- Highly trustworthy and credible people believed it at the time (Criteria 3), and

- We had direct personal experiences (Criterion 4), which we interpreted as supporting the belief at the time (i.e. we witnessed on a repeated basis what we interpreted as the sun rising in the East and setting in the West).

However, what became known as the Copernican Revolution led humanity to a different belief, i.e. that the earth actually revolves around the sun, and moreover, it rotates on its axis, creating the "false" impression that the sun revolved around the earth. Employing the steps laid out in FACT, Copernicus engaged in Criterion 5, and using logic (Criterion 1) and evidence (Criterion 2, e.g. seeming complexities and "anomalies" in the evidence which had either been ignored or dismissed by the mainstream scientists of his day), Copernicus (1) developed an alternative theory which (2) made new predictions which were (3) subsequently confirmed with the development of the telescope (as revealed through discoveries made by Galileo).

Once we understand this historical and logical fact and honor this lesson, we can become more effective and responsible truth seekers concerning the process of our adopting and holding beliefs. FACT can be thought of as a "work in progress:" though the future may reveal that we need to add additional criteria to the framework (and give up the acronym in the process), learning and using some version of the current FACT holds the potential to improve our personal and species' ability to engage in responsible and accurate truth seeking (Bourey and Schwartz, 2016). Doing so could provide a common path to reaching accurate and responsible beliefs, and in the process foster the evolution of peace and well-being personally, institutionally, and globally.

References

Banerji, D. (2012). Seven Quartets of Becoming: A Transformative Yoga Psychology Based on the Diaries of Sri Aurobindo. D.K. Printworld.

Beitman, BD (2011). Coincidence Studies. Psychiatric Annals, 41, 561-571.

Bourey, A, Schwartz, GE (2016). Responsibility to Truth: An Enlightened Path to a Hope Filled Future. Vancouver, Canada: Param Media, in press.

Chalmers, D.J. (1996). The Conscious Mind: In Search of a Fundamental Theory. New York, NY: Oxford University Press.

Chopra, D. (2014). The Future of God: A Practical Approach to Spirituality for Our Times. New York, NY: Harmony.

Davids, P, Schwartz, G (2016). An Atheist in Heaven: Compelling Evidence for Life After Death from a Life Long Skeptic. Los Angeles, CA: Yellow Hat Press, in press.

Dossey, L (2013). One Mind: How our Individual Mind is Part of a Greater Consciousness and Why It Matter. Carlsbad, CA: Hay House.

Haisch, B. (2010). The Purpose-Guided Universe: Believing in Einstein, Darwin, and God. New York, NY: New Page Books.

Jung, C. (1972). Synchronicity—An Acausal Connecting Principle. London, United Kingdom: Routledge & Kegan Paul.

Nelson, R, Bancel, P (2011). Effects of mass consciousness: Changes in random data during global events. EXPLORE: The Journal of Science & Healing, 7(6); 373-383.

Radin, D, Michel, L, Johnston, J, Delorme, A (2013). Psychophysical interactions with a double-slit interference pattern. Physical Essays, 26(4), 553-566.

Schwartz, GE (2006). The G.O.D. Experiments: How Science is Discovering God in Everything, Including Us. New York, NY: Atria Books.

Schwartz, GE (2007). The Energy Healing Experiments: Science Reveals Our Natural Power to Heal. New York, NY: Atria Books.

Schwartz, GE (2011). The Sacred Promise: How Science is Discovering Spirit's Collaboration with Us in Our Daily Lives. Hillsboro, OR: Beyond Words.

Schwartz, GE (2014). God, synchronicity, and postmaterialist psychology: Proof-of-concept real-life evidence. Spirituality in Clinical Practice, 1, 153–162.

Schwartz, GE (2015a). God, synchronicity, and postmaterialist psychology II: Replication and extension of real-life evidence. Spirituality in Clinical Practice, 2(1), 86–95.

Schwartz, GE (2015b). God, synchronicity, and postmaterialist psychology III: Additional real-life evidence and the higher power healing hypothesis. Spirituality in Clinical Practice, 2(3).

Schwartz, GE (2016). Synchronicity and the One Mind: How the New Self-Science of Super Timing Can Transform Our Lives. Vancouver, Canada: Param Media.

Strobel, L (2004). The Case for a Creator: A Journalist Investigates Scientific Evidence That Points Toward God. Zondervan.

Dr. Gary E. Schwartz, Dr. Ernest P. Schloss, Robert Cook, MS, Alan D. Bourey, JD

Dr. Gary E Schwartz is a professor of psychology, medicine, neurology, psychiatry, and surgery at the University of Arizona and director of its Laboratory for Advances in Consciousness and Health. He is also corporate director of development of energy healing for Canyon Ranch Resorts and the author of several books, including *The Sacred Promise.* Gary is also a co-founder of the Campaign for Open Sciences, as well as a co-editor and contributor to a forthcoming Param Media anthology on Post-Materialism. Gary's next book, *Synchronicity and the One Mind: How the New Self-Science of Super Timing Can Transform Our Lives*, will be published by Param Media in 2016.

Dr. Ernest P Schloss is a retired assistant professor of public health policy and management at the University of Arizona Mel and Enid Zuckerman College of Public Health. He continues to teach undergraduate and graduate courses in strategic planning and religion, spirituality, and public health. Ernie has over 40 years of experience in health care, management, and education. He has worked in both the public and private sectors. His executive positions have included serving as the executive director of a non-profit health planning agency and the vice president of planning and marketing at an academic health center. In addition to a PhD in educational administration, Ernie holds masters degrees in Anthropology, Counseling Psychology, and Divinity, and is an ordained interfaith minister.

Robert Cook has wide-ranging community-related planning experience working in the private, public, and non-profit sectors. He is President of NEST, Inc., a non-profit community development organization operating in Tucson since 1989. Robert co-founded Sustainable Tucson in 2006, and currently serves on the Pima County Planning & Zoning Commission. He is the co-author of two books on environmental design and planning and large-scale renewable energy development (based on research conducted in collaboration with American visionary R. Buckminster Fuller.)

Alan Bourey, JD is an attorney and counselor with over 38 years of experience, primarily in litigation. Currently restricting his practice to mediation through his company, A.C.C. (Affordable, Creative and Compassionate) Mediations, he recognizes that every case is different and that many cases are only resolved by using creative solutions. Alan has been able to settle 90% of all the cases that he has mediated, and he also serves as a parenting coordinator and decision maker assisting parties who have difficulty working together for the benefit of their children, and as an arbitrator rendering decisions in place of court proceedings. He is the author of *A Common Path: The Future of Religion, Science and Spirituality*.

Dr. Gary E. Schwartz, Dr. Ernest P. Schloss, Robert Cook, MS, Alan D. Bourey, JD

Enlightening Understanding: A Twelve Dimensional System for Fostering Personal and Planetary Peace, Wellness, and Hope

TRUTH-SEEKING, UNDERSTANDING, PEACE

Peace cannot be achieved through violence,
It can only be attained through understanding.
Ralph Waldo Emerson

I do not want the peace which passeth understanding,
I want the understanding which bringeth peace.
Helen Keller

Introduction

The challenge of fostering and sustaining human understanding and peace has existed since recorded history. As Michael Shermer writes in his 2015 book *The Moral Arc: How Science and Reason Lead Humanity toward Truth, Justice, and Freedom,* the preponderance of the evidence indicates that we are living in the most moral period of our species' history. History shows us how the evolution of the scientific method and increased knowledge over the past two centuries is paralleled by a similar increase in social justice and freedom as expressed in present day democracies. Moreover, as Stephen Pinker writes in his 2011 book *The Better Angels of Our Nature: Why Violence Has Declined* violence has decreased both in the short term and longer term, and this is something to be acknowledged and celebrated.

However, the fact remains that *as a species* we have yet to collectively achieve a peaceful coexistence (1) with each other, (2) with animals and plants, and (3) the environment and planet as a whole. Quite the contrary, the history of world warfare in the twentieth century, plus the evidence of aggression and violence—physically, emotionally, and / or ideologically:

- within families
- between political groups,
- among extremist fundamentalist groups (as well as with "militant atheists"), and
- between nations and nature (i.e. the emerging climate change crisis),

is alarming and often disheartening. Moreover, what Bourey and Schwartz refer to as "truth abuse" in their forthcoming book *Responsibility to Truth* (Param Media, 2016) is rampant not only in present day politics, but in traditional and online media as well.

Bourey has written about how the process of searching for *A Common Path* (the title of his 2011 book) holds the promise of healing extremist conflicts between (and within) science and religions, and in the process, of providing a more accurate and integrative spirituality for humanity.

We must ask ourselves:

- Is it possible to develop a common path to truth seeking?
- Is it possible to derive a set of general principles for fostering the process of forming and adopting accurate and responsible beliefs, and the making of adaptive and wise decisions?
- Is it possible to discover, validate, and implement an integrative collection of universal (meta-cognitive) tools which can together provide a consensually agreed upon common path for raising questions and seeking answers to life's challenges, both great and small?
- If such a holistic integrative framework is consensually employed in situations involving strong differences of opinion and belief, will the use of this generic common path framework foster increased mutual understanding in the service of peace and well-being?

We believe the answer to these questions is yes. The purpose of this chapter is to introduce the reader to what we formally term the "**Dimensions of an Enlightening Understanding System**" (or **DEUS** for short). We illustrate how DEUS is a highly useful collection of universal conceptual tools for increasing human understanding and action.

As you will see, DEUS can expand our understanding in any area of knowledge—be it at the micro, moderate (meso), or macro levels of scale. DEUS can be applied to any field of knowledge, from physics and chemistry, through biology and psychology, to ecology and astrophysics. DEUS can be applied to personal decisions or to global situations such as issues of human rights and environmental sustainability

DEUS fosters big picture thinking and it sheds light on both the parts and the whole, thereby becoming a practical means of enlightening our way of understanding. We propose that the effective application of DEUS provides an essential conceptual tool for understanding and solving humanity's problems, both great and small, through what can be called the DEUS Hypothesis.

Twelve Dimensions of an Enlightening Understanding System

The twelve dimensions in DEUS are graphically displayed around a circle which can be used to draw individualized star graphs. This DEUS diagram reflects the current evolution of common universal tools for understanding nature and the cosmos, what Stephen Pepper originally called *World Hypotheses* (the term he proposed in his 1942 book of the same title).

Figure 1
DEUS circle displaying the Twelve Primary Dimensions

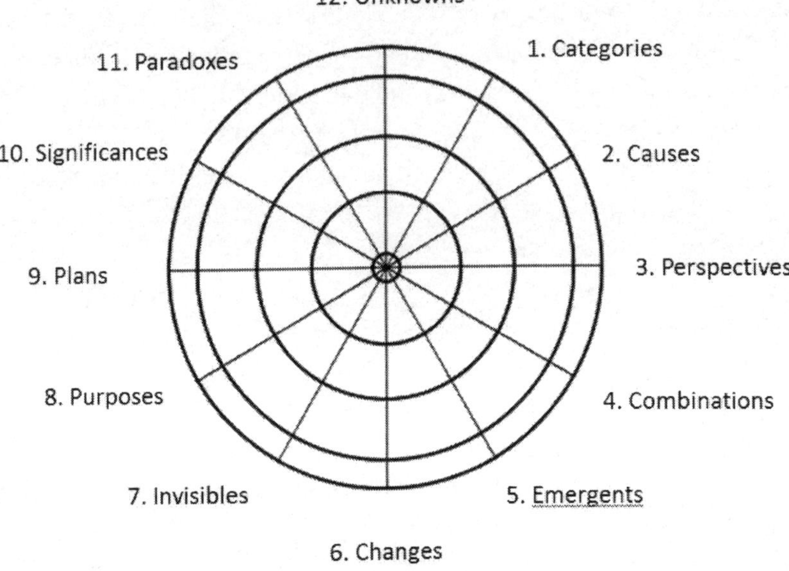

Pepper writes that there are four World Hypotheses which express universal assumptions for collecting and interpreting evidence as employed by scientists and lay persons alike. His four hypotheses are termed (1) Formism, (2) Mechanism, (3) Contextualism, and (4) Organicism. Because these are universal assumptions about nature and the Cosmos, World Hypotheses are considered to be content free and therefore are applicable to any question in any area or domain of life.

Being an academic philosopher of science, Pepper's terminology, as well as his writing style, was not readably comprehensible to most academics or the general public. What is important to know for our purposes—as well as to honor—is that Dimensions 1- 3 of DEUS in Figure 1 are derived from Pepper's World Hypotheses 1-3, and Dimensions 4 – 6 of DEUS come from Pepper's World Hypothesis 4.

In 1997 Schwartz and Russek explained how the total number of World Hypotheses could be justifiably and responsibly increased from 4 to 8, and in 2006 Schwartz and Schloss further expanded the total to

9. As of the date of this publication, we see substantial value in increasing the total to 12, recognizing that future advances in science and philosophy may justify increasing the total even further.

To make DEUS more understandable, we have labeled each of the twelve dimensions using terms most readers will understand. As you will see, the core concepts underlying each dimension are not new. *What is novel and useful is their integration into an organized system for creating a universal, common path framework for truth seeking and understanding which transcends content, education and culture.*

What is a Dimension?

A major difference between DEUS and Pepper's World Hypotheses is our addition of the concept of dimensions. Whereas Pepper viewed his World Hypotheses in terms of simple categories, we view DEUS in terms of dimensions.

What is a dimension? There are two basic meanings of dimension: (taken here from The Oxford Pocket Dictionary of Current English, 2009)

1) *An aspect or feature of a situation, problem, or thing. For example, "sun-dried tomatoes add a new dimension to this sauce."*
2) *A measurable extent of some kind, such as length, breadth, depth, or height. For example, "the final dimensions of the pond were 14ft. by 8 ft."*

Our use of the term dimension involves both of these definitions: (1) the more general, abstract concept (aspects or features), and (2) the more specific, concrete measurement (extent).

Each of the Twelve Dimensions of an Enlightening Understanding System can be thought of varying along the two continua of:

1) Levels of scale, and
2) Degrees of complexity.

First consider levels of scale—we can think of this as varying magnification all the way from a microscope (looking at the very small) to a telescope (looking at the very large and very distant). We can think of this as being a "mind-scope" or "meta-scope" of the mind. Figure 1 displays levels of scale as the length of the lines moving out from the center of the circle.

Conceptually we can adjust our mind-scope from the microscopic to the telescopic, and think about levels of scale such as:

1) Photons (e.g. ultra small "massless" particles)
2) Subatomic particles (e.g. electrons, protons)
3) Atoms (e.g. hydrogen, oxygen)
4) Molecules (e.g. water, carbon dioxide)
5) Biochemicals (e.g. DNA, RNA)
6) Cells (e.g. neurons, amoebas)
7) Organs (e.g. brains, hearts)
8) Organisms (e.g. humans, giraffes)
9) Groups (e.g. families, friends)
10) Institutions (e.g. universities, businesses)
11) Cultures (e.g. Hopi, Basque)
12) Nations (e.g. United States, China)
13) Global (e.g. climate, internet)
14) Solar System (e.g. sun, earth)
15) Galaxies (e.g. our Milky Way Galaxy, Andromeda Galaxy)
16) Super Clusters of Galaxies
17) Universe as a whole

Each DEU can be extended from the very tiny to the super large in terms of levels of size and scale.

In addition, each DEU can vary along the dimension of degrees of complexity. For example, consider organisms. Organisms vary not only in their scale (in terms of number of cells and size), but in their complexity (in terms of structure and function) as well.

For example, in terms of scale, birds have more cells and are typically larger in size than insects, and mammals often have even more cells and are typically larger than birds. In addition, in terms of complexity, the *organization* of their anatomies can vary; the organization of neurons in a bird's brain is typically more complex than in an insect's brain, and the organization of neurons in a mammal's brain is often more complex than in a bird's brain.

On the surface, DEUS may appear to be superficially simple, and yet it is actually super-complex. Our goal is on the one hand to make DEUS as simple as possible, and yet enable it to be sufficiently robust so that it can address any topic of any size, and of any complexity.

This is certainly a tall order; some might say it is a grandiose order. However, we believe this is not only an achievable task but is also essential to the survival and evolution of the life and knowledge of our species and planet.

Simply and metaphorically stated, the goal of DEUS is to shed light on any topic, and in the process, provide us with more to see. This is what we mean by "enlightening" understanding.

You can think of each dimension of DEUS as a separate source of light (a sort of spot light), enabling us to see more of what exists within a gigantic room filled with information. Each dimension explored sheds light on an aspect of knowledge. The more light we have to shine (within limits), the more we can see. Spotlights can also combine into a floodlight of experience.

At the same time, our challenge here is to not bring so much light to the room of information so that we become blinded by the intensity of the light and complexity to the point where it becomes blinding. It is valuable to remember the universality of the inverted U-shaped function, whereby—beyond some optimal limits, as with any system, our perceptions, understanding, and performance will be impaired.

Each of the twelve DEUs can be likened to one of the twelve colors on a color wheel; DEUS fosters "full spectrum envisioning."

Twelve Dimensional Understanding Envisioned through Twelve Core Questions

To develop twelve dimensional thinking, it is helpful to first learn how it is possible to pose each dimension as a question (which is revealed in detail below). It follows that with each question, more light is shed, and more information is revealed. As we examine each dimension, and review each question, you will see how the emerging picture becomes ever more expansive and illuminated. The twelve core questions are summarized in Table 1 below. The term X used in this Table refers to any domain we wish to understand.

Table 1
Core Questions Associated with Each of the Twelve Dimensions

DEUs	Descriptors	Questions about X
DEU 1	Categories	What are the essential categories for defining and describing X?
DEU 2	Causes	What are the essential causes that generate changes in X?
DEU 3	Perspectives	What are the different ways of viewing X, and why are they essential for understanding X?
DEU 4	Combinations	What combinations of DEUs 1 -3 above (and the DEUs below) are essential for fully understanding X?
DEU 5	Emergents	What novel or unique properties of X appear when these essential combinations occur, and how are they essential for understanding X?
DEU 6	Changes	What changes in X occur over time, and how are they essential for understanding X (both short term and long term)?
DEU 7	Invisibles	What factors invisible to our senses and consciousness need to be inferred in order to understand X?
DEU 8	Purposes	What functions and purposes are associated with X, and how are they essential for understanding X?

DEU 9	Plans	What creative plans and intentions are associated with X, and how are they essential for understanding X?
DEU 10	Significances	What meanings and significances are associated with X, and how are they essential for understanding X and its effects?
DEU 11	Paradoxes	What seeming paradoxes are associated with X, and how are they essential for understanding X?
DEU 12	Unknowns	What unknown (and possibly unknowable) factors are associated with X, and how are they essential for understanding X?

To encompass the full scale and complexity of DEUS, it is helpful to provide core examples of each of the dimensions. These are provided in Table 2 below.

Table 2
Core Examples Associated with Each of the Twelve Dimensions

DEUs	**Descriptors**	**Core Examples**
DEU 1	Categories	Properties, distinctions, groupings, qualities, characteristics, appearances
DEU 2	Causes	Physical, biological, psychological, social, political
DEU 3	Perspectives	Philosophical, cultural, education, allegiance-based
DEU 4	Combinations	Linear summing of categories, causes, perspectives, plus DEU's below

DEU 5	Emergents	Novel properties, surprises, interactions of combinations, nonlinear effects
DEU 6	Changes	Dynamics over time, history, development, learning, memory, evolution
DEU 7	Invisibles	Energy fields, unconscious processes (including thoughts, feelings and intentions), hidden variables, spiritual forces
DEU 8	Purposes	Functions, uses, applications, rationales, missions
DEU 9	Plans	Designs, creations, intentions, goals, motivations, strategies
DEU 10	Significances	Meanings, importance, symbols and signs, consequences
DEU 11	Paradoxes	Conflicts, inconsistences, contradictions, counter intuitive instances, seeming impossibilities
DEU 12	Unknowns	Unmodelable, unmeasurable, and unpredictable phenomena and change, unanticipated consequences, uncertainties, mysteries

With this overview in mind, we will briefly introduce each of the twelve dimensions and illustrate how collectively they shed light on one of the most complex and important challenges facing humanity and the planet today—climate change. In the process, you will see how DEUS makes it possible for us to become "Twelve Dimensional Thinkers," and thereby expand and elevate our consciousness accordingly.

In light of the history of Pepper's original concept of World Hypotheses, and in the spirit of asking universal questions, we will introduce each DEU as a hypothesis and follow it with its respective question from Table 1. To facilitate your learning these twelve dimensions, we will also cite the core examples from Table 2.

The First Dimension: Categories

DEU 1 Question: *What are the essential categories for defining and describing X?*

DEU 1 Examples: *Properties, distinctions, groupings, qualities, characteristics, appearances*

DEU 1 concerns categories. This is the most fundamental of all of the cognitive hypotheses, and most of us typically assume that DEU 1 is true. Most of us believe that categories exist in nature and that they accurately reflect how the universe works.

When Pepper proposes that there are four basic World Hypotheses, or when Schwartz et al propose that there are twelve essential DEUs, we are using DEU 1.

As explained above, all dimensions can vary in both levels of scale and degrees of complexity, and this also applies to DEU 1.

For example, depending upon our mental and visual proclivity, we can think in terms of three, seven or twelve basic colors (a relatively simple set of categories), all the way to sixteen million plus colors (the total number of discernible colors possibly displayed on a contemporary RGB monitor with 0 – 255 intensities for red, green, and blue respectively – 256 x 256 x 256 = 16,777,216).

The question then becomes, how many categories do we need to define and describe a given area? For example, consider climate change. How do we define climate? And how do we define change?

According to www.dictionary.com, climate can be defined as follows: "the composite or generally prevailing weather conditions of a region, as temperature, air pressure, humidity, precipitation, sunshine, cloudiness, and winds, throughout the year."

Notice that included in this definition is a sizable collection of DEU 1 categories:

1) Composite (combination—which in our terminology applies to DEU 4)

2) Generally prevailing weather conditions (implying average around a mean)
3) Region (a measurable quality)
4) Temperature (a measurable quality)
5) Humidity (a measurable quality)
6) Precipitation (a measurable quality)
7) Sunshine (a measurable quality)
8) Cloudiness (a measurable quality)
9) Winds (a measurable quality)

This is already a sizable list. However, is it complete?

Do we need to refine or expand this list to consider (1) prolonged storms (e.g. of rain or snow), (2) the precise frequency, severity, and location of hurricanes (which include rain and wind), (3) the precise frequency, severity, and location of tornados (which also include rain and wind), or (4) the degree of unpredictability and extremes in these patterns?

In order to fully understand climate, we would first need to create the essential list of all categories associated with term.

Now, what about change?

In the simplest sense, climate change means change in climate; however, how is change in climate to be defined? Is the criteria defined in months, years, decades, centuries, millenniums, or eras? Should we consider micro changes as well as macro changes?

Reaching consensus about these basic questions is essential for having constructive and responsible conversations about the causes and consequences of climate change. For example, if we are speaking about long term climate changes, then short term deviations (e.g. in a given season) in the "generally prevailing" conditions of climate change patterns observed over decades or centuries, should not be interpreted as evidence that there is no long term climate change.

The Second Dimension: Causes

DEU 2 Question: *What are the essential causes that generate changes in X?*

DEU 2 Examples: *Physical, biological, psychological, social, political*

DEU 2 concerns causes, and by extension, their effects. DEU 2 can vary from (1) the simplest instance of single cause / single effect, through (2) complex chains of causes, to (3) even more complex patterns of multiple causes, in parallel, having multiple effects. In principle, any single category (DEU 1) can have one or more causes, and evidence one or more effects.

To fully utilize DEU 2, we would need to rigorously apply it to each of the categories specified in DEU 1. In the case of climate change, let's consider just one of the categories, temperature.

We would need ask ourselves, what are the essential causes that increase and / or decrease climate temperature? This would result in our creating as complete a list as possible of known causes of environmental temperature. These would include:

1) Dynamics of the sun
2) Distance of the earth from the sun (which changes over the course of a year)
3) Degrees of cloud cover
4) Concentrations of different kinds of molecules in the atmosphere, including carbon monoxide, carbon dioxide, methane, ozone, etc.
5) Presence of dark surfaces (e.g. roads)
6) Presence of light surfaces (e.g. ice)

This list immediately shows us that the question of relationship between the measured increase in carbon dioxide observed in the atmosphere—especially over the twentieth and twenty-first centuries—and the observations of the apparent increase in global warming during this same time period, may only account for a portion of the total increase in global temperature.

Moreover, the measurement of increased carbon dioxide levels in the atmosphere, one of the major causes of atmospheric warming, does not in and of itself tell us what is causing the increase in atmospheric carbon dioxide in the first place. We would need to repeat the analytic process and systematically apply DEU 2 to the question: what are the essential causes that increase and / or decrease carbon dioxide in the environment?

With a topic as complex as climate change, it becomes immediately obvious using DEUs 1 and 2 that responsibly pursuing a big picture understanding of climate change will result in the creation of a very big picture indeed.

The Third Dimension: Perspectives

DEU 3 Question: *What are the different ways of viewing X, and why are they essential for understanding X?*

DEU 3 Examples: *Philosophical, cultural, education, allegiance-based*

DEU 3 concerns perspectives. This is the hypothesis that when people look at anything, they bring their world views, expectations, understandings, and outlooks to whatever it is they are observing. The phrase "it depends upon the way you look at it" expresses this property of perception and understanding, as does the concept of seeing the glass as half empty, or half full. Another example is the story of the three blind men examining different parts of an elephant, with each "seeing" only a portion of the creature and thus coming to different conclusions about the animal, which reminds us of the core message of DEU 3.

The rigorous application of DEU 3 requires that we systematically put on different conceptual hats and determine what new information or ideas can be revealed.

When we apply this to the area of climate change, we immediately come to appreciate how different people tend to see only a portion of the big picture, and tend to favor one cause over another (e.g. carbon dioxide versus methane).

DEU 3 encourages us to honor as many different perspectives as possible in order to increase the totality of our understanding of the topic in question.

The Fourth Dimension: Combinations

DEU 4 Question: *What combinations of DEUs 1 -3 above (and the DEUs below) are essential for fully understanding X?*

DEU 4 Examples: Linear summing of categories, causes, perspectives, plus DEUs below

DEU 4 focuses on linear combinations and sums. It hypothesizes that in order to understand the full extent of a given area, it is essential to add up all of the relevant factors—both positive (i.e. increasing factors) and negative (i.e. decreasing factors).

This is one of the core premises of complex conceptual models like general systems theory, including contemporary computer modeling. Along with DEU 5 (see below), these models attempt to combine factors / variables to better explain and predict patterns of effects such as the weather.

The process of combining components within and between DEUs is the complex task of DEU 4.

The Fifth Dimension: Emergents

DEU 5 Question: *What novel or unique properties of X appear when these essential combinations occur, and how are they essential for understanding X?*

DEU 5 Examples: *Novel properties, surprises, interactions of combinations, nonlinear effects*

DEU 5, the hypothesis of emergent properties, is one of the hallmarks of systems thinking. This is the idea that whole is greater than the sum of its parts. It recognizes that at every level in nature and the universe—from subatomic particles to super clusters of galaxies—novel properties emerge and express nonlinear properties. The classic example is how hydrogen and oxygen are individually gases at room temperature, but collectively they can evidence surprising properties (e.g. the ability to form snowflakes) when they join forces and become the molecule called water.

Nonlinear interactions (sometimes referred to as chaos) is well known in the modeling of weather, and is included in complex climate change models. What DEU 5 reminds us to do is to be open to the surprising interactions that can emerge when combinations of factors are present.

The Sixth Dimension: Changes

DEU 6 Question: *What changes in X occur over time, and how are they essential for understanding X (both short term and long term)?*

DEU 6 Examples: *Dynamics over time, history, development, learning, memory, evolution*

DEU 6 is the hypothesis which encourages us to look for evidence of change in the structure and functioning of a given topic or area. Whether the changes are rapid and variable, reflect learning, are developmental in nature, or extend over long time frames (e.g. are historical or evolutionary), they are all important to consider.

DEU 6 inspires us to ask whether there are any historical, evolutionary, or developmental changes occurring in the emergence of climate change which may be important to understanding its nature and consequences. Are there emergent properties (DEU 5) affecting rate of change over time (DEU 6)?

The Seventh Dimension: Invisibles

DEU 7 Question: *What factors invisible to our senses and consciousness need to be inferred in order to understand X?*

DEU 7 Examples: *Energy fields, unconscious processes (including thoughts, feelings and intentions), hidden variables, spiritual forces*

DEU 7 is the hypothesis which postulates that in order to understand nature and the cosmos, it essential to infer the existence of things (matter, energy and information) which are normally invisible to our senses and consciousness. This includes raising questions about the potential role of invisible fields and other unconscious processes in the functioning of a given process.

Whereas most of the descriptors of climate (DEU 1) can be known to our physical senses (e.g. cloudiness, rain, winds), the causes of these changes are often invisible to our senses (e.g. the concentration of carbon dioxide in the atmosphere). The rigorous application of DEU 7 encourages us to ask questions about potential invisible processes in areas such as climate change and our acceptance (or denial) of it. The role of the unconscious processes of bias, for example, is especially important at the human scale and is a critical factor in how humans understand (or misunderstand) climate change and the human role in causing it.

The Eighth Dimension: Purposes

DEU 8 Question: *What functions and purposes are associated with X, and how are they essential for understanding X?*

DEU 8 *Examples: Functions, uses, applications, rationales, missions*

DEU 8 and the higher DEUs become ever more novel and challenging for us to consider. DEU 8 hypnotizes that in order to understand nature and the cosmos, it is necessary to consider potential functions and purposes associated with the areas or topics under investigation.

The eighth dimension applies not only to purpose at the human level, but in principle applies to all systems at all levels. For example, it raises the challenging question: does the emergence of climate change have any functions or purpose at the species level, and even potentially at the global level? Is there an invisible "wisdom in climate change," possibly expressing the planet's effort to self-regulate for the purpose of reducing human population with its associated polluting and depletion of the earth's resources? DEU 8 inspires the raising of such deep questions.

The Ninth Dimension: Plans

DEU 9 Question: *What creative plans and intentions are associated with X, and how are they essential for understanding X?*

DEU 9 Examples: *Designs, creations, intentions, goals, motivations, strategies*

DEU 9 raises even deeper questions. It hypothesizes that in order to understand nature and the cosmos, it is necessary to consider the potential roles of intention and intelligence in their creation, evolution, and sustainability.

At the human level, the importance of our raising questions about intention and intelligent planning is self-evident. Considering climate change, for example, the pressing need to consider how we as a species intend to understand its causes and consequences, and how we plan to adjust to its effects (as well as potentially reverse them) is becoming increasingly recognized.

However, at environmental and global levels, it is rare for us to entertain potential hypotheses such as the possibility that the earth system has been "designed" to actively counter life threatening imbalances in populations of species through self-regulatory feedback mechanisms at a planetary scale, and that these intelligent mechanisms might involve alterations in climate patterns. DEU 9 encourages the asking of such profound questions.

The Tenth Dimension: Significances

DEU 10 Question: *What meanings and significances are associated with X, and how are they essential for understanding X and its effects?*

DEU 10 Examples: *Meanings, importance, symbols and signs, consequences*

DEU 10 hypotheses that in order to understand nature and the universe, it is essential to consider potential meanings and significances expressed in their existence and dynamics.

Humans are a highly meaning and symbol focused species. The meaning and significance we place on climate change, for example, can have profound effects not only on how we understand climate change, but also how we respond to it. Exploring the meaning and significance of climate change holds the promise of inspiring the public to better comprehend and address this challenge. For example, can climate change take on the significance of bringing the human species together toward the common goals of survival and well-being?

It is valuable to point out that DEUs 7-10 inspire the raising of questions which are spiritual and meta-physical in nature. For example, Schwartz's research documenting complex chains of synchronicities in daily life (Schwartz, 2014; 2015 a-b; 2016) requires the hypothesis of the presence of some sort of higher or universal intelligence and energy playing an invisible orchestrating role in nature and the cosmos.

The Eleventh Dimension: Paradoxes

DEU 11 Question: *What seeming paradoxes are associated with X, and how are they essential for understanding X?*

DEU 11 Examples: *Conflicts, inconsistences, contradictions, counter Intuitive instances, seeming impossibilities*

DEU 11 hypothesizes that in order to understand nature and the universe, it is sometimes essential to consider how seeming paradoxes (at a given level) may nonetheless be valid observations and need to be accepted as true.

Sometimes paradoxes cannot be resolved by (1) simpler explanations, or (2) more complex explanations. One of the best examples of DEU 11 in contemporary science involves paradoxical phenomena in quantum physics. For example, as revealed in the double-slit experiment, light can (1) under some conditions (e.g. a single slit) be described as being a particle, localized in space, and (2) in other conditions (e.g. a double slit appropriately positioned), have statistical properties best described as if it were a wave, distributed in space. This repeatedly documented paradox has not been resolved by the math involved; it has merely been described by it.

Learning how to accept inherent paradoxes reduces the inclination to reject evidence and knowledge if it does not fit a given theory (or even world view). When people learn to raise and ponder DEU 11 questions, they become more tolerant of seeming conflicts and contradictions. In the process, they become freed to see the bigger picture as it really is.

The Twelfth Dimension: Unknowns

DEU 12 Question: *What unknown (and possibly unknowable) factors are associated with X, and how are they essential for understanding X?*

DEU 12 Examples: *Unmodelable, unmeasurable, and unpredictable phenomena and change, unanticipated consequences, uncertainties, mysteries*

DEU 12 may be the most difficult hypothesis for people to understand and accept. This hypothesis proposes that in order to understand nature and the cosmos, it is sometimes necessary to accept not only that (1) certain information is unknown, but that (2) it may be unknowable, and can only be inferred indirectly.

DEU 12 is more than just a recognition of the holes in our current knowledge of a given topic or area. It actively seeks to comprehend the missing aspects in our current knowledge which may be inherently "inconceivable" except in a vague or metaphorical way.

Examples of such unknowns are abundant in mathematics. The concept of "infinity" is wholly abstract; though infinity can be expressed with an abstract symbol, and it is possible to create a mathematical strategy for manipulating the infinity symbol, this does not mean that we really know what these infinities are. It is difficult enough to imagine how big a single infinity is; it is conceptually impossible to visualize what infinity plus infinity is, or even more abstractly, what infinity times infinity is.

In string theory, physicists speak about structures comprised of ten or eleven dimensions. Conceptually we are spatially limited to experiencing only four or five dimensions. Similarly and metaphorically speaking, we are suggesting that to fully implement DEUS understanding, it is essential to integrate all twelve dimensions of questions and information in terms of twelve dimensional thinking.

Schwartz and Schloss (2006) originally called this hypothesis the 9th World Hypothesis (as mentioned above, there were 8 specified World Hypotheses at that time). However, they pointed out that no matter how many future World Hypotheses might be specified in the future, the last hypothesis would always be the "Unknown" hypothesis, and hence it could be termed the "n^{th}" hypothesis.

DEU 12 fosters open mindedness as well as humility. It mindfully leaves spaces in the emerging big picture puzzle for information that is currently not known, and may never be known precisely. Specifying what the holes are in our knowledge are about a given topic or domain such as climate change reminds all of us about what we can and cannot conclude at any given moment. We cannot see the whole without seeing the holes. In fact, inside the word whole is the word hole.

We should note that DEU 12 is implicit in DEU 5 (Emergents) since they are both concerned with nonlinear effects which often are not known until manifested under the right conditions.

From Twelve Dimensional Understanding to Peace, Wellness and Hope—The DEUS Hypothesis

To the best of our understanding, the current list of twelve DEUs captures the core conceptual hypotheses people use to explain nature and the cosmos. Most of us employ combinations of these DEUs, but we do so mindlessly in the sense that we use them (1) implicitly, (2) unconsciously, (3) spontaneously, and (4) automatically.

To the best of our knowledge, we are not aware of anyone who mindfully employs all twelve DEUs (1) explicitly, (2) consciously, (3) systematically, and (4) intentionally. The reason for this is straight forward. Most of us have not been formally educated to see the big picture which provides a comprehensive understanding of human understanding. Moreover, prior to the writing of this chapter, none of its authors had been educated to see a comprehensive and integrative system of twelve dimensions of an enlightening understanding system.

However, we believe that just as humans have invented (or in another sense, discovered) mathematics and the philosophy of logic and science, two beacons of universal understanding, humans also have the capacity to develop integrative "meta" systems for enhancing universal understanding. DEUS is one such attempt.

Can you imagine a world where people are educated to adopt a common set of truth seeking conceptual tools which transcend specific world views, cultures, and religions (or anti-religions)?

Can you imagine a world where people understand that these core meta-conceptual tools are the very means by which they learned, and adopted, their historical world views, cultures, and religions (or anti-religions)?

Can you imagine a world where we elect public officials who are formally trained in DEUS-like thinking, and all employ the identical set of meta-tools for addressing challenges and conflict?

If people voluntarily adopt a common path meta-strategy for seeking understanding, will this help us resolve our most pressing human problems? Our prediction is yes.

This is the basis of what we call the DEUS Hypothesis. It is essential to remember that DEUS's twelve dimensional tools of understanding are intended to be generic / universal; they are free of subject matter and cultural biases. As far as we can tell, they represent a family of common "meta-friends" for all truth seeking human beings regardless of sex, race, religion, culture, or world view.

We might say that they are "meta-beacons" of mind.

References

Bourey, A (2011). A Common Path: The Future of Religion, Science and Spirituality. Boulder, CO: A Common Path.

Bourey, A, Schwartz, GE (2015). *Responsibility to Truth: An Enlightened Path to a Hope Filled Future.* Vancouver, Canada: Param Media, in press.

Pepper, S (1942). *World Hypotheses: A Study in Evidence.* Berkeley, CA: University of California Press.

Pinker, S (2011). The Better Angels of Our Nature: Why Violence has Declined. New York, NY: Penguin Books.

Schwartz, GE, Russek, LG (1997). The challenge of one medicine: Theories of health and "eight world hypotheses." *Advances*, 3(13), 7-23.

Schwartz, GE, Schloss, EP (2006). World hypotheses and the evolution of integrative medicine: Combining categorical diagnoses and cause-effect interventions with whole systems research and nonvisualizable (seemingly "impossible") healing. *Explore: The Journal of Science and* Healing, 2, 509–514.

Schwartz, GE (2014). God, synchronicity, and postmaterialist psychology: Proof-of-concept real-life evidence. *Spirituality in Clinical Practice, 1,* 153–162.

Schwartz, GE (2015a). God, synchronicity, and postmaterialist psychology II: Replication and extension of real-life evidence. *Spirituality in Clinical Practice, 2,* 86–95.

Schwartz, GE (2015b). God, synchronicity, and postmaterialist psychology III: Additional real-life evidence and the higher power healing hypothesis. *Spirituality in Clinical Practice,* in press.

Schwartz, GE (2016). Synchronicity and the One Mind: How the New Self-Science of Super Timing Can Transform Our Lives. Vancouver, Canada: Param Media.

Shermer, M (2015). The Moral Arc: How Science and Reason lead Toward Truth, Justice and Freedom. New York, NY: Henry Holt and Co.

Bhava Ram

Bhava Ram is the author of the highly acclaimed memoir on the healing powers of Yoga: *Warrior Pose, How Yoga Literally Saved My Life.* A former NBC network news war correspondent, Bhava self-healed from stage four cancer and a broken back through Yoga. He now devotes his life to sharing the miracle of self-healing with others, believing fully that we all have the inherent power to take charge of our destiny, heal ourselves, and effect lasting personal transformation in our lives.

Interview

TRANSFORMATION, YOGA, REALITY VS ILLUSION

Param Media: How would you define intuition? And reason?

Bhava Ram: We dismiss intuition as being variable and not necessarily based in fact, when in truth, to me, it is the wisdom of the whisper of our soul, of a deeper knowing that we all have inside of us. Just as in every acorn there is a mighty oak tree, we hold within each and every one of us all the intelligence of humankind throughout the ages. It's encoded inside of us, and the more we become present and aware of our inner being, the more that inner wisdom arises. When we're just experiencing little glimpses of it, it might be referred to as intuition, gut feelings, or "aha" moments. But ultimately, it's the wisdom that we were born with, and to which the practice of yoga guides us.

Reason, such as inductive and deductive reasoning, is, of course, a more rational process. It's a beautiful process, and a great exercise for the mind; it can bring us to a high degree of intelligence, but it has its inherent limitations, because oftentimes we can't impose reason on circumstances that are really, truly far beyond our grasp in their depth and complexity. Ultimately, blending intuition and reason together—having a grounded cognitive reason to rely on, while also listening to our deeper intelligence, and blending the two of them—I think is a powerful pathway.

PM: You gave a very moving presentation for TEDx, in which you described a life-changing moment where you made a shift from illness to a state of beginning a journey to wellness and wholeness. Was this shift of an intellectual nature, or was it based in emotion? Would you describe it as a spiritual awakening, or somehow a combination of all these things?

BR: It was absolutely a spiritual awakening. When my son implored me to live as I lay there dying, deeply crippled and in pain, it cracked something open in me that, before that moment, I didn't really know I had within me. I had only had glimpses of it throughout my life. After that moment, I began to hear an inner voice, despite being a jaded and cynical war correspondent who thought he had seen all of the evil side of humankind around the world and wasn't one prone to trusting. And yet, I trusted that voice. It was that inner voice that guided me to change my life, and is truly the reason why I'm alive today.

PM: How were you able to come to terms with that shift, in terms of your more everyday conscious or reasoning faculties? How did you integrate that awakening into the rest of your life once the shift occurred?

BR: I would characterize it more as coming to terms with the ego. We in the West are a very ego-based, individualistic culture, unlike many Eastern cultures that, I think, have a greater understanding of the oneness of the world. Here in our Western culture, it's truly all about us: what's in it for us, our individual likes and dislikes, and so forth. We always struggle with that when we are faced with something new, because the ego-mind does not like change, and it will find reasons to torpedo something that the deeper parts of ourselves might otherwise want to embrace. I have done this all too often. Yet for me, the quality that impressed me most about my awakening was the sudden discovery of a realm of spiritual wisdom that always had been there, despite my eyes somehow being closed to it, to which my inner vision was now opened. It was utterly bedazzling. And yet, one still needs to apply reason and logic to that spiritual process; it's essential. This is truly the essence of the deeper practices of yoga, because yoga is a spiritual science.

In the New Age movement, for instance, many people think, "If I just love everybody, if I just draw a picture of what I desire and put it on my vision board, it will come true!" The deeper science of yoga teaches us that it also takes dedication and consistency, because your thoughts do create your actions and form your habits, which ultimately give you your character, and that, in part, determines your destiny. And so, by changing your thoughts, you change your actions. Action is the key; that's the rational part of it. Yoga is based on something called *tapas*—self-discipline—and on *sadhana*—daily practice. Along with the spiritual awakening has to come a very pragmatic attitude, because you've now seen the top of the mountain, but you still have to climb it.

For me, it still is not easy. I have fallen down the mountainside many times.

PM: How can we show that true spiritual awakening does require this aspect of action, which has to be integrated with rationality? Conversely, how can we avoid being engrossed in the importance of the brain, or "stuck in our heads," so to speak?

BR: That kind of attitude, being "stuck in our heads," is a bit like fundamentalism. One aspect of the ego is that, when I am engrossed in my individuated ego, I have to be right; if you don't agree with me, then you must be wrong. From this frame of mind, we can muster a lot of facts, and we can cherry-pick those facts that support the reason why we're right and everyone else is wrong. We see this in religious systems all the time, as well as in politics, in nationalism, and in spirituality.

I'm not here to try to convince anyone to see things my way; I'm here to devote myself to teaching others that which has transformed my life. Through the Deep Yoga School of Healing Arts that my wife Laura and I founded, we have seen thousands of people undergo transformation. This is not because we are gurus—because I believe that *the guru is you*, and that the power is inside of you. We are here to help people unlock their own inner power through the deeper mind-body-spirit sciences of Vedic wisdom, from which yoga and Ayurveda arise. If someone is finding some kind of genuine sustenance in the New Age movement, then God bless them. If someone is finding what they need in Hinduism, Islam, Judaism, Christianity, Buddhism, or atheism, then God or the gods bless them; Buddha bless them; the void bless them. I am not seeking any primacy for what I believe and what I teach.

PM: Do you have any advice for those who are looking to make a conscious shift into a more spiritual way of life, or who are looking to integrate their intuitive and reasoning parts? Can any sort of advice or instructions be given to help facilitate that shift, or does that kind of transformation have to come solely from within each person?

BR: We all need guidance, and these ancient, time-tested spiritual sciences are so profound partially because they have lasted so long throughout our history. They have been carried forth by humankind for millennia—they are certainly not faddish or trendy. However, over the course of time, some teachings have become over-codified and overly structured, and one has to be mindful of that. I would say that anyone who is coming to spiritual awareness is inherently suffering; we all experience a certain level of suffering in our lives. The first thing to consider is that this suffering presents such an opportunity for positive change, in that all of our obstacles are truly opportunities. The second thing to consider is that no matter what, you have the power inside of you to heal to your maximum potential, and ultimately to transform your life. Whatever path you choose up the mountain, the fact remains that you must choose one; you can't simply keep stepping onto different paths, or you will just keep getting lost and you'll never make the ascent. Another way to think of it is that you can dig a lot of shallow wells without ever quenching your thirst, but if you dig a single deep well, clearing away all of the rocks and other blockages, then ultimately you will find water and you will be nourished.

PM: Your analogy of climbing a mountain is a good reminder that we're all on the journey together; perhaps we could say that different people are at various stages of the climb, yet it's a similar journey for everyone. A powerful part of that analogy is the fact that there *is* actually a mountain in reality, and you *do* have to climb it at some point; you can't walk down the mountain because it's easier and then pretend that you made the ascent. Our actions do have objective consequences.

It can seem that we are living in a rather relativistic society, where many people think that they can change the meaning of a concept simply by redefining the terminology. Could you expand upon the role of objectivity in our society today?

BR: Let me do my best to answer that question through Vedic wisdom, which was codified in the Yoga Sutras of Patanjali some twenty-five hundred years ago (but which predates even that time, because you find elements of these precepts in the Bhagavad Gita, the Upanishads, and the Vedas). Patanjali talks about the *kleshas*, the five reasons why we suffer, the first of which is called *avidya*, which means "we have forgotten." We have forgotten—or never were aware in the first place—the fact that we, and all of life, are interwoven. It truly is a *uni*verse, not a *multi*verse; it's a single song of life. When we're in that state, the second *klesha*, called *asmita*, takes hold, which is when we become overly self-identified or individuated. This leads to the next two *kleshas*, which are called *raga* and *dvesha*, meaning "attraction" and "aversion," respectively.

When I forget that you and I are the same, that we hold the same light of spirit within us and that we are in this together, then it becomes all about me, doesn't it? Suddenly I'm immersed in my own movie that replaces what reality truly is. And guess who the star of my movie is? It's not you—it's me, and I'm the director, the cinematographer, and the film editor. I'm stuck in my likes and my dislikes, in *raga* and *dvesha*. I want everyone to really like me and respect me, to admire me and treat me well. I don't want to be stuck in a traffic jam or in line at the bank, and if I do find myself in a traffic jam, then it's every other person's fault for being there… except mine! Many of us go through our entire lives like this, and that causes the final *klesha—abhinivesha—* which is the fear of death of the ego, of losing control… and this is the very definition of stress.

In our modern world, we are over-inundated with mass media to the point where our minds are controlled by it. Almost everything on television, radio, and on other media platforms—unless you are very conscious about your choices of media consumption—is causing these *kleshas* to arise in us; it's disturbing us and giving us a false image of reality, one where each one of us is the central star of our own reality-movie. This form of media plays to the fact that we often get affected by our likes and dislikes, which causes us to feel stress; in an attempt to alleviate that stress we go shopping, or we drink too much, or we take pharmaceutical medications, and subsequently fall prey to a whole host of products peddled by various multi-billion dollar industries. All of this arises from the illusion that there is more than one reality. If I consider my own personal movie to be the truth, with me in the starring role, then that requires there to be seven billion alternate universes for every single ego-soul out there in the world.

Understanding that there is one unified reality allows us to see that the totality is bigger than each of us, that we are all threads woven into this multicolored, magical tapestry of ongoing and expanding life. In this context, from a rational and pragmatic perspective, this does not imply that we should simply give in to the divine and say, "Whatever, I'm not the star of the movie." We must learn to truly act skillfully toward manifesting our deepest, most authentic aspirations, while letting go of the need to always control the outcome. The outcome can be placed in the hands of a reality over which we ultimately do not have control. The essence of yoga in this respect is called *abhyasa* and *vairagya*, which means to practice every day with deep devotion, and to always be detached as to the outcome. Just sing your song, and don't worry whether or not it becomes a top forty hit. Keep singing, and you will find rhythm and harmony, and beautiful things will happen.

PM: It's so refreshing to witness such passion for the pursuit of foundational reality, because unfortunately there are major factions within the scientific and academic community that have been misinterpreting quantum physics. The multiverse interpretation of reality, where it is argued that we are all authors of our own reality, obviously suffers from serious rational shortcomings.

BR: We are all authors of our own illusion.

PM: Perhaps it's partly a question of convenience; society as a whole seems to not want to challenge itself, and we seem to have a certain resistance to learning who we really are, and what reality truly is.

BR: At one point in our not so distant history, people were executed for saying that the earth was round and that it circled around the sun. And when ultimately it was discovered that this was, in fact, the case, those who had previously denied the truth were quick to say, "Look what we've discovered!" Only then did it become officially recognized as truth. There have been so many modern scientific discoveries that were known through Vedic wisdom for thousands of years. All of this talk about the matrix and about quantum physics, all of that is encoded in the ancient Vedas, in Samkhya philosophy. They knew the distance from the earth to the sun and the moon, the interplay of the planets, how human consciousness was woven together, and how your thoughts can create neurochemicals in your body that either support you or harm you, all of which is now starting to become a part of more mainstream mind-body medicine (although there is still tremendous resistance). They knew all that before the Western world knew it.

PM: Why do you think these teachings are becoming more a part of the accepted mainstream now?

BR: I think, in great part, it's because of the surge in the popularity of yoga. And when I say yoga, I don't just mean people doing warrior pose in the spa or at the gym, although that's fantastic. In fact, doing warrior pose with your arms up in the air has finally been shown by modern science to create more testosterone in your body. If, instead, you have a more withdrawn posture, it creates more cortisol and adrenaline in your body. Simply by taking a posture of expansiveness, you start to change your inner chemistry and, ultimately, you change your destiny; you will start to perceive yourself in a more positive way, and so will those around you.

The science of yoga has now infused Western culture, and more and more of my clients or students in our Mastery of Life training program are doctors, physicists, psychologists, psychiatrists, oncologists, and lawyers. These are generally very intelligent, professional people, who are realizing that this science is transformative, and it is changing their lives. So many highly accomplished people are now bringing these teachings to the greater public, like doctors Dean Ornish, Deepak Chopra, David Frawley, and so many others far, far wiser than I. Of course, it is going to meet with great resistance—as deep change always does—but we are reaching a tipping point where suddenly everybody is saying, "Oh, I thought of that first."

PM: It's incredible to see yoga and Ayurveda becoming such a part of the mainstream. In what ways could these ancient traditions be further developed to help us progress in the modern world?

BR: I do my best to bring this profound body-mind-spirit science forward in a way that is relevant to a Western experience, rather than keeping it overly esoteric. In this process, I do not use imagery involving the archetypes, the deities, the language, and the mantras of yoga. I do my best to present the science in an applicable and relevant way without the elements that some might find too far out for them at this time in their lives.

The science of yoga and Ayurveda is so utterly practical, you know. Boiling it down, if you eat pure, natural food from Mother Nature, you will be healthier than if you eat nothing but junk; that's pretty simple. If you think positive thoughts and choose love and the answer "yes" more than negative thoughts and the answer "no," your inner chemistry will be different and you will be likely to have a better life. If you do yoga *asanas* every day based upon your personal capabilities and physical limitations (such as any injuries you may be experiencing, or limitations due to your age), you will be more detoxified, stronger, more flexible, more balanced, and you will ultimately live a healthier life. These are pretty pragmatic, simple things.

If you repeat something every day, the whole world will rise up to support you in that pursuit—although you still have to climb the mountain. If every day you say to yourself, "I don't like people and they don't like me," the whole world will give you back that energy every day, guaranteed. If instead you say, "I really do have the capacity to live the life that I really aspire to, and at the deepest part of my being I affirm this intention," the universe is going to rise up and support that idea. Those are two completely different journeys, and it's up to each one of us to decide which one we want to undertake.

PM: Many people seem to operate under the misconception that these ancient practices and teachings can't fit into their lives, but when it's presented so simply, it's hard to deny the fact that you can actually implement them in certain ways and undergo a transformative shift.

How can the practices of yoga and Ayurveda help people to find their "authentic self?" And what is the "authentic self?"

BR: The Yoga Sutras of Patanjali start in Sanskrit with "*Yoga Chitta Vritti Nirodhah Tada Drastuh Svarupe Vasthanam.*" Yoga is the practice of the journey from a distracted, over-stimulated, ego-based, externalized mind down to the deeper self that is one with all that is—to our inner guru, to the soul. These practices bring us more into the present moment. Part of yoga, too, is called *pratyahara*, which is withdrawal of the senses. When we finally awaken to this, we realize that all the television we're watching, all the hate-talk we listen to on the radio, and the overstimulation from the media at large is really destroying our minds. We can't even hold a single thought for thirty seconds. When we learn to still our minds, that's when we begin, through a contemplative, meditative experience, to hear the whisper of our inner wisdom with greater clarity. Ultimately, the whisper becomes a voice, and then we can have dialogue with that intelligence that has always been inside of us. That intelligence is our authentic self.

PM: Would you say that an interplay between reason and intuition is part of finding your authentic self?

BR: One can delude oneself greatly through the rational mind, or through reason. Again, I've done it far too often in my own life. Likewise, one can delude oneself greatly through embracing spirituality without truly understanding it. All of our faculties need to come together if we want to achieve true understanding. These ideas, again, are thousands of years old; *manas* (the externalized mind) and *buddhi* (the inner, deeper knowing) all bring us toward *atman* (the soul). It is a process of slowing down, being present, closing our eyes and looking within, realizing the miracle of our breath and our bodies, and how Mother Earth is in every cell of our being. Fully coming into the present moment, stilling our minds, and remembering, again, the *vidya*— the wisdom—that we are all truly connected and that we are all filled with possibility and potential. The more that we do that, the more those little "aha!" moments and epiphanies will begin to transform into a constant sense of knowing how we will choose to live our lives.

PM: In the more mainstream realm of yoga (and in New Age movements in general), you rarely hear people address anger, fear, and other similar emotions, which are so common to the human experience. If anger or fear do come up, it's usually only to admonish us not to let fear or anger hold us back. Do you think that anger and fear, as natural human emotions, can be used to help us transform in a positive manner, or assist us in our journey up the mountain?

BR: We can call anger or fear the fight or flight response, which is a tremendous mechanism to have when our lives are threatened and we need to vanquish or escape that threat to our life. This is part of our primal structure, and all animals and plants have this instinct. When that impulse arises in us, adrenaline and cortisol become positive neuropeptides that course through our veins, drawing energy from our immune and digestive systems and causing a great deal of blood to flow to our limbs so that we can fight or flee. This is a very positive reaction to have if we are facing a serious threat or challenge, or have a great task to accomplish, because in those moments we need that adrenaline and cortisol to totally wake us up and bring us fully present into the moment. Unfortunately, we live in a culture that stimulates perpetual fight or flight; mass media knowingly stimulates this response in us on a constant basis, so that we are stressed out and become consumers purchasing things in hopes that they will alleviate our angst, which they never do. As a result, we are no longer masters of our own destiny, but rather we become tools of a corporate destiny.

There is far too much anger and fear being incited by our media, and it is unnecessary. It has been tailored to us, although many are not even aware of the instinct that it creates within them; they might just think it's their normal state. If the fight or flight instinct serves as a catalyst for something very important, then it's a positive thing, but if it's with you all the time, then it becomes poison, and we have to be able to differentiate between those two things.

When I was healing myself from stage-four cancer, a broken back, and failed back surgery, after I had gone through the detoxification I was a little bit delirious, having emerged out of that process after fourteen years of extremely heavy medication. After all that, I was still left facing a marriage that was clearly falling apart, and a number of social, emotional, and financial challenges surrounding that. Sometimes, when it was three in the morning and I wanted to get up to do my practice, there was a side of me that said, "Oh, just forget about it. Just pull the covers up and snuggle in and sleep." I'd actually get a little angry sometimes, and say, "You know, there are some people who want me to fail. And I'm not going to." I'd use that as a catalyst to empower myself. So anger and fear are not always negative things. They can help…

but only in small doses, and they are no match whatsoever for the power of love!

Laura Plumb

Laura Plumb is trained in Classical Yoga, Ayurveda, Vedic Nutrition, Herbology, and Jyotish. Her mastery of Ayurvedic Medicine and the Vedic Sciences are showcased on her highly acclaimed blog, Food-A Love Story. She combines this deep knowledge with a devotion to nature's own wisdom, offering seasonal cleanses and detoxification programs, online programs and workshops, and consultation in Ayurvedic Medicine for university medical schools and corporate clients.

Interview

WELLNESS, AYURVEDA, ANCIENT WISDOM

Param Media: How would you define reason, and how would you define intuition?

Laura Plumb: Generally we might look at right-brain thinking versus left-brain thinking and call them reason versus feeling, or being more mathematically-minded versus being more creatively-minded. To me, intuition is where they unite. Reason and intuition are not opposites; they're not black and white. Intuition is when you bring it all together, when you're operating from your whole mind. We can feel something—which is its own way of perceiving—so we can ask ourselves whether we are perceiving more from the right-brain or the left-brain, or whether we are perceiving from all of our faculties as a whole.

I do use the word intuition in my work, but I often stop and ask myself, "What does that really mean?" For instance, if I'm offering a cleanse, I want to be able to say to my clients, "Here's a chart that shows in a rational and precise ways the steps I want you to follow for this cleanse." But then I want to say, "Follow your intuition." Following your intuition does not mean simply doing things on a whim. Rather, through Yoga and Ayurveda, intuition can be applied to help people connect to what is right for them and listen to what their body is telling them. When I tell my clients to choose intuitively, what I mean is that they should pay attention with their whole self, their whole mind—especially their innate and inherent intelligence—and bring their awareness to what is happening in their body. Then they are able to feed their body according to what its needs are. That's what we mean when we say something is "holistic."

Intuition is extremely valuable. It means that we take everything we've learned from our studies, from our life, from paying attention, and we fully integrate it; we become so present, so awake, so clear-minded and clear-hearted that we are able to spontaneously respond to the needs of any moment as they arise.

In Ayurveda and Yoga, it is understood that there are four aspects to the mind: *ahamkara*, the sense of "I-ness," that part of us which understands us to be unique and distinct from others. There is *citta*, which is the storehouse of memories, wounds, and even family patterns and what is often causally called *karma*. *Citta* relates to the subconscious mind.

Thirdly, there is *manas*, the outer mind, which perceives the world around us. *Manas* mediates the outer and the inner experience, and our awareness of our relationship to nature, the things and people who surround us. Through *manas* we perceive and process sensory perception, and so *manas* gives what we call the mental or emotional response to that life and what happens. That is where most people live day to day.

The inner mind, which we refer to as the reasoning mind, is called the *budhi*. That's where Buddha got his name. That inner, reasoning mind requires concentration and focus, and it is the gateway to the inner self, to the interior mind, which gives wisdom and stillness.

In Yoga and Ayurveda psychology, we are seeking to move from the often volatile outer mind to the quieter, more refined inner mind. The inner mind takes you to the deeper mind, which is peaceful, creative, spontaneous intelligence. The outer mind is the emotional, the inner mind is the reasoning, and the interior mind or the inner self is intuition, the intuitive being.

The inner mind rests on all of the reasoning we've already done in terms of our studies, our experience of thinking through problems, all of our sensory input, and all of our direct experiences of life. It is an integration of all four aspects of mind, but with the *citta* having been transformed from weight and wounds to a very beautifully bearable lightness of being. When all of this comes together—your knowledge, your life wisdom, your inner freedom and clarity, and your sense of belonging to the world and the cosmos—then you have a powerful, sure knowing, a connection to intelligence, to the intelligence before, between, and beyond all things. That, to me, *is* intuition.

PM: Could we say that if you genuinely tap into intuition, it almost transcends the reasoning capacity? That intuition is compatible with reasoning, yet it somehow transcends it to a level higher of functioning?

LP: Intuition transcends reasoning, but it also subsumes it. We want to be careful not to imply that we don't need reasoning; we need both reasoning *and* intuition. We need the outer mind to tell us if there's a fire endangering our safety or a stoplight we need to pay attention to, or to let us know that somebody has just stepped on our foot. We need to be able to know these things are happening, and we need to be able to respond. Our emotions can provide useful information about our outer world, too, about whether or not we are safe.

The inner, reasoning mind—which is deeper, and requires more thinking and processing—has to be strengthened like a muscle. We have to have a strong mind muscle to be able to concentrate on problem solving, on making a clock, or making a book, or starting a company. These kinds of tasks are undertaken by the reasoning mind, but then there's a place where it all comes together, and either in a flash or in a moment of depth, all of a sudden it feels whole and complete. In that moment, everything comes together as one. It's like your outer mind (your outer experience, your outer processing) and your inner mind (your deep thinking that combines everything you've learned) unify, and then something inside of you says, "This is my own personal expression of that unity." It's a journey inward.

PM: How can Ayurveda help us on this journey?

LP: Ayurveda is the oldest and most comprehensive form of natural medicine on earth. It's called the Mother of all Medicines, and the Mother of all Healing Systems, for two reasons. The first reason is that Ayurveda is a profoundly comprehensive system. The second reason is that it is a very inclusive system. As Ayurveda grew through time, if it came across something that worked—like the fact that blue is a color that soothes somebody who's enraged, or that a certain herb tends to ease inflammation—it integrated that knowledge. It is able to integrate all this because it's based on a very simple understanding of nature, namely that all of nature—everything in the material world, everything that is alive—is made up of the five elements: space, air, fire, water, and earth. And if you understand those elements and their dynamic properties within you, you will understand yourself; you will understand your place in the world, you will understand how the world is impacting you, even how the weather is affecting you. You will understand when you're out of balance and what to do to bring yourself back into balance.

Ayurveda is a system of medicine that has a different approach for each individual. In Ayurveda, we don't treat a disease; we treat a human being. Ten people can come to you with diabetes, and there isn't one single treatment for diabetes. There will be a treatment for person one, and person two, etc., and each treatment might look radically different from the others. How can we have a system of medicine that has seven billion different pathways to health and wellness? Because it's based on a very simple principle; it's really about understanding nature in the individual and taking into consideration all aspects of their lives, from age, occupation, gender, physiology, psychology, discipline, fears, angers, resistance, and determination.

The energy of nature is in constant motion; it's constantly changing. Ayurveda is really about learning to align with that movement of energy. And how do we align ourselves with that movement, when there's no pause button on nature? There's no pause button on the cycling of seasons; we can't just say, as we're moving into autumn, "Stop! I didn't finish with summer—I need to cool down before I move into this season!" The best way to have peace and balance, to achieve health and wellness, is to learn about the dynamism of nature and to move with it. When we move with it, surprisingly and amazingly, we feel ourselves at peace, in a state of quietude, open and available to life, with clarity and vibrancy. We find that we have everything we need—not just to feel healthy in our body, but to really feel healthy in our mind and be ready for our life and all of its demands.

Ayurveda comes out of the Himalayas, and is one of the Vedic sciences. It is said to be an *Uppa Veda*, which mean a supporting science; *Veda* means science, and *Uppa* means to support. Ayurveda is a supporting science to the Prime Veda, which is Yoga. It's a beautiful understanding that even health and wellness are not the prime goal of our life; health and wellness are essential to support the prime goal of our life, which is self-realization. Ayurveda seeks to help people get healthy so that they can live according to nature, and by virtue of that come to understand who they are, and that they are, at a deeper level, something beyond nature. They are something that is beyond change, something that is unchanging, eternal, and infinite—the true self. Understanding Ayurveda in this way is also helpful, because sometimes we have to help people who may not be "getting better," so to speak. Sometimes it's about helping people make peace with chronic illness, or with the challenges in their life, and fortifying them to face those challenges, rather than just trying to medicate them.

Ayurveda also comes out of the shamanic traditions. Shamanism, as a healing system, reaches back fifty or sixty thousand years, while Ayurveda is about twelve thousand years old. We don't know if there was ever a break between shamanism and Ayurveda, or if it was one uninterrupted flow, like the river Ganges. Ayurveda is a comprehensive system that involves all the different ways in which we can perceive and experience the world around us. It's a system that's been written down, tested, tried, and proven to be true. As such, we can say that it's the oldest comprehensive system of healing, truly time-tested and evidence-based. Sadly, it went underground, so to speak, during the British occupation of India, but now it's coming back with a force—particularly in the west, because that's where it's needed so badly. We in the west are so disconnected from our own nature and from the natural world that it's very comforting, in Ayurveda, to remember that we don't have to go on holiday to find nature, that it's there within us. The more we can remember and learn from nature and live according to its energy, the healthier and happier we're going to be.

In India, Ayurveda has taken on a kind of British format, so that it's very westernized in many ways. There is a certain focus on doling out herbs and herbal medicines, and while this is an important part of Ayurveda, the primary focus is to understand that the individual is the healer. Nature is healing, but the true healer is inside of you. An Ayurvedic practitioner can provide you with food recommendations, meal plans, herbs, exercises, or anything else, but that's not being the actual healer. Those things are there to help reignite your own inner healer. What's been happening in the west with Ayurveda is beautiful; while they've embraced a more westernized approach to it in India, in the west we're actually embracing the ancient approach, which is to recognize that it's a spiritual science, and to renew and really ground or anchor into the idea that the healer is inside of you, inside what we would call consciousness.

In Ayurveda, there is this great underlying wisdom that says that most suffering, most pain and illness, is caused by a break or a cessation of your own inner knowing. For instance, somebody might ask, "How did you break your leg?" And the person replies, "I knew I shouldn't do such-and-such, but I did it anyway, and I fell." Or, "I knew I shouldn't have eaten that meal last night; I did it anyway, and now I've got a stomachache." Often, we really do know what we should and should not be doing, but we don't listen to our own inner knowing; we are not fully present to the depth of wisdom within us. This is what intuition is on some level; there's an intuitive or instinctive voice, something inside of us that represents a different layer of knowing. Whether we're using intuitive knowing or reasoning knowing, suffering comes because we're not listening to our own inner knowing; there's a break between what we know and what we do. Ayurveda provides a beautiful understanding of that and a stricter pathway to coming more fully into pure presence.

A lot of times, people come to me and say, "I didn't come to you for three weeks because I knew what you were going to tell me." So they come to see me just so that I can remind them of what they already know, so that they can hear it from outside of themselves from somebody with "authority," mirroring it back to their own inner knowing! If there's one thing I hope people get from a one-on-one session with me, or from the workshops and classes that I teach, is that they learn to value quiet time and inner listening on a more consistent basis in their lives. I hope they learn to really listen to themselves, to listen to their bodies and their hearts, to what's being said inside of them, because that deep knowing is infinitely intelligent. But they also need to bring some reasoning power to that deep knowing. To me, reasoning happens once you have the inner knowing, and now it's time to problem solve. If you don't get enough exercise in the day, for instance, ask yourself: can you walk to work, or take a walk on your lunch break? You've got to reason through that problem and find a solution. But it comes from your intuition first, from asking yourself what the problem is, whether it's that you're not getting enough exercise, you're not in a good relationship, or that you're thinking all the time and need to start feeling more. Your inner self will tell you what the problem is, if you have the courage to listen and then act on it. And most people don't want to act, and so they don't want to find the solution... yet it is so simple! All wellness is based on the simple principle of applying opposites. Eat too much? Eat less! Into junk food? Eat pure food! Not enough exercise and time in nature? Exercise and get into nature!

When I teach longer Ayurveda workshops, for a weekend or a whole week, I always start by saying, "You're going to hear what, somewhere inside of you, you already know." It's like taking the wisdom inside of you and putting it out in front of you, reflecting back to you what your body already knows how to do. Our great-grandparents lived this way, because they just paid attention; they got up with the sun, they went to bed when the sun went down. They ate food that was grown in season, from the earth, right outside their door. Nowadays, we often hear people say, "Eat local, eat seasonal, eat organic," and that's all anybody ever knew before the advent of factory foods, fast food, additives, and preservatives. That knowledge is inside of us; we just need some help remembering it.

PM: Can you offer an example from your own life of how you used reason and intuition before you became involved with Ayurveda and Yoga? How might that have shifted once you began your practice? For example, did your approach become more focused on intuition, or did both your reasoning and intuitive capacities become stronger?

LP: When I was growing up, I felt like I had a good sense of knowing how to take care of myself. For instance, we lived not too far from Lake Michigan, and whenever I was going through difficult times in my life, I would go to the beach, way out on the edge of the pier, and I would just sit there looking at the water until I felt better. When I look back now, I realize that I was kind of meditating, and I was using the effect of the water to wash over my sorry heart. Then I went through a period in my life where I lost my father and I lost some friends, and I had about a five to ten year period where things seemed very bleak and challenging. I felt as though I needed to be rearranged at quite a deep level, because the things that had supported me in my life were not there anymore. I needed to find that support within myself, and now I've reached a point where I not only know how to listen to myself, but I really believe in it. Before, I would go to the beach and sit on the pier all by myself, and I wouldn't tell anybody I was doing it. I could do what I needed for myself, but I wasn't going to stand in front of a group of people and advocate for it or argue for it. But now I do, and I feel like studying Ayurveda really strengthened this for me; it really proved to me that a lot of what I was already living, feeling, and believing was true, and that I could use it to help other people.

I used to be surrounded by people who would say things like, "Well, I'm an empirical person, so I don't believe in that," and so I feel like I went into Yoga and Ayurveda always with a voice saying, "Where's the proof?" I needed evidence-based medicine and science, I needed to know the reasoning behind things. And then, after I had been studying Ayurveda for a few years, I went to India on a ten-day intensive training conference, with molecular biologists, organic chemists, and other people with decades-long careers in the sciences. One of my favorite teachers there would start every day with a meditation where he would recite scripture, and every time I saw him, he had this giant smile on his face. At the end of the conference, I said to him, "Oh, doctor, are you returning to Kerala [where most of the doctors had come from]?" He said, "Oh, no, my dear. I'm going to Delhi." I replied, "I didn't know you were from Delhi," and he said, "My dear, I work for the Prime Minister." It turned out he was the head of the Institute of Science for the government of India, and every day, he wakes up, meditates, and recites scripture. He told me that he didn't see science and spirituality as separate; he didn't see the Vedas and Yoga as not being part of science. There's proof that it works, however you want to look at it, whether it's from the eastern perspective or the western.

PM: What are some ways that the traditions of Ayurveda and Yoga can be further developed and integrated into our modern lives?

LP: Social media can be a great way to share the message of these traditions, and it can make us feel empowered as we continue to look for more and more creative ways to share this information and these teachings. This is why I have a blog called "Food-A Love Story." Secondly, I think it's important that we invite people to participate in Yoga, meditation, and Ayurveda without relying too heavily on Sanskrit terminology, that we use language in a way that's easily accessible to people and meets them where they are. The third thing is that we really need to educate people, to let them know that whatever their spiritual background, these practices can help them heal, find vibrancy and wholeness, and further their spiritual growth.

PM: There will be a certain sector of people who hold to a more traditional understanding or appreciation of traditions like Ayurveda and Yoga. What would you say to the traditionalists who may feel that the tradition is being degraded in the west by trying to integrate it into our modern ways of life?

LP: Taking Yoga as an example, a lot of people say things like, "I can't do Yoga because I'm not flexible enough." A lot of people understand Yoga to be about becoming more physically flexible. Hopefully, it makes us more flexible not just in a physical sense, but also in terms of our minds, our hearts, and our approach to life. The opposite of flexibility is fundamentalism, and I think it's very important that we avoid fundamentalism, whether it's in Yoga or Ayurveda or any other tradition.

I do admire and value purists when they're coming from a place of devotion—devotion to a teacher, or a certain lineage, or the tradition as a whole—because devotion is a powerful quality. Because that devotion is so powerful, it can help to bring these teachings and traditions to a greater number of people; I like to think of it as the Ganges River flowing out of the Himalayas to the oceans of our world. While the purists have really helped that river of the teachings flow onward, everywhere that Ayurveda spreads it is going to have to adapt to the local culture if it is going to have a deep impact on people. For example, a lot of people come to me with a list of groceries given to them by a traditional Ayurvedic practitioner in India, and some of these items aren't even available where they live; they don't know where to find them, and they wouldn't even know how to cook them if they could. They end up telling themselves that they're not able to apply Ayurveda to their lives right now, because they don't have access to these ingredients—but that's not true Ayurveda. There's a local, cultural aspect of Ayurveda; we can adapt the list to fit our environment while still basing it on the same principles, which is the magic of nature. Nature always brings forth the right nourishment for the region and climate in which you live. This is why we always urge people to eat local and eat seasonal.

When we talk about being a purist, I hope that we can all be purists to the truth that is Ayurveda, while also being able to adapt—because Ayurveda teaches us to adapt to the needs of the individual. This is the balance we seek: to be true to the truth, true to the fundamental principles of Ayurveda, while always being able to adapt it to the needs of the individual. I think the west is really reflecting back to India the power of Ayurvedic science, and I think this is helping the tradition to grow even more in India.

I feel very positive and hopeful about the future of Ayurveda. Seeds are being planted in different parts of the world, and I think those seeds will take root and grow into a strong and flourishing garden. And in order for those seeds to grow strong in the soil in which they're planted, the tradition is going to have to be adapted to the local climate.

PM: Are there any other messages you'd like to share?

LP: Ayurveda includes many categories or schools, from surgery to acupuncture to various treatments for chronic illness and rejuvenation therapies. Especially in terms of rejuvenation—addressing ideas of anti-aging, for instance—Ayurveda teaches that you're only as young as the sharpness of your senses, the health and balance of your body, and the clarity of your mind. In this way, Ayurveda utterly embraces the cultivation of our reasoning faculties; making sure these faculties are clear and vibrant, so that we are perceiving properly. Armed with a strong reasoning and perceiving capacity, we can live our lives more fully and move in the direction of our dreams. We can have the health and wellness that we seek, and also have the joy that we desire. Being in touch with that joy, with our life purpose even, requires intuition. I really think that Ayurveda teaches that—return to wholeness, listen deeply, and believe in your intuitive mind. With sharp reasoning coupled with powerful intuition, we can truly have it all.

Prof. Sir Roger Penrose (OM FRS)

Prof. Sir Roger Penrose (OM FRS) is the Emeritus Rouse Ball Professor of Mathematics at the Mathematical Institute of the University of Oxford. He was awarded the 1988 Wolf Prize for physics with Stephen Hawking for their contribution to our understanding of the universe. He is the author of several books, including *The Road to Reality: A Complete Guide to the Laws of the Universe.*

Interview

THEORETICAL PHYSICS, DISCOVERY, PLATONIC FORMS

Param Media: What do you mean by the "three worlds" and the "three deep mysteries"?

Roger Penrose: The three worlds you refer to here are the *physical* world, the *mental* world, and the world of *Platonic absolutes.* By the physical world, I mean things like tables and chairs, planets, galaxies, and people: what we normally think of as the inhabitants of the world. Then there is the mental world, which is the totality of mental activity: our perception of the real things in the world, our thinking about them, and that kind of thing. And finally there is the Platonic world of absolutes; most particularly, I think about *mathematical* absolutes. I claim that all these worlds have an existence, and although sometimes philosophers or others worry about them (particularly, they worry about the Platonic world), in my view, they all have a kind of reality, a different kind of reality each.

Now, the three *mysteries* are the connections between these three worlds. One of these mysteries is the fact that all actions of the physical world, as far as we understand them, seem to depend very precisely on very subtle, sophisticated mathematical laws. Without mathematical laws, we seem to have no ultimate way to understand how physical things behave.

Another of these mysteries is how our consciousness comes about from physical things. We have our physical brains, and those physical brains somehow seem to evoke conscious experience. So there's the world of mentality, which seems to emerge in some way from the physical world. The third mystery is how our conscious understanding can have access to the world of mathematics. Their interrelationship can be viewed as a triangle, where we have the mysteries as the sides of the triangle, and the three worlds—the Platonic, the mental, and the physical—are the vertices of the triangle.

So, in a certain sense, I think of these worlds as separate, but also, in another sense, I think of them as deeply connected. On the one hand, we have the fact that certain parts of the world of Platonic absolutes and, in particular, absolute *mathematical* laws, govern the behaviour of the physical world. When we understand mathematics, we see that it does control physical things extremely precisely, and how it does that *is* a mystery.

How we come to find truth in mathematics is also something mysterious; it has to do with what is involved in the word *understanding*, or in the word *insight*. What is it that leads us to these truths? There are deep theorems that we have in mathematical logic, which tell us that our understanding of mathematics cannot just be following rules. This implies that there is something deeply mysterious involved here. And there is something else—a fourth mystery, if you like—which is how all these things can somehow depend on each other in this cyclic way; there is something additionally mysterious about that, too.

PM: Could you elaborate on your view that we *discover* physical and mathematical truths, rather than merely inventing them?

RP: I do take the view that we can discover mathematical truths, which are out there in the (Platonic) world, in a sense. It's a bit more like archaeology than perhaps people normally think. These things are out there, and what mathematicians do is to discover truths. Now, I would perhaps slightly qualify that, because there are things in mathematics that are more like inventions and less like discoveries. I think this is more likely to happen in *proofs* of results. Say a mathematician is trying to find out whether or not some mathematical assertion is true, and this mathematician finds that there is some way of establishing this which involves making some rather arbitrary construction, which could have been achieved in different ways. This suggests that it's more like an invention; it's like constructing some kind of object that does a job. In such cases, I think the mathematics is a little bit more like an invention than a discovery. So I think it's not such a clear-cut thing. And you might say also that, in a subject like engineering, where you want to make some kind of an engine or a motor or something like that, and there turns out to be some particularly elegant, unexpected solution, then you might say that the elegant solution is "out there" in the world already, and that this is like discovering that solution rather than inventing it. So I'm not sure that the two words are quite as opposite as they are presented as being. Nevertheless, I do think that in mathematics, we are basically discovering truths which are out there.

Now, when it comes to, say, physical laws, again I would say yes, it is a matter of discovering and not simply a matter of describing. I think you often find that people say: well, all we're doing is finding mathematical *descriptions* of what's going on in the world. They say it's just that human beings have this way of formalizing things in mathematical terms, and that's their way of understanding what's going on, so it's not really "out there" in nature; it's just that mathematics is our way of understanding things. I very much disagree with that; well, I disagree with it if we're thinking about the *basic* laws of nature. When we're thinking about things which are secondary or tertiary, which aren't really the fundamental laws, then maybe we *are* finding mathematically convenient descriptions. For example, in biology one may categorize things in one way rather than another, and to some extent that may be just the way that our human minds can better cope with understanding such things.

On the other hand, when you're looking at basic physical laws, I really do believe that with mathematics we are discovering something which is out there already. I think that one of the best examples of this is gravitation. Kepler discovered how the planets move round the sun and satisfy certain laws, and then it took Newton to realize that these empirical laws could be explained in terms of some very simple mathematical principles, which gave not only the Kepler laws about how planets move round the sun, but also how the moon goes round the earth and how deviations from the elliptical orbits come about because of the interrelations between different planets, and so on. It's not as though Newton found that the inverse square law was a good way of describing things because human beings could understand that better than something else; rather, there is something out there which Newton discovered, that was there already.

Now, along comes Einstein, and Einstein has a different theory of gravity. So you might say, well, this is now showing that Newton was just describing things. But it's not like that, because Einstein's laws were built upon Newton's. The Newtonian theory is a limiting case of Einstein's theory. When velocities are small compared to the speed of light and gravitational potentials are not particularly big— they're relatively small in the solar system — we get the Newtonian limit of Einstein's theory. Newton's theory resides within the more precise Einstein theory. So I would say that these fundamental mathematical laws really *are* out there in nature, rather than being creations of our minds.

PM: Would you be able to say a bit about the roles of reason and logic, as well as intuition and insight, in the process of discovery, perhaps illuminating your view with a personal example?

RP: I think it's very difficult to talk about intuition in particular; we know more about logical reasoning than we do about what intuition means. I would say that when we use the word *intuition*, we're referring more to those kinds of insights which are not logical progressions, where there may be some feeling about something which one might have for one reason or another, maybe after building up a lot of experience in some area, and then feeling that some kind of idea should be appropriate in that area. That's very difficult to describe, and it's very difficult to analyze, I'm sure. In the case of logic, it's much clearer because there are rules of logic. You can question whether verbal statements are logical by asking whether assertions follow logically from one another. Are they perhaps blatantly disobeying the rules of logic at some point? And, at a more sophisticated level, can we find mathematical descriptions of such logical rules which are precise and, according to which, following the rules gives us a good theory of what's going on?

On the other hand, I think what we call intuition is, to a great extent, built up from experience, and it may be experience from areas which are not exactly the ones that we are thinking about at the time. For example, a certain type of unifying idea in one area might well be appropriate in a somewhat different area. To some extent, the essence of the meanings of intuition and insight may be describable in terms of anecdotal experiences that might have more general implications of some sort, but I'm not sure. At least I can perhaps give an anecdotal experience which, whether it helps or not, at least is an experience.

In the later months of 1964 I had been interested in black holes—or what we *now* call black holes. At the time, I don't think we had a good name for them. A black hole is what happens when a body gets too large and concentrated and can't hold itself apart, so it collapses under its own gravitational attraction. People had been worrying about these things particularly at that time, because of the discovery of the first of the objects that came to be known as *quasars* — found and analyzed by the Dutch astronomer Maarten Schmidt. This had provided strong evidence for actual situations in which such gravitational collapse might well be taking place. I had been influenced by John Wheeler, of Princeton University, who had pointed out the importance of the question of the *singularities* which seemed to arise. When I say the word singularity, I mean a place where the equations break down. You follow the equations and you find something that becomes infinite, and since it becomes infinite, the equations just don't work anymore, and this is what the word singularity usually means in this context, in mathematical physics.

Now, in the case of the black holes, there had been a very important piece of work done by Oppenheimer and Snyder just before the war in 1939, where they examined what would happen to a very idealized star. It was idealized because the material that the star was made of was what we call dust; it didn't have any pressure, and it was exactly spherically symmetrical. It was considered to be falling inwards under its own gravitational attraction. This was the model that Oppenheimer and Snyder were studying. Now, the thing is, in this model, because of the symmetry, everything was falling in a straight line to the centre, and since it was all heading for this one point in the middle, and there was no pressure, the density would become infinite at the centre. Accordingly, this singularity might have seemed to be a fortuitous result of this symmetry assumption. A lot of people were very suspicious of this singularity, particularly some very distinguished Russians who had concluded that, in the general case, you wouldn't get these singularities. They had actually, as it turns out, made a mistake in their calculations, but this was not clear at the time. Now, I began worrying about this: to what extent would these idealizations really represent the reason that you got singularities, so that if you removed the idealizations you wouldn't get a singularity? Maybe if you had, say, not just dust, but some pressure in the material, so it would start to push itself back out again and maybe bounce outwards. Or maybe, because of irregularities, as the stuff collapsed it would swirl round in some complicated way and then come swishing out again. None of that seemed at all unreasonable. But I began worrying about this question, to see whether you could make a general argument.

In any case, the anecdote here is that I was in conversation with a colleague (Ivor Robinson) who tended to talk a lot, although in very interesting ways, so if he was talking you would be bound to listen to what he was saying. And we were talking, walking along beside the street, and although I'd had this problem buzzing around in my head, I wasn't particularly thinking about it, certainly, because I was listening to what he was saying. Well, we came to this spot where we crossed a road; it was just a side road, basically, but we had to be careful not to ignore the traffic, and so he stopped talking at that point. And evidently, when we were halfway across the road, a certain idea came to me about how to characterize the collapse in such a way that it reached a point, a point of no return, in a sense. Well, this idea came to me, and then when we got to the other side of the road he started talking again and, of course, the idea was blotted from my mind, and I didn't think more about it at the time; I just was interested in talking with him.

Later in the day when he'd gone off and I returned to my office, which was in this area, I had this strange but definite feeling of elation; I felt somehow cheerful in ways that I couldn't quite attribute to anything. I don't know why I should have wanted to attribute it to anything, but I had found it a little bit odd that I was feeling more elated than I would have expected from the things that had happened to me during the day.

So I went through my recollections of the day, starting at the beginning and going through everything that had happened to me to see if I could find out what the source of this elation was, until finally I got up to the point where we were crossing the street, and I then retrieved this idea, which now we refer to as a *trapped surface*, which was a characterization of a collapse which is somehow, in a certain sense, irreversible, but in a way which does not depend on details of the matter distribution there and does not depend on anything to do with the symmetry, but can apply in very general circumstances. And I was then able to bring together ideas that I'd been working on several months earlier on a completely different problem, which enabled me to sketch a proof of the result that these collapsing matter configurations had to become singular, and that under very general circumstances you could not avoid these singularities. It wasn't a question of solving complicated differential equations. You see, that's what people would normally be doing in these situations. If you have a simple problem where it's very symmetrical, you might be able to solve it fairly easily. If it was very complicated, then there would be no hope. People do it numerically nowadays using computers, of course, but in those days one wouldn't have the mathematical techniques telling us how to treat these equations in a way which could solve them, even just numerically, in an approximate way. So the arguments that I was using were of a quite different kind, where you talked about these things in very general ways.

But anyway, the point I'm trying to make is: what kind of an idea could I have had crossing a street? Certainly it wasn't a calculation. It was some kind of feeling, an intuitive feeling, and I don't know how to describe that, really. An intuitive feeling that here was an idea of just the right kind that could be used to characterize the irreversibility of its collapse, and would be of the kind that you could then apply the mathematical techniques that I'd been working with in this other context, and maybe give a general argument to prove the result I was looking for. So there's the intuition: why did I feel that this idea was just the key to this? It's very hard to say. It seemed to fit in with certain criteria, I suppose; I knew I needed a criterion that was not purely a *local* thing; it had to be something dependent on some global properties. My thought had just the right kind of characteristics that I was, in a sense, looking for.

Often you're looking for things and you have no idea whether the thing you're looking for exists or not, but you know the kind of characteristic that that thing should have and, well, that's a kind of quality one tends to describe as intuition. I'm not altogether sure I like the word intuition in this context, because it has a sort of connotation that these are ideas which come to you out of the blue, and which are sort of glorified guesswork, whereas I think I prefer to use a word like *insight*, which is maybe some kind of understanding of what's going on which goes a little bit beyond the understandings that had been evident to people prior to this. If that's intuition, well, fine. But I think you need that in order to make these steps which go beyond the kind of thing which you'd been doing before; but then it's not any use unless you can tie it all together in a very logical way. So the strictly logical work comes later, and you can use this insight or intuition or whatever it is to develop it into a rigorous argument which is logically watertight. Perhaps this illustrates a difference between intuition and logic; at least it's an example which may give some insight, if you like, into what's going on here.

PM: Many people may find it odd for a physicist to use the term *beauty* when talking about discovering fundamental laws of nature. However, I'll read a quote from your book *The Road to Reality*: "Beauty and truth are intertwined, the beauty of a physical theory acting as a guide to its correctness and relation to the physical world." Would you be able to clarify what you mean by that?

RP: Well, I suppose it's partly an empirical fact that we do seem to find laws which are very, very precise in the way they describe the world, and at the same time they seem to have this quality, an aesthetic appeal about them. Is this an accident? Is it even *true* that there is fundamental beauty in these equations? Or is it because we have this feeling that the laws *should* be beautiful that we, therefore, find the beautiful ones, whereas there are a whole lot of other laws which are hideous, and we haven't found them yet because we're not so good at finding ugly laws? All these options are possibilities, but my own feeling is that none of them offer a proper explanation of the intertwining between truth and beauty that is out there; but if we want an explanation for that, I can't give one.

I would say, however, that it is *true* that there is a particular kind of beauty in the physical laws, at least in those that have been discovered, and this is a beauty which resides within the mathematics. Or, perhaps one should say that it is true that the way in which a certain mathematical idea which has a particular power and is beautiful as a piece of mathematics may also find its role in the laws of physics. But beauty on its own is certainly not a reliable criterion, partly because there is an enormous amount of extremely beautiful mathematics that has (so far) found no role whatever in physical theory. Moreover, often you find things that at least may be viewed as beautiful by particular physicists but turn out not to have any connection with the physical world.

Let's consider the Dirac equation for the electron, which was an extremely important development, and enabled physics to leap forward. When people asked Paul Dirac how on earth he found that equation, which was of quite a different kind from the equations that people had been playing with, he is alleged to have said, "Well, I have a very keen sense of the beautiful, and when I found my equation and I saw its beauty, I knew I was right." Now, this may not be quite what he said, but there is something of that which I think, in a sense, was true. He did have this ability to perceive the beauty within this equation, which went beyond its simplicity, because in a certain sense it's simple, and in another sense it's not so simple; it is rather unusual, and you have to understand quite a bit about what's going on before you can really appreciate it. But at some point you say, gosh, that's a wonderful idea, how these things can twist around and fit together in a way, and that very fact depends on some kind of symmetry in it, and the whole theory depends on this, and there is something marvelous about that. It's a hard question; not a question that I can see how to answer, but I do believe that the question contains more than a grain of truth. I think there's a lot of truth in it, that beauty and the very basic laws which govern the world are intertwined in a very mysterious way.

PM: Do you believe that robots or computers will ever have the capacity to become self-aware or have consciousness or experience inner states, and why do you hold the view that you do?

RP: To me, a robot is some kind of machine that is controlled by a computer, so it's a computationally-controlled device of some sort. And the arguments that I've made in the past are to do with whether the quality of human understanding is something that could be achieved by a purely computational entity, where the computational rules are to be of the character that they could be checked by a machine to see whether or not they've been followed correctly. Of course, the checking machine would not be required to have any understanding of what it's doing; it just checks mechanically.

My argument that human understanding cannot be achieved by such a robot comes from a theorem due to the great logician Kurt Gödel, as re-interpreted by Alan Turing. Let's suppose that we are given a certain set of computational rules that can be used to establish mathematical theorems of some specific, well-defined type. Suppose, also, that you understand what the rules are saying, and are thereby convinced that the rules are *sound*, in the sense that any theorem established by their correct application must be actually true. Then, from the detailed form of these rules, you can construct a specific mathematical statement, of the general type to which the rules can be applied, but which *cannot* be established using the rules, yet which nevertheless can be seen to be actually true on the basis of one's understanding of the soundness of the rules. I always thought this was extraordinary and remarkable, because it's telling you that the understanding that we have is not constrained by any set of computational rules whatever. If we trust the truth of theorems obtained by *use* of the rules, then we can see how to *transcend* the power of the rules. There is something else other than the following of computational rules that is going on in our conscious understanding.

I had held this view for a long time, and didn't think to do much with it, but then people started talking about when computers were going to exceed human abilities at understanding, and so on, and it seemed to me that that's ridiculous, because the computers are simply following rules. Of course there are lots of quibbles and counter-arguments that people make concerning this, which I don't want to go into here, but the basic argument is that understanding, whatever it is, is something which goes beyond rules. Although it isn't that rules, if they are sophisticated enough, may, or may not, be able to simulate *parts of* genuine understanding, it's that understanding is needed to tell us which rules to choose. So the understanding is something not driven by rules, and it's not driven purely by computation —although computation can certainly provide an *aid* to understanding.

When I say rules and things like that, I really mean things which you could put on computers. Clearly computers can be programmed to be very clever at doing certain things. For example, we know that they can be extremely good at playing chess, but they do it in a very different way from the way that human beings play chess. Basically it's just that they run through all the possibilities, and this is quite different from the way that humans play chess. But the trouble with things like chess, for my arguments, is you can't so easily make this difference clear-cut, because chess is a finite game, after all, and maybe eventually it will be totally solved by computational procedures, whereas in mathematics, the things we're talking about here involve the infinite in one way or another.

But then some people object and say, how can you know anything about the infinite? Well, how do we know that when you add two even numbers together, you always get another even number? The fact is, that's a statement about an infinite number of things, and it's something which we can fully appreciate. So I'm saying we *can* appreciate things about the infinite; that's not the problem. The problem is that the way in which we appreciate things about the infinite cannot be encapsulated in a finite set of rules. And that's what the computers do; they chug along according to a finite set of rules. Ok, there are lots of quibbles, and lots of people do make arguments about these things, but it does seem to me quite clear that what we do when we understand something is different from simply following the rules; it's almost the antithesis of that. It is our understanding about what the rules *mean* that tells us whether they're good rules in the first place.

Now, we should ask whether or not computers will be able to have this quality of *understanding* — I think that's a good distinguishing word here. Will computers ever understand what they're doing? It's certainly not what we *use* computers for. We don't use computers to tell us what they understand. In fact, we use our understanding to guide us in making the computer's program in the first place, and when the answer comes out, we use our understanding to interpret that answer. Understanding is what the computer doesn't do; what the computer does do is the computation in the middle. So it's different, that's all I'm saying. I'm not even saying our understanding is superior; I'm just saying it's different.

I'd also say that, whatever understanding is, it's something which involves awareness. But in a sense, I'm here using two words where I don't really know what either of them means, so that's sort of curious. I mean, how can I say anything about understanding if I don't really know what understanding is? And how can I say anything about awareness if I don't really know what awareness is? But nevertheless, it seems to me that the implication between these two things is, in my view, pretty clear. It would be a bit absurd to say that an entity understands something if it's not even aware of it. That's not what I would mean by understanding, anyway. It seems to me that understanding is something, a quality, or whatever it is, that depends on awareness. So, in that sense, I would say a robot, a computationally-controlled entity, does not, will not have the quality of awareness, as it cannot have the quality of understanding.

However, I want to be clear that I do not mean that it would be impossible for some latter-day Frankenstein to construct in the lab some entity which has consciousness. I do believe that whatever is going on in our heads is something which is acting in accordance with physical laws. I happen to believe that it's acting in accordance with laws that we don't fully understand. I happen to believe that there is something physical going on there in our heads which we do not yet have the physical theory to explain. This doesn't mean that it's not physics, that it's not science. I think it *is* physics and it *is* science; it's just not the physics and the science that we have now. That's saying perhaps quite a lot, if you like. It's also saying that there's something else going on apart from simply the connections between neurons, and I would also say that it has something to do with quantum mechanics and, moreover, that it has something to do with where quantum mechanics is *limited.* It's to do with the boundary between quantum mechanics and the classical world, which is not fully understood. In fact, not just not fully understood; it's completely *un-understood.* So I think that we are completely missing something in the physical world, which is what is being made use of when we are conscious. Often people think this is a wild speculation; maybe it is, but it is based to a large degree on completely logical arguments, and these arguments, many of them going back to Gödel, seem to me to show that understanding is something which cannot be described in terms of entirely computational procedures, so that if we're going to understand what consciousness is, ultimately it has to depend, in my view, on a physics which we don't have yet. It *will* be physics, but some essentially new physics.

PM: Is there any advice you would like to give to philosophers specializing in the philosophy of science?

RP: Well, I was recently part of an Oxford Union debate which, in this case, was about whether philosophers were of any use in science. And when I spoke, I addressed the question by saying, well, I'm not so sure about philosophers themselves; occasionally they make significant contributions to science, but not very often. But *philosophy,* definitely— I think scientists often have their philosophies and I think this can be important in the way they do their science.

I was commenting on the Oxford philosophers, who I think, among probably any group of philosophers in the world, understand science, and particularly quantum physics, better than any other philosophy department I know of, anyway. I think they are very well up on physics, and particularly on quantum mechanics. Now, the point I was making here was, well, I think they have missed a big trick. You see, what is the role of philosophers in science? Well, it could well be to stop shoddy thinking among the physicists and other scientists. And here is a particular case where I thought they really missed what they should have been doing in this regard. And what I was talking about was quantum mechanics. Quantum mechanics is a subject which, in my view, has no clear ontology; that is to say, you have the theory, but it's not at all clear how it corresponds to the world. And you have people arguing about what on earth it means, and it seems not to make sense when you try and say, what part of this theory corresponds to the real world? And the philosophers should have said, look, your theory needs changing, because it doesn't have a sensible ontology. And that seems to be a job for a philosopher of science, to see where some theory doesn't satisfy the sort of criteria that you would think a philosopher would insist upon in their professional discussions.

The problem, in my view, is that quantum mechanics is basically inconsistent with itself. For example, the Schrödinger equation says that if you have a system, it evolves in time in a very, very precise way following the Schrödinger equation. Now, the thing is, with that equation, it doesn't give you what happens in the world, and Schrödinger was very clear to show this with his famous cat-in-the- box thought experiment. The cat, according to Schrödinger's own equation, would evolve in this particular situation into a superposition of a dead and a live cat, so the cat would be dead and alive at the same time. That's clearly not the right ontology; it's not dead and alive at the same time, and you should have thought the philosophers would point that out and say, well look, this is ridiculous, you got your theory wrong. Instead, what they do is they follow what the physicists say; they say, well, you know, it's all complicated in one way or another, and it's the environment that's come into it, and you haven't taken that into consideration, or something else, or ultimately what it is, is you're lead to the view that when some conscious observer—forget about the cat, whether it's conscious or not—some other observer comes along, looks at the cat, and that observer somehow splits, or the consciousness of that observer splits, into one which sees the live cat and the other which sees the dead cat, and somehow these two coexist in the world. To me, that's not the ontology of the world we want to describe, and the philosopher ought to tell us, your theory, you physicists, is not right, and you should be doing something about it. And it seems to me that the job of the philosophers should have been to tell the physicists that their theory was not good enough, and they missed a trick in not doing this.

PM: What do you think the physics of the future may look like in ten years? One hundred years? One thousand years?

RP: I really haven't the faintest idea. There are ways in which I can think I would *like* it to look, one way or another, but what it *will* look like even in ten years— well, maybe it won't change much in ten years. One hundred years? No idea. One thousand years? Not the foggiest.

Klaus Oehr

Klaus Oehr has developed and sold products based on his winemaking and grape-growing hobbies on both a wholesale and retail basis in 3 countries. He also financed the development of his own mercury pollution control invention, which he licensed to an American company with $4 billion in annual sales. Klaus is the co-winner of the 1996 Financial Post Gold Environmental Improvement Award.

Klaus Oehr

If I Pretended That I Could, What Would I Do?

INVENTION, ECO-CONSCIOUSNESS, SYNCHRONICITY

The purpose of this chapter is to describe the factors that I believe foster transformational creativity, the dramatic deconstruction and reconstruction of perceived reality. An example of perceived reality is that chemicals are required to remove lubricants from wires manufactured from rods pulled through telescopic dies (circular diamond cutters). However, by moving beyond this limited perception, in 1996 I co-invented a process that eliminated the use of chemicals in the high speed cleaning of wires.

As a successful, self-employed scientist and entrepreneur with multiple commercialized inventions, I have been asked about my process of discovery, which is not about collecting and managing information on a purely deductive or scientific basis.

Here are fourteen key factors that I use to facilitate transformational discovery in any endeavor.

1. Discover benign purpose/intention

At a time in late 2001 when I had no customers for my business, I remember sitting in my basement den in my favourite rocking chair and writing the following question in my diary:

"What is my purpose?"

Answer: "Create ecological joy."

Next question: "How?"

Answer: "Pretend that you can."

Next question: "If I pretended that I could what would I do?"

Answer: "Control mercury in coal-fired electric power plants."

Mercury is a nerve toxin, and coal-fired electric power plants are the largest source of mercury pollutants in North America, releasing about 50 tons per year into the atmosphere. At the time of my intention, mercury capture was extremely expensive.

Following my intention of "controlling mercury in coal-fired electric power plants," I successfully developed the cheapest way to prevent mercury air pollution in these plants and was able to reduce mercury capture costs fivefold to tenfold. That single intention resulting in a transformational discovery has made me financially independent, while removing 90% of the mercury from coal-fired plants in multiple locations, including Portland, Oregon.

Today, if I ask myself the question, "What is my purpose?" the answer is:

"Heal environments by co-creating ecological joy as a rational visionary in ecological collectives," while practicing discernment (low level of emotional distraction for me) instead of judgment (highly emotionally distracting for me). "Ecological collectives" refers to teams of kindred spirits i.e. soulful, compatible, independent thinkers who I trust emotionally and intellectually with the power to implement benign change on an environment.

I believe that benign intention fosters helpful synchronicity, which will be discussed later.

2. Work off your strengths and park your weaknesses

Ever since I was a young child and learned how to read, I would spend lots of time in libraries. My two favourite locations are the ocean and quiet libraries. As an introvert, I learned to hyper-focus in quiet, un-distracting environments, hardly ever looking at my watch. If something really interested me, I'd study it without consideration of how long the exercise would take. If I felt information/discovery flowing, I would just let the flow flow. I never worried about hitting dead ends. Just as when I was a child, when I am emotionally and physically undistracted, I find it easy to be peaceful, playful, and joyfully diligent. This has always been my strength. My latest co-invention, the recycling of waste latex paint, took five angst-free years to manifest with a three-year time lag in the middle due to a dead-end (more on this later).

As a young adult, I had to develop my extroverted side. This was necessary to develop emotional empathy for others, a connection to others and the world around me. The challenge of course was to separate "judgment" from "discernment", because empathic people are magnets for others, especially "needy" people. So I've had to park my extroverted/people side when learning how to create transformational ecological science. Empathy should have its time separated from creative time. Conventional brainstorming may suffer from extrovert control, causing emotional distraction in introverts or less powerful extroverts. This can result in frustration of the extroverts (e.g. ideas come too slowly or aren't good enough) or the introverts (e.g. "I need time to think"). Distraction slows down the creative spirit.

My central processors, the brain and heart, don't function well when they are running too many programs (distractions) at the same time. For me, creativity and multi-tasking don't go hand in hand.

If I'm trying to create at a really deep level, I can't be thinking about:

- Time—looking at my watch, thinking about when I will be able to finish a process.
- Ultimate goals—where I'm at and where I'm going.
- Social media and entertainment - TV, newspapers, Email, social media, phones, mementos, photos.
- Hunger or thirst for anything—speed of process, food, water, money and emotional relationships, including those with people or the environment (where people can be family members or complete strangers, and the environment can be as simple as desk clutter or a pet).

3. Synchronize with energy

My creative brain works best early in the day, from about 8 AM until about 2 PM. After that I need to recharge by going to the YMCA to exercise, working in the garden, or going for long walks with my wife. Then I just let things happen any way they do. This is when I allow for distractions, work or play with minimum angst. My wife is a night owl and I'm an early riser, so we sleep in separate rooms so that sleep is deep and continuous and we feel energized on waking. Don't worry: we are lovers on many levels, including environmental/ecological.

4. Consciousness inhaled and exhaled meets the art of pretending

I always imagine that the first part of information is either a collection of electrons as particles (sheepdogs speaking dog language) or waves (sheepdogs speaking dog or sheep language). I imagine the second part of information as photons (sheep) being herded by unbonded electrons (untethered sheepdogs) into internal (e.g. hemoglobin, proteins, junk DNA) and external holograms (invisible fields of coherent light or another sentient being's sheep pens). The difference between particles and waves is that waves need time to propagate, or flow.

Imagine that a wave (like a camcorder recording) collapses into a particle (like a pause or stop button on the camcorder resulting in a single image like a camera shot) when it is acted upon by a thought (i.e. thoughts are things – streams of particles) e.g. is/isn't, true/false, black/white, good/bad thinking collapses flow. Pretend that the act of pretending, i.e. suspending judgment as long as possible, allows information to flow in or out of your body through the skin, eyes, ears or into and out of the blood via the lungs on inhale and exhale e.g. via hemoglobin in the blood. Pretend that untethered electrons flowing as waves can encode or decode photon flow as waves. Pretend that the "sheep pens" or holograms can be acted on by benign internal and external sentience, i.e. consciousness is everywhere and may be accessible from places outside the human brain. Deep synchronicity proves that consciousness is accessible from outside the human brain since it can occur with or without the result of a personal intention. Experimental data shows that the heart can register an intuition a few seconds ahead of the brain (e.g. hemoglobin is a molecule loaded with untethered "sheepdog" type electrons which may collect information photons from any source. DNA and proteins are molecules also loaded with untethered "sheepdog" type electrons which may collect information photons from any source). I think of oxygen molecules as surfboards carrying surfers (external sheep). I think of exhaled carbon dioxide as surfboards carrying surfers (internal sheep).

5. Feeding networks

I imagine my highest function to be that of a benign switchboard connecting at a fifth sensory level (personal seeing, feeling, touching, hearing, tasting) with other people, and at a sixth sensory level (intuiting and transpersonal seeing, feeling, touching, hearing, tasting) with external sentience, including holograms (universal and/or transpersonal). My role is to be an open conduit for benign healing via ecological transformation anywhere, anytime. Having been fed holographically via multiple deep solicited and unsolicited intuits and synchronicities, my role is to enhance the healing sixth sense in myself and others anywhere, anytime. Highly improbable events on a fifth sensory level may be common on a sixth sensory level. Fifth sensory perception is about "me consciousness," while sixth sensory perception is about "we" consciousness.

My first synchronicity occurred on a tour bus in Majorca, Spain in 1972. I felt nauseous and my back suddenly starting sweating, along with the accompanying thought, "I need to get off this bus!" The sensation was so strong that I actually started walking up the bus aisle towards the driver. Halfway up the aisle I saw the same model and coloured tour bus (white and blue) on its side, facing towards me on the shoulder of the other side of the road. I went back to my seat feeling stunned, but didn't understand the significance of the event until twenty-nine years later while sitting in the University of British Columbia science library, experiencing the exact same nausea and sweating symptoms. This time I had the feeling that "I am missing a reference on mercury chemistry," a reference that I would need in order to develop the mercury control concept. I pretended that the nausea and back sweating were really telling me that a missing reference existed, and I then felt prompted to enter the next room where, to my amazement, I found this missing reference in the table of contents of the only scientific journal that was in the room un-shelved. The odds against chance of finding this vital reference sitting there on a cart, as if waiting for me to find it, are astronomical, and this event triggered an avalanche of subsequent synchronicities that greatly facilitated my capacity to develop the mercury control concept. It is as if the universe is programmed to interact with sensitive intended, benign intended, human switchboards at a simultaneous fifth sensory and sixth sensory level. I am certain that humanity is not alone, and that transformative consciousness is everywhere.

6. Curiosity (or questions and answers)

Creative people tend to be curious. Rather than just asking questions and leaving those questions unanswered, they try to patiently answer questions. Here is an example:

"Why is basement cement cool and damp?"

Answer: "It is porous and evaporates water, which cools it."

Next question: "Why is cement porous?"

Answer: "Under a microscope, cement looks like a box of fuzzy ping pong balls with lime water between the balls."

Next question: "How could I fill the spaces between the ping pong balls to prevent salt water from road de-icers corroding reinforcing steel (called 'rebar') and causing the cement to crack due to swelling of the corroding rebar?"

Answer: "Add fine coal fly ash to the cement, which can chemically react with the lime water to make marble-sized fuzzy ping pong balls and fill up the gaps between the large balls."

Next question: "How could I fill the remaining spaces between the ping pong balls and marbles?"

Answer: "Add a waste product that acts like gelatin or custard, i.e. starts off liquid and ends up as a flexible solid that can act as a salt water barrier."

Final question: "What waste product acts like gelatin or custard that won't damage cement?"

It took me five years to answer this last question when, whether by accident or synchronicity, one of my best friends told me that he was working with waste gelatinous material (latex paint) in cement without the ash (marbles).

Today, we are close to developing the world's lowest cost, lowest porosity cement from two waste sources: coal fly ash and latex paint. We have the potential to recycle over three billion liters per year of waste latex paint worldwide, with an equal volume of waste coal ash, to prevent the corrosion of cement or the drying of cement (e.g. toxic mold growth prevention).

7. Fostering creativity

Here is a list of good intentions and good deeds to foster creativity:

- playfulness
- peacefulness
- diligence
- discernment
- curiosity
- benign intention
- switch-boarding
- forgiveness
- gray thinking
- thought/question/answer/intention/incubation

Here is a list of intentions and deeds that hamper creativity:

- judgment
- emotional distraction, including grudges
- physical distraction, including multitasking, clutter, and pets*
- black-and-white thinking
- lack of thought/question/answer/intention incubation (e.g. hyper-speed brainstorming and rigid goal-setting, especially in extrovert-controlled environments)

*I close the door on a very loving female cat when I'm in deep thought that requires the use of my laptop computer, because I can't type properly when she is sleeping on my lap. If I'm reading or using a notebook, sometimes I'll let her in. When I'm done working, I always let her in. Perhaps giving attention to pets will help foster your creativity in the moment, but not for me.

8. Working with Artists, Craftsmen, and Technocrats

One of the most useful books that I have ever read is "Artists, Craftsmen and Technocrats" by Patricia Pitcher. In a nutshell, this is what I learned:

Artists – deconstruct and reconstruct reality (e.g. manufacture of coherent light via the laser, filmless cameras vs. film cameras, wireless vs. land-line communication).

Craftsmen and craftswomen – streamline existing and reconstructed reality (e.g. Apple's evolution of Xerox's graphic user interface on Mac computers).

Technocrats – control existing reality (e.g. societal decision makers allowing high toxicity water fracking instead of low toxicity carbon dioxide fracking).

Artists are perceived as anarchists by Technocrats.

Technocrats respect competent Master Craftspeople.

Only Craftspeople can interact simultaneously with Artists and Technocrats.

Being successful in implementing transformational creativity (i.e. benign anarchy) requires that Artists or Artist/Craftspeople ("Creatives") suspend judgment of Technocrats by developing skill as "Master Craftsmen/Craftswomen."

The weakness of Artists is that they sometimes live by "I think, therefore it is" or "Can't you see it?" or "Don't you just love it?" i.e. their sometimes manic/manic depressive emotional behavior interferes with a possibly calm/cool and collected detached initial audience to their art e.g. a compassionate Craftsperson.

The strength of Craftspeople, especially Master Craftspeople, is that they tend to do experiments, simulations, or build prototypes, thereby making the creative transformation more real and less ethereal or risky, especially to a more open-minded Technocrat with power to mobilize resources including money, people, and equipment. The best Craftspeople are curious and are able to compassionately interact with Artists.

The bottom line is that Artists partially disguised as Master Craftspeople are respected by any personality type or network. So you should aspire to develop your craft (i.e. learn for life) along with your creative art in order to have the maximum impact on your audience. I'm blessed to be married to a Craftswoman who helps me craft my art (e.g. she acts as a proof-reader, curious skeptic, and simplifier). As an Artist, I aspire to be a Master Craftsman as well.

9. Recurring dreams

When I was a child, I was always dreaming about flying and having to flap my arms and move quickly to get off of the ground. In these dreams, once I was up in the air I could hover.

Once I had learned how to swim at the age of fourteen, these dreams stopped.

As an adult, I have had literally hundreds of dreams about missing flight connections in airports. Sometimes, I'd be the last person off a plane when the cleaners came on board and sometimes I couldn't find the right terminal or departure gate.

I pretend that my subconscious is telling me that if I wanted to fly, then I would need to get rid of excess baggage in the form of emotional or physical distraction to the maximum extent possible, especially when incubating creativity.

Once I created my mercury invention, I started having recurring dreams about travelling by passenger train to Washington, D.C. Unlike in the airport dreams, I always got my ticket on time and made it onto the train. I asked a friend what he thought the dreams meant. He said, "That's easy. You are obviously on the right track!"

Surprisingly, soon after this conversation there was a mercury pollution control convention in Washington, D.C. I attended the convention, thinking that I would find myself in a sea of strangers, and yet my dreams were urging me to go. When I arrived at the hotel where the convention was staged, I walked into a mercury tradeshow room and heard somebody call out my name. I turned around to face a smiling exhibitor, the Vice-President of a company and a person who I had met about three years before. How he had remembered my first name, I have no idea. When he asked me why I was there, I explained that I had just received government acceptance of my mercury control invention as unique and belonging solely to me and was looking for a sponsor to help develop and market it. Three months later, his company licensed my invention and has since commercialized it in Canada and the United States.

10. Online/Offline

Although, like most people, I read a lot online, I am careful to manually search un-hyperlinked, non-electronic information, including old archived information, and I use statistical software when analyzing complex interactions between multiple input variables to optimize an output variable. In fact, I used this software to design coal ash grinding recipes—minimization of marble sizes in the ping pong ball field—that increased the speed of grinding by up to 24X the prior art. Although there is nothing inherently less biased about printed material over online material, neither source should be treated as an only source or "island unto itself."

11. Work vs. play

I try to turn work into play as often as possible to make it as much fun as possible. This is necessary to weather the emotional impact of hitting temporary or permanent dead ends when undergoing the creative process. The deeper the exploration, the more likely it is that dead ends will occur. Shallow exploration, such as hyper-speed, time-constrained brainstorming, results in fewer dead ends, but also tends to bring shallower results. I like to imagine myself as a blissful astronaut flying into the unknown. Deep, playful exploration is like the ancient game of snakes and ladders: if you stop rolling the dice, you can't move forward, and therefore you can't win. If you roll the dice, you may also lose, but moving forward is the only possible way to win. If you lose one game, you may win another game. A dead end may be a lost game, or merely a snake in a winning game. Dead ends often lead to new beginnings.

12. Feedback loops

Try to think of holograms, synchronicities, peer review, and outsider curiosity as a way to magnify your internal consciousness (e.g. thinking, biases, concepts, logic, experience) and chances of success. For instance, it can be very useful for very creative people to interact with other Artists or Craftsmen anyway they can, especially to add structure to vague or semi-vague concepts. Get feedback anyway you can. Remember not to judge feedback too quickly. It doesn't have to stick to you if you ultimately judge it as un-useful in whole or in part. Let it flow, let it flow, let it flow...

13. Brainstorming

I'll use brainstorming when I'm in a hurry brought on by a crisis, but never when I have ample time. The weakness of brainstorming is that it doesn't allow sufficient time for subconscious incubation of ideas, synchronicities, or input from creative introverts who may be timid.

14. Ego management

A human "switchboard" can interact with itself and others at a fifth or sixth sensory level.

A human ego interacts with itself at a fifth sensory level.

Transformational creativity is enhanced by the suspension of the ego to a less dominant role as often as possible to maximize deeper fifth sensory perception plus sixth sensory perception from any source.

Final Words

Try to develop a "loose", camcorder-like relationship with potentially transformational information by playfully, peacefully, and diligently letting it flow as long as possible. Intuition and synchronicity require unregimented free flow of information (e.g. let the untethered "sheep-dogs" talk to the "sheep" as long as possible).

Dr. Lou Marinoff

Dr. Marinoff is Professor and Chair of Philosophy at The City College of New York, and President of the American Philosophical Practitioners Association (APPA). He has authored several books, including the international bestseller *Plato, Not Prozac!: Applying Eternal Wisdom to Everyday Problems*, which has been translated into 27 languages.

Interview

CRITICAL THINKING, ETHICS, PHILOSOPHICAL COUNSELING

Param Media: How would you define "philosophy"?

Lou Marinoff: The standard definition of "philosophy" is uncontroversial, and flows from its Greek etymology: "love of wisdom." Defining wisdom itself, along with defining what it means to love such a thing, is a more difficult task, and much less agreed-on.

The ancient Greek philosophers espoused four cardinal virtues: wisdom, courage, justice, and temperance (i.e. moderation). If we attempt to define any one of these virtues, via formal and robust methodologies, we quickly discover that they are interrelated. For example, one usually requires some measure of wisdom, courage, and temperance in order to be just. Similarly, people who regularly exercise injustice are also likely to be unwise, uncourageous (i.e. either cowardly or reckless), and intemperate. Exactly like virtues, vices are interrelated.

If you wish to define "philosophy" in more colloquial or operational terms, ask this: What does a philosopher do? Answers to this question are bound to be more diverse, more controversial, and less agreed-on by philosophers and non-philosophers alike.

PM: What are the most important guiding philosophical principles in your life?

LM: While I do not believe it is such a simple matter to say that one's life is guided by a set number of principles, I do think that certain guiding principles (truths, or ideas) tend to have an important influence on our lives. Siddhartha Gautama needed four noble truths to reveal an eight-fold way to summarize Buddhism; Euclid required five postulates to generate plane geometry; Moses delivered ten commandments to forge his covenant; the American Bill of Rights consists of the first ten amendments to the U.S. Constitution. I will here mention four that have been important for me.

The first is from Chinese philosophy's *I Ching*, or *Book of Changes*, an anonymous work that exerted seminal influence on both Lao Tzu and Confucius. Its central tenet: change is inevitable, and so our primary challenge is to make the best of changes, instead of the worst. We cannot necessarily or at all control change, but we can control what we make of it. (This principle is also shared by the Stoics.) Second is an idea from early Buddhism, expressed for example in the *Dhammapada*: we co-create salient aspects of our reality with our thought-forms. "As you think, so shall you become." This is part of a larger doctrine on karma, which asserts that our thoughts, words, and deeds are like pebbles cast in a pond: they exert ripple effects, and the ripples eventually reflect back upon us as well. (This was echoed by Ecclesiastes.)

Third, I long ago took to heart the importance of encouraging and promoting individual merit, and of not allowing individualism to be devalued, constrained, prohibited, or trumped by collectivism. In support of this social axiom I incorporate teachings from Western philosophers including Aristotle, John Stuart Mill, Ayn Rand, and Karl Popper, among others, as well as cautionary tales from Johann Wolfgang von Goethe, Gustav Le Bon, George Orwell, and Eric Hoffer concerning the suppression of individuals by collectives, which potentially degenerate into mobs. With respect to the conduct of his or her own life, the individual is either a sovereign or a slave, and sovereignty is infinitely preferable to slavery. Of course this does not preclude rendering services to others, and to society: service-providers are not slaves, because they willingly and often gladly choose to provide services, whereas slaves have no choice in the matter.

The fourth guiding principle would be this: all great things are the sum of many small ones. As Lao Tzu said "The longest journey begins under your feet." This is empowering, because most of us can manage to take one step now. What prevents some people from embarking on important journeys is their anticipated length: "It's too far." Nothing is too far, if you take one step at a time. Therefore, if you aspire to lead a great life, by manifesting your inner greatness, do not think about how difficult it is to be great. Think only about how easy it is to be small, and also about where you will find the patience and perseverance to do many small things, repeatedly and well.

PM: Could you give a brief clarification of the terms "reason", "logic," and "critical thinking," as well as "intuition," "insight," and "emotion?"

LM: I can try, although some of these terms are easier to clarify than others. First, it is helpful to appreciate that the human brain is bicameral; that is, consists of two hemispheres. The left hemisphere is generally responsible for language, as well as logical, mathematical, and scientific thinking. The Greeks called this *logos*: the faculties of speech and reason. Reasoning ability, both logical and empirical, is based here. The right hemisphere is generally responsible for creative functions: musical, artistic, and other aesthetic pursuits. The Greeks called this *mythos*: the faculties of imagination and intuition.

Reason is a versatile vehicle. Its engine runs on deduction, induction, and (when all else fails) statistics. Reason conveys us to novel destinations on the map of understanding, in such a way as to blaze trails that others can follow. The products of one person's reason are generally intelligible to another person's reason. Reason operates in both internal and external domains. Internal reason we call logic; external reason, science.

Logic is mainly concerned with the internal consistency of arguments, which are valid or invalid according to their structures, and virtually independent of their contents (except in notorious cases embodying sell-referential premises.) An argument is deductively valid if and only if it is impossible for the premises to be true and the conclusion false. Since deductive validity depends upon logical structures only, it does not require that any of the premises actually *be* true, only that the conclusion would have to follow if they *were* true.

For example, the argument "All As are Bs; all Bs are Cs; therefore all As are Cs" is deductively valid according to its structure, no matter what A, B, and C stand for. So the argument "All dogs are cats; all cats are birds; therefore all dogs are birds" is deductively valid, because if the premises were true, the conclusion would also be true.

Science demands something stronger: arguments that are both deductively valid, and whose premises are true in extra-mental reality.

Such arguments are called "sound." For example, "All dogs are mammals; all mammals are warm-blooded; therefore all dogs are warm-blooded" is a sound argument, because it is both deductively valid, and its premises are true in extra-mental reality. A sound argument delivers a truthful and therefore useful conclusion about the world. Any science that embodies one or more false premises will necessarily be wrong in its deductions, and misguided in its applications. The history of science is rife with examples.

When we attempt to reason about the external world, more often than not we are endeavoring to explicate chains in the causal nexus. Deductively valid arguments are acausal. They transcend space-time, and are therefore valid in any place and at any time, whereas reasoning about cause and effect is necessarily bound up with space-time, within which the flux of events is subject to lawful change, and likewise to capricious interpretation. Even when we enlist reason to elucidate objective empirical facts -- such as the structure of DNA, or the shape of the benzene molecule -- we see from the history of science that such enterprises are fraught with uncertainty, prone to trial and error.

Scientific breakthroughs are not made by unaided reason alone; they require insight, intuition, and frequently accident. Fleming's discovery of penicillin, and Penzias's and Wilson's discovery of the cosmic "echo" of the Big Bang, were unintended by-products of experiments consecrated to other purposes. Crick and Watson, who discovered DNA's "double helix," were not blinded by received dogmas. Kekulé famously realized the shape of benzene immediately upon awakening from a sleep; it was a sudden insight, not a protracted deduction. Scientific success is not simply or purely a function of left-brain reason; rather, it frequently requires right-brain insight, or imagination, which can then be tested by left-brain rigor.

I would propose the following distinction between *intuition* and *insight*. First, intuition is the faculty of knowing something without knowing how one comes to know it. Reason can always give an account of how it comes to know something, whether a logical truth or an empirical fact. Intuition can never give an account of how it comes to know something, except by an appeal to intuition itself (e.g. typically:

"I don't know *how* I know; I just *do*.") Second, insight is the faculty of making a cognitive breakthrough after having thought about a problem rationally for some time. The insightful moment is instantaneous, just as the intuitive one is, but in the case of intuition there is not normally a history of prior contemplation, whereas in the case of insight there is.

All this underscores the importance of *critical thinking*. Its main aim, as taught in the universities, is to make non-philosophers aware of logical fallacies and empirically dubious claims encountered in everyday life. Students who take critical thinking are better-positioned to assess the validity or soundness of arguments propounded by the media, by advertisers, by politicians, by fanatics, by family members, by friends, by whomever. In the absence of critical thinking, people remain vulnerable to every conceivable kind of brainwashing, whether motivated politically, religiously, economically, or in any other way. Indeed, an educational system which emphasized critical thinking would inculcate healthy skepticism in a broad spectrum of the population. Yet every generation of humanity in recorded history has succumbed to some litany of nonsense or other, and is ever-ready to persecute truth-tellers. One reason for this is the power of *emotion*, particularly when aligned in herd-like mass-movements.

This brings us to the last term on your list, namely "emotion," about which we know least of all -- notwithstanding an enormous proliferation of literature in many fields. Some of the earliest scientific studies of emotion were undertaken by physiologists (e.g. Canon and Sherrington), because they recognized its connection with the central nervous system and the most evolutionarily ancient part of our brains -- the limbic system. Indeed, Darwin had posited that emotions must play some salutary role in our survival as a species, or they would not have been selected for with such intensity and ubiquity across our species. Contemporary neuroscience informs us that hormones and neurochemical transmitters also play vital roles in mediating emotion, which has led to the flooding of consumer markets with mood-enhancing pharmaceutical formulations. Psychotherapies of many kinds deal primarily with "feelings," which are the cognitive echoes of emotions, powerful enough to overrule reason and govern people's lives, for better or worse. Positive emotions can be strongly motivating; negative ones, strongly debilitating.

In the short run, our strongest emotions can and do override our capacity for reason. The source of primitive emotions appears to be the limbic system, the most ancient part of the brain in evolutionary terms. The limbic system is pre-verbal and pre-conceptual, so is not directly amenable to the linguistic and conceptual faculties of the neo-cortex, our newest module. This is why negative emotions (e.g. anger) cannot be dispelled simply by telling oneself that one is better off not being angry. Similarly, positive emotions (e.g. love) cannot be dispelled by reason either; so, for example, you cannot reason your way out of unrequited love, even though you know it may be a bad emotional investment. Emotions undoubtedly played a vital role in our natural history, and contributed to our survival and evolutionary success. But they are a two-edged sword, or zero-sum game, such that every positive emotion we can experience is counterbalanced by a potentially negative one.

Absent a "grand unified theory" of the emotions, the benefit of hindsight allows us to appreciate their original "survival value," from the perspectives of human sociobiology and evolutionary psychology. But at times, our emotions are simply too numerous and too powerful for our own good. This compelled political theorists like Hobbes, and psychologists like Freud, to assert that human civilization cannot be peaceful and harmonious unless citizens are willing to renounce or rein in their strongest desires, for the sake of civil society itself. In evolutionary terms, that's a tall order.

Western and Asian philosophers alike have long grappled with this problem, or at least have identified salient components of it. The Stoics realized that negative emotions cannot be dispelled by reason alone, and so they sought brilliantly to finesse them by correcting negative judgments, which are amenable to reason. Spinoza later accomplished a similar mission. Indian philosophy long ago asserted that desire is mankind's greatest enemy, and developed yogic practices that allow one to control it, and ultimately to conquer it. Buddhists have identified "three poisons" -- anger, hatred, envy -- that are emotionally toxic to happiness and well-being, and have similarly developed practices for transforming them into wholesome mind-states -- kindness, love, compassion -- which are essential to happiness and well-being.

Current neuroscientific work (such as that by D'Amasio) suggests that the distinction between emotion and reason is not black-and-white, and that we require emotional inputs to be fully functional: e.g. to formulate goals, and to achieve them. This would help account for the fact that while computers have surpassed human beings in executing purely logical programs, from crunching numbers to playing chess, computers have not (yet) surpassed human beings in social or civic interactions, which have significant emotional content.

Notwithstanding their disadvantages and drawbacks, the panoply of human emotions is also a source of pride (another potentially dangerous emotion) as a unique characteristic of *being* human. Since we are stuck with our emotions, we may as well make the best of them.

PM: In what ways can philosophy be applied to help us envision and implement better approaches to doing business locally, nationally, and globally?

LM: I will list below ten different ways in which philosophy can be and has been applied to ameliorate approaches to business. Before doing so, I must offer a couple of overarching points.

First, there is an ongoing debate about the moral status of "business ethics" -- the most dubious among subjects in the applied ethics stream. Most people appreciate the moral and practical necessity of biomedical ethics, engineering ethics, environmental ethics, and so forth. At the same time, textbooks on legal ethics are vanishingly thin, while those on political ethics are non-existent -- unless you consider Machiavelli a political ethicist. Bertrand Russell didn't: he once called *The Prince* "a handbook for gangsters." Similarly, business ethics often attracts criticism from cynics, who maintain that since the main objective of business is to maximize profits, ethics are irrelevant if not oxymoronic. With this view I beg to differ.

Money itself is morally neutral; it is inherently neither good nor evil. Love of money is another matter entirely, and one can see how it leads to evil. But merely observing that someone is wealthy, or for that matter impecunious, entails no moral judgments about that person's character. The operative question, from which moral judgments do follow, is this: *how* does a given person earn their money? If a person or organization earns money by providing beneficial products or services, then by and large that is morally reputable; whereas if a person or organization earns money by providing harmful products or services, then that is morally disreputable. Of course, this distinction is far from black-and-white, since benefits and harms are not mutually exclusive and are often entangled (for example, as in risks of harmful side-effects from medications that may be helpful). But this is at least a first-order way of assessing the moral status of business profits. Do you profit mostly from helping, or from harming others? This is a weighty question.

The second overarching point has to do with local, national, and global contexts. The internet and cyberspace have largely transcended these boundaries. Any business with a website is global in terms of its potential exposure, even though it may confine itself to offering goods or services exclusively in a local or national marketplace. "Act locally, think globally" has become a maxim for doing business in today's global village.

Here are ten ways in which philosophers can work with businesses:

1) Helping craft mission, vision, or values statements.
2) Helping draft and implement manuals of best practices and/or codes of ethics.
3) Advisement on social responsibility and philanthropy.
4) Advisement on environmental responsibility.
5) Advisement on socially responsible wealth ownership and stewardship.
6) Advisement on patronizing the arts.
7) Helping cultivate leadership and entrepreneurship.
8) Helping to educate for innovation.
9) Conducting motivational events.
10) Conducting workshops, e.g. Socratic dialogue, dilemma training, strategic gaming.

As you may know, philosophical practitioners render these services to a variety of organizations worldwide. I would like to see the establishment of "Philosopher in Residence" programs, in which philosophers could render such services to organizations as in-house providers, for fixed periods of six months to one year. Such programs would greatly ameliorate the quality of life within organizations, and would make for more ethical and values-oriented organizational cultures. Virtuous cultures are happier than vicious ones, are more productive, and (I would hazard to guess) not less profitable.

PM: Can we talk intelligibly about social justice without first having some idea of what true justice really is? How can we know justice itself?

LM: To your first question: no, we cannot talk intelligibly about anything, unless we first have some idea as to what it is -- unless we depend on blind luck, and hope that the arrow of intuition finds the bull's-eye of inquiry, even though the archers are blindfolded by ignorance. Ignorance is removed only by arriving at true ideas as to what something is, as opposed to false ones, or to none at all.

To your second question: you can begin to know justice itself by studying foundational philosophical treatments of it. The most important ones have been implemented in various ways at various times, so one can weigh their empirical effects in addition to evaluating their hypothetical merits.

That said, the answers that you get to these two questions depend fundamentally on what kind of philosopher you ask. For example, Plato's *Republic* is devoted to addressing precisely these two questions. It begins with Socrates eliciting an assortment of half-baked opinions as to what justice is, from citizens who speak unreflectively from their immediate experiences and emotions, without connection to any transcendent or universal perspectives. The result is that their naive definitions of justice are easily exposed by Socrates as self contradictory (i.e. as producing injustice), and therefore are unsatisfactory.

The most troublesome and troubling definition is put forward by Thrasymachus. He is neither untutored nor naive; rather, observant and cynical. He claims that justice is nothing but "the interests of the stronger." This is not entirely sophomoric, and so Plato needs a whole book to refute him, advancing his own theory in the bargain.

Plato's answer is that what you call "true justice" is essentially a "Pure Form" or "Eternal Idea" of justice, which resides outside space-time, in the realm of Forms or Ideas, which are non-material and immutable, but which can be apprehended by the human mind.

According to this rather elegant theory, societies which are profoundly unjust are governed by rulers and legislators who have not glimpsed the Pure Form of justice, and are therefore incapable of imbuing their governance models with its essence. On the other hand, societies which are reasonably just are governed by rulers and legislators who have at least glimpsed the Pure Form of justice, and are therefore capable of imbuing their governance models with its essence.

On Plato's view, what prevents most people from apprehending the Pure Forms is their literal or figurative enslavement by rulers, power-brokers, and culture-makers, who keep them chained to the cave wall, where they can see only shadows and misrepresentations of things, and can only guess at their true origins and compositions. In today's parlance, the masses are brainwashed from cradle to grave by regnant dogmas, ideologies, and untruths -- and in every nation of the world, some more, others less.

For Plato, it is the philosopher's duty to descend into the cave, sunder these shackles, and lead people into the light of day, i.e. of pure contemplation, where they can apprehend the Forms and thus be liberated from the illusions and delusions imposed on them by others. Socrates was martyred for doing just this.

Aristotle took issue with Plato's theory of justice, which is why he did not succeed Plato as head of the Academy, and was obliged to found his own school, the Lyceum. He also had no desire to be martyred, as Socrates was, and so Aristotle fled Athens when vacillating popular opinion eventually turned against all things Macedonian, including him.

Aristotle was adamant in his refutation of Plato on this point, insisting (for example) that people do not become good by contemplating

Goodness, rather by doing good deeds. Similarly, we become courageous by exercising courage. One of the flaws in Aristotle's theory is precisely the point you raise in your question: he presupposes that people already know the difference between good and evil, justice and injustice, without requiring deep contemplation. They only need to be persuaded that their happiness depends on the exercise of virtues instead of vices, and then they will exercise virtues according to Aristotle's "manual" of virtue ethics. Since justice is one of the cardinal virtues, Aristotle believed that justice is attainable by regular practice, rather than by pure contemplation.

What Plato and Aristotle hold in common is that a just state requires just citizens; that is, citizens who have balanced the rational, emotional, and instinctual aspects of their souls. They differ only on how this is to be accomplished: for Plato, primarily through contemplation of the Forms; for Aristotle, primarily through exercise of virtues.

A third major theory of justice, which is theological, emerged in Augustine's *City of God*. In essence it asserts that all attempts to create and sustain just societies on earth (the *City of Man*) are doomed to fail. For Augustine, and indeed for billions of adherents to Abrahamic faiths, true justice can only be divine, not man-made. On this view, life is a preparation for divine judgment, culminating either in salvation or damnation, and therefore the attainment of eternal justice (in the *City of God*) comes through a life of piety, devotion, and prayer in the *City of Man*.

These three classical theories were harmonized in Raphael's 1510 painting known as "The School of Athens," which was originally entitled *Causarum Cognitio* (Knowledge of Causes). Its centerpiece depicts Plato and Aristotle standing together, each holding a book, and gesticulating in different directions. Plato holds his *Timeaus* (his cosmology), and points skyward, toward the heavens, where supposedly the Forms reside. Aristotle holds his *Ethics*, and points outward, along the earth, indicating that we are embodied beings (in addition to contemplative ones), and thus need to exercise our virtues. These two giants share the center stage, not in opposition, but in orthogonality: literally, their arms are ninety degrees apart. This defines a plane, not a contradiction.

Moreover, the painting was commissioned by Pope Julius II, and is on public display in the Vatican, the "halfway house" between the City of God and the City of Man. The Roman Church of the Italian Renaissance was humanistic, and approved of Greek philosophy.

Subsequent centuries have witnessed a great proliferation of theories of justice and its administration: from contractarian to utilitarian to communitarian; from the Divine Right of Kings to the General Will of the People to the Dictatorship of the Proletariat; from anarchism to objectivism to utopianism. More recently, globalized theories of justice are often expressed in terms of human rights, via instruments such as the Millennium Development Goals. Animal rights are also bundled with some contemporary theories and practices of justice, as are many aspects of environmentalism. Add to this a congeries of populist conceptions of justice, usually with parochial and mutually contradictory single-plank agendas, such as "Pro-Life" versus "Pro-Choice", and we can easily see that there are, indeed, many different notions of, and often dogmatic or unconscious assumptions about, the nature of justice.

Sometimes, we know justice best by experiencing injustice. Only then are we moved to contemplate both deeper and more universal aspects of the human condition, to become philosophers instead of perpetrators, victims, or parrots of an ideology-of-the-month.

However, no matter how you construe justice, and no matter in which sphere or stratum you may seek it, at any given moment the world always appears unjust to some, and just to others. In this world, there is no time and place in which perfect justice prevails. Justice systems do not produce justice as car factories produce cars. Injustice is often a byproduct of justice systems themselves.

If people desire that the virtue of justice prevail, at least partially, and if they wish to serve its cause, then let them heed Plato: they should spend some time contemplating justice, with the guidance of a philosopher, before they embark blindly on its practice -- or malpractice, as the case may be.

PM: Is there an underlying metaphysical or spiritual system of values across the world's religious/spiritual traditions, and how is philosophical understanding essential to any sort of interfaith dialogue?

LM: These are two good questions with which to conclude our interview.

First, you seem to be seeking a common denominator that undergirds the world's religious and spiritual traditions (à la Joseph Campbell?). Before approaching that, we must distinguish between religion and spirituality. By a "religion," I understand a set of beliefs about the supernatural and our relation to it, subscribed to by sufficient numbers over sufficient time to acquire (in global parlance) a "brand" name. There is now a recognized set of so-called "world religions" -- e.g. Judaism, Christianity, Islam, Hinduism, Buddhism, Sikhism, among others -- which have had millions or billions of adherents over centuries, and across oceans and continents. They are almost all characterized by a scripture and associated worshipful practices, which bind them to their respective Godhead. (Buddhism differs in that it posits no external Godhead, but it is nonetheless a religion.) To be robust in a religious sense, a scripture must contain a "theory of everything," to help its believers feel secure. The etymology of "religion" is the Latin *religere*, to bind, and religions indeed bind believers to their particular Godhead, by means of their particular "theory of everything."

Thomas Hobbes, whose far-sighted and witty philosophical vision brought several death sentences upon him, which he managed to evade until the age of ninety-one when the Grim Reaper finally took him, defined *religion* as "tales publicly allowed"; *superstition*, as "tales not publicly allowed." In other words, all religions are based on superstitious tales, only some are publicly approved or sponsored, while others fall under suspicion or are prohibited and often are characterized as "cults". In popular imagination, a "cult" is morally suspect, whereas a religion is trustworthy. Hobbes made the telling point that *all* religions are cults, whether publicly approved or not.

Philosophers have constantly been in trouble with organized religions, because we are resistant to brainwashing, immune to proselytization, and not shy to say why. Philosophers know better than most people that there is no complete, consistent, and coherent "theory of everything" -- on the contrary, we're lucky if we can develop a complete, consistent, and coherent theory of *anything*. Most philosophers would rather live with the discomfort of doubts, rather than be anaesthetized by dogmas.

Today, many Churches are in crisis, and we are witnessing a widespread secularization of formerly devoutly religious populations. Millions of Americans now identify themselves as "spiritual, but not religious," signifying that they sustain some mystical state of awe, wonder, and appreciation of the amazingness of our universe and all it contains, but don't need and don't want to be party to religious organizations and their concomitant dogmas. "Spiritual but not religious" is a beautiful phrase to me.

To conclude, you ask "How is philosophical understanding essential to any interfaith dialogue?" This is a great question.

To begin with, and from what we have seen thus far, it should be clear that a secular philosopher is the ideal person to facilitate an interfaith dialogue. Many philosophical practitioners -- present company included -- regularly facilitate dialogues for all kinds of groups, and plurality of opinion in a group is always a virtue at the beginning. Plurality becomes transformed into consensus by the process of dialogue itself.

Second, secular philosophers are much more likely to be neutral (that is, equitable) facilitators of an inter-faith dialogue, precisely because they have no theological stake in any of the religions themselves. To borrow Bertrand Russell's unvarnished vocabulary, the philosopher regards each religion as "a brand of sacred nonsense," and so favors none. As Russell pointed out, each brand of sacred nonsense regards itself as the absolute truth, and the others as damnable heresy. As one discovers in a practical vein, this gives them at least as much to talk about as to quarrel about; that is, when their leaders are willing to talk instead of quarrel.

In fact, the faithful in such a convention suddenly become aware that a true heretic is in their midst: a philosopher, who doubts or disbelieves or disavows all their most cherished articles of faith. Theologically, the philosopher is clearly further apart from them than they are from each other. Thus, the very presence of such a philosopher makes them feel closer with one another. This is beneficial to their dialogue.

On one such occasion, I found myself in a room with leaders of some world religions, who had convened to search for common values. They were motivated to do for both acute and chronic reasons. Acutely, they were all concerned that 9/11 and its aftermath had diverted the world into a perilous course -- theologically, politically, and economically. Believing that peace is preferable to war, they sought political stability, and were hopeful that interfaith dialogue would help pacify their adherents. Chronically, they all felt threatened by globalization itself -- its allure of secular materialism, social and sexual radicalism, moral relativism, and spiritual bankruptcy. They wanted economic prosperity for their adherents in addition to political stability, but feared that the faithful would melt away if they became "too globalized." Their challenges were great: How can major world religions enact reforms in order to keep up with the times, yet not lose their fundamental identities in the process?

Since theologians and philosophers are both concerned with moral questions, the search for common values touched on the idea of a moral compass for humanity. All religions offer moral guidance to their adherents, and engage in charitable works, all of which are of increasing value in a globalized and secularized world that is habitually driven by predatory and opportunistic capitalism. Philosophy helped these religious leaders to contextualize their problems, thus allowing them to see that their noblest virtues are all cut from the same human cloth, no matter which God (if any) wielded the scissors.

Dr. Samir Mahmoud

Dr. Samir Mahmoud is a Visiting Assistant Professor in the Department of Architecture & Design at the American University of Beirut. He received his PhD from the Faculty of Divinity, University of Cambridge, researching comparative aesthetics (Western and Islamic). In addition to his several publications, he has also founded a unique touring company, Mediterranean Cultural Academy, and Placemaking Lebanon, a design and strategy consultancy for public spaces in Lebanon.

Dr. Samir Mahmoud

Tasting Reality: An Islamic Mystic's Perspective on Direct Intuitive Knowledge

DIVINE INSPIRATION, CREATION, RENEWAL

There is a banyan tree outside my office, and as I write this chapter I cannot help but contemplate its majesty: it began its life as an epiphyte, its seeds germinating in the crevice of an old, dry stone wall that once helped to support a cascade of terraces on the northern slope of a Beirut hill overlooking the Mediterranean. It is a remarkable tree, with its deep green leaves, hollow core, and serpentine aerial roots sprouting out of every branch and meandering back into the ground. It has stood there for over a century, both serving as a witness *to* and being witnessed *by* a myriad of life forms, including myself on this sunny spring morning. Its life has been repeatedly replenished since it came into existence. What stories it could tell, if only it could speak!

I could describe this tree from a detached perspective, using statements like 'this tree is a particular instance of a banyan tree, which belongs to the fig family of trees', and then go on to recite the scientific data I can find in the annals of botanical journals. In a related fashion, I could enter into the realm of abstract thought, making logical categories and distinctions and reducing the tree to a universal type. What characterizes this rational approach is a withdrawal away from the phenomenon of *this* particular banyan tree. There seems to be a direct relation between the degree of reliance on reason and abstract thought to know reality on the one hand, and the degree of denigration of the appearance of things and their singular uniqueness on the other. In other words, the more rational and scientific our approach to knowledge of trees in general, the less we know about the uniqueness of any one tree in particular.

Likewise, one could say that the greater the degree of reliance on immediate experience or intuition, the higher the degree of taking the singular uniqueness of things and their appearances seriously. At least this is the opinion of the author I will be considering in this chapter, *Ibn ʿArabī,*[47] one of Islam's greatest mystics. Ibn ʿArabī spent most of his life defending the path of immediate experience or intuition, taking the plunge into things in the manner in which they appear through their sensible appearance.[48]

For Ibn ʿArabī, taking his cues from the Quran, all things pulsate with a unique praise (*tasbīḥ*)[49] of the Divine Being that sustains them.[50] Only Prophets, and often mystics, have been gifted with understanding the tongue of trees, birds, and nature, but this is a gift that ordinary human beings can also acquire. The banyan tree is more than just a particular instantiation of a universal type or species. It stands alone,

---

[47] His full name is Muḥammad b. ʿAlī b. Muḥammad Ibn al-ʿArabī al-Ṭāʾī al-Ḥātimī (1165-1240), but he is known as Ibn ʿArabī. He is considered Islam's greatest mystical philosopher, which earned him the honorific Doctor Maximus (al-Shaykh al-Akbar), and his name is associated with the famous doctrine of the 'Oneness of Being' (*waḥdat al-wujūd*). Born into a noble family of Arab descent in Murcia in 1160, he turned to the contemplative life early on in life as a result of a number of personal mystical experiences. He is best known for his visionary work 'The Bezels of Wisdom' (*Fuṣūṣ al-Ḥikam*) translated by Ralf Austin, *Ibn Arabī: The Bezels of Wisdom*, New Jersey: Paulist Press, 1980 and his magnum opus 'The Meccan Revelations' (*al-Futūḥāt al-Makkiyyah*), both of which were written as a result of direct experience or intuition. In terms of the details of Ibn ʿArabī's life, see Ralph Austin, *Sufis of Andalucía: The Rūḥ al-Quds and al-Durra al-Fākhira of Ibn ʿArabī*, London, George Allen & Unwin, 1971 and Claude Addas, *Quest for the Red Sulphur: The Life of Ibn ʿArabī*. Cambridge, UK: The Islamic Texts Society, 1993.

[48] For an excellent exposition of the relation between intellect and intuition in Islam, see S.H. Nasr, 'Intellect and Intuition in Islam: Their Relationship from the Islamic Perspective,' *Studies in Comparative Religion*, Vol. 13, No. 1 & 2 (Winter-Spring), World Wisdom, 1979. See also Sajjad Rizvi, 'Mysticism and Philosophy: Ibn ʿArabī and Mulla Ṣadra,' *The Cambridge Companion to Arabic Philosophy*, ed. Peter Adamson and Richard C. Taylor, Cambridge University Press, Cambridge, 2005. For a look at another Islamic author who placed immediate experience and non-discursive modes of knowledge at the heart of his philosophy, see Samir Mahmoud, 'Suhrawardī and Plotinus on Self-Knowledge as Illumination,' *Selections from the Prometheus Trust Conferences, 2006-2010*, edited by Linda H. Woodward, The Prometheus Trust, 2013.

[49] Q (17:44): "The seven heavens and the earth and all that is therein praise Him, and there is not a thing but hymneth his praise; but ye understand not their praise. Lo! He is ever Clement, Forgiving."

[50] The Divine Being, the Compassionate One, or the One all refer to God.

unique, and like no other. To know it in its uniqueness, one must plunge into it, and not withdraw from it into a realm of abstract ideas and constructed scientific categories. But what does it mean to "plunge into things," and what kind of knowledge can be gained from such an approach? We shall turn to this at the end of the chapter, but first let us explore Ibn 'Arabī's extraordinary view of reality and existing things.

The Breath of the Compassionate One (*Nafas al-Raḥmān*)

Ibn 'Arabī's mystical intuition of reality provides a most ingenious image to depict existence, namely the image of the great respiratory cycle of breathing in and breathing out (*tanaffus*). For Ibn 'Arabī, the world is breathed into existence by God through what he calls 'the Breath of the Compassionate One'. God knows and embraces all the latent possibilities within His own Reality, as if drawing a deep breath.[51] He then feels sadness (*karab*) towards them because their state of non-manifestation is like a constriction of the breath, an extreme compression of non-manifestation that needs to be alleviated. So God exhales in the same manner as one would to relieve holding one's breath, showing compassion (*raḥma*) towards the latent non-manifest possibilities, and thereby manifesting them and giving birth to the cosmos in the process, while also relieving His own constriction. The Divine Being breathed, and by so doing externalized the inner realities within Him.

The image of breathing helps clarify an important aspect of Ibn 'Arabī's view of creation. It is not a creation from nothing (*creatio ex nihilo*) that explains creation, but theophany or Self-disclosure (*tajallī*), which is a passage from the state of being hidden, latent, and in potentiality to the luminous, manifest, revealed state. Since *theophany* refers to God becoming visible to humans, we can say that Ibn 'Arabī's creative ontology proceeds with a *theophanic* conception of things. In other words, every individual process or thing is conceived as a manifestation,

---

[51] In Islam, the Divine is neither masculine nor feminine. The Quran is quite clear on this. However, Arabic, like many gendered languages, uses masculine or feminine nouns and pronouns to refer to God. For example, the unknowable Divine Essence is referred to in the feminine while God is referred to in the masculine.

expression, or creation of the Divine Being who manifests Himself in the infinite multiplicity of His creations.

It is this perpetual breathing in and breathing out of things that accounts for the fact that things continue (or appear to continue) to exist from one moment to the next. However, it is neither the breathing in nor the breathing out that captures the essence of reality here. Instead, the essence of reality is the moment when things emerge out of the Breath—the original matrix that brings the world into existence—or the moment they sink back into it. It is not in relation to the category of being (or nothingness) that reality is truly revealed, but in the *continual process* of beings emerging forth in their perpetual state of becoming and withdrawing, or what Ibn ʿArabī calls *renewed creation.*

Renewed Creation (Khalq Jadīd)[52]

The respiratory cycle, this process of creation/theophany, is not an event that happens once and for all. On the contrary, this cycle or process is forever recurring at every instant, faster than the blink of an eye. The world is forever resorbed back into the Divine Being, and emerges anew at every instant, this pulsating movement repeating itself perpetually. Every thing comes out of non-existence and into existence before returning back into non-existence, and this eternal emergence continues infinitely (*ad infinitum*). Ibn ʿArabī derives this principle from the Quranic verse (50:15): 'But they [the creatures] are unaware of the renewed creation'.

Renewed creation does not mean that the same thing is *re-created*, but rather that with every new creation it is both the same and not the same. Although the existence of each particular thing is forever replenished and renewed, it is never repeated, and so even if something seems identical from moment to moment, in reality it is not so. There is no repetition (*lā tikrār*) in creation, which means that the Divine Being never manifests Himself in the same form twice. The breath that gives

---

[52] William Chittick, The Sufi Path of Knowledge: Ibn al-ʿArabī's Metaphysics of Imagination, Albany: State University of New York Press, 1989, p. 96-112 (Henceforth SPK).

each thing its existence at every instant is not the same breath that gives a thing its existence in the next instant. Therefore, the things that appear to us in the cosmos are perpetually re-created, giving the illusion of permanence and stability. Each newly changed state or transformation that happens to a thing in existence is actually a new creation.[53]

For Ibn ʿArabī, what is primary in existence is the new, the act of creation, a dynamic and active process perpetually unfolding. In other words, the *act of creating* is primary, not *the created.* As such, Ibn ʿArabī insists that existence or the cosmos is in perpetual flux, always being created and re-created. Therefore, creativity is really all that there is and all that there can be, and individual aspects of the cosmos are differentiated as so many distinct acts of perpetual creation. Indeed, in the Quran, when the Divine Being wills to inaugurate existence, He says *Kun* (Be!) in the imperative, and existence comes to be.[54] The Arabic imperative, KN[55], is the Quranic language of creativity, which can only be expressed through verbs, rather than nouns. Verbs refer to flux and movement, while nouns refer to static entities, but nothing in creation is static.

---

[53] SPK, p. 96.

[54] Does this imply that the Divine Being did not exist prior to uttering 'Kun'? This is an interesting question. If existence is equated with the cosmos, and if the Divine Being willed the cosmos, then the Divine Being was in reality prior to the cosmos or existence. And so what, according to Ibn ʿArabī, was (or is) the ontological status of the Divine Being? If the Divine Being willed existence (or the cosmos) into reality, then wouldn't the Divine Being have been (or be) beyond existence, and hence in a realm of pure being? At the very least, if the Divine Being has the power to will existence into reality, then the Divine Being is something other than existence or the cosmos, which may seem to entail an unavoidable duality. However, for Ibn ʿArabī, the initiation of existence is one of manifestation, not *creatio ex nihilo,* which means that the Divine Being manifests Himself in and through existence. Ibn ʿArabī's doctrine of the Oneness of Being means that existence consists of manifestations of the Divine Being. There is naught but the Divine Being, whether before or after creation. What changes is the state of things: before creation, they were in God but not manifest externally, and after creation, they are manifest externally, but still in God. I refer the reader to p. 4 above and note 16 below for more on the question of the state of things before they came into existence.

[55] Quran, 3:47.

Ibn ʿArabī often employs the image of the day and night to refer to the nature of things. From our human phenomenological point of view, the sun rises every morning and spreads its warm light over things, rendering them visible. Gradually, things emerge from the twilight of their haziness with their contours becoming fully visible at the sun's nadir at mid-day, when shadows disappear. As the sun descends across the sky and sinks into a red sea on the horizon, things shed their forms, appear hazy once again, and then disappear under the cover of darkness. Likewise, each thing among the innumerable things of the cosmos has a daytime existence and a nighttime existence. Its daytime existence refers to its existence in the open, luminous world that we are able to witness around us. Its nighttime existence is when it exists within the Divine Being as a latent hidden possibility, waiting for the Divine Breath to bring it forth into the daylight. At every instant, everything comes forth into the daylight of existence and is resorbed back into the nighttime of non-existence. The transformation involves the end or death of one form and the birth of another. Ibn ʿArabī refers to this process for each thing as its *term* (*ajal*), and with every renewed creation a thing's form is also renewed.

The Sensible World (*ʿĀlam al-Ḥiss*)

Everything, from the highest spiritual world down to the sensible world, is a pulsation of the Divine Breath, a manifestation of the Divine Being. But isn't there a contradiction here? How can the things we witness as multiple and diverse be only part of a single force that permeates them? Is their distinct sensible difference a mere illusion? According to a certain reading of Plato, which made its way into Islamic philosophy, a fundamental dualism separates 'being' from the sensible appearances.[56] Wherever its traces can be found, this view is characterized by 'an opposition between the multifarious appearances involved in perpetual change and an immutable realm of existence, forever persisting in strictest self-identity'.[57]

For Ibn 'Arabī, one of the most ardent defenders of the reality and dignity of all the multiple things of this world, the Divine Being is manifest in the manifold things called creatures, and demands the radical singularity, individuality, and 'oneness' of every creature and every act of creation. According to Ibn 'Arabī, an individual is only truly unique (*fard*) and one (*aḥad*) if its manifestation is the result of an Unlimited and Uniquely One (*Fard*) individuating power, the One (*al-Aḥad*). 'It is evident', Ibn 'Arabī insists, that in our everyday experience of things '*this* is different from *that*'. There is no denying this point. 'This is a truly fundamental fact', Ibn 'Arabī insists, for the doctrine of no repetition and renewed creation 'necessitates that there is no similitude between the existing things and that similitude is merely conceptual and imaginary. If similitude did exist, then no single thing would be distinguishable from another thing similar to it [i.e. belonging to the same species or genus]'.[58] Therefore, there is no thing that is identical or even similar to another thing. Each possesses a uniqueness and singularity not shared by any other thing; otherwise, if similitude existed, that would limit the Divine limitlessness. 'Similitudes are conceptual and not existential'[59] in the sense that they do not actually exist in the 'real' world, but are merely conceptual categorizations of reality provided by

---

[56] I have insisted on the phrase 'a certain reading of Plato', because Platonism does not claim that transitory things are illusory. They are less real than what is eternal and unchanging, precisely because transitory things are constantly changing, and so they never remain themselves for any length of time, not so unlike the conclusion reached by Ibn 'Arabī. Also, the differences between things are not excluded from reality according to Platonism, as Proclus, for example, makes clear in his meticulous exposition of the Platonic dialectic in his Commentary on Plato's Parmenides.

[57] Aron Gurwitsch, *Phenomenology and the Theory of Science*, Evanston, Illanois: Northwestern University Press, 1974, p. 51 (Henceforth *PTS*).

[58] Ibn 'Arabī, *al-Futūḥāt al-Makkiyya*, Vols. 1–8, Beirut: Dār Ṣādir, 2008, Vol.1, Chapter 35, p. 268 (Henceforth *FM*).

[59] *FM,* Vol.1, Chapter 35, p. 269.

reason, which do not necessarily correspond to the things as they really are (*al-ashyā' kamā hiya*). For Ibn 'Arabī, who has experienced and savored the true nature of things, it is precisely our unique individuality that differentiates us from other human beings, that makes each human being one, unique, and like no other.

To further illustrate this point, Ibn 'Arabī turns to a Quranic verse that is central in Islamic theology and philosophy for explaining God's Incomparability, i.e. His utter transcendence. The verse Q (42:11) reads: 'There is no-thing like Him', meaning that there is nothing in existence that God can be compared with in terms of similitude. However, Ibn 'Arabī uses this verse in a surprisingly new way: 'Since the fundamental principle [*al-aṣl*] of our act of existing is God and He is [described as being] *there is no-thing like Him*, then *everything* that issues forth from Him cannot but be upon this [governing] reality'.[60] This means that *everything* in existence is similarly described as 'there is no-thing like it', and therefore the singular uniqueness and unity of *everything* points to the singular uniqueness and unity of God.[61] Ibn 'Arabī often repeats the Sufi adage: 'In everything He has a sign that points to that He is One'.

For Ibn 'Arabī, this radical individuality of everything even extends to the state when things were still with the Divine Being before becoming manifest by the Breath, what Ibn 'Arabī calls their immutable enti-

---

[60] *Ibid.*

[61] William Chittick, *The Self-Disclosure of God: Principles of Ibn al-'Arabī's Cosmology*, Albany: State University of New York Press, 1998., p. 44.

ties (*'ayān thābitah*), which is comparable to, but distinct from, the Platonic Forms or Ideas.[62] The essences or immutable entities provide the things of the world 'with an "essential" fixity which keeps them from disintegrating. To use our example from earlier, *this* banyan tree is different from *that* banyan tree, and each has its own distinct, unique essence, Form/Idea, permanent archetype, or immutable entity. Therefore, each immutable entity allows the Breath to manifest the Divine Being differently, leaving a unique trace in existence, which we call

---

[62] The immutable entities (a'yān thābita) for Ibn 'Arabī are forever non-existent. They possess what Ibn 'Arabī calls immutability (thubūt) or they are immutable (thābita) but not existent (mawjūda). Immutability is their state within God's knowledge, but not yet manifest externally in existence. The very notion of something possessing 'immutability' but not 'existence' is a contentious one to say the least. The key to understanding the nature of the immutable entities, then, is to understand the notion of the Supreme Isthmus (Barzakh), which stands in between Absolute Being and Absolute Non-Being. Explaining the nature of the Supreme Isthmus, Ibn 'Arabī says: 'It has a face towards Being and a face toward nothingness. It stands opposite of each of these two known things in its very essence. It is the third known thing. Within it are all possible things [that have yet to manifest]. It is infinite, just as each of the other two known things is infinite. The possible things have immutable entities within this Isthmus in the respect in which Nondelimited Being looks upon them. In this respect the possible things are called "things." When God wants to bring a "thing" into existence, He says to it, "Be!", and it is. In the respect in which nondelimited nothingness gazes upon the Isthmus, it has no existent entities. Hence God says "Be!", which is a word denoting existence. If the thing had already come to be, He would not have said to it "Be!" [...] The possible things exist in respect of this Isthmus. Through them God has a vision of the things before they come to be [...] In relation to the entities which are embraced by this Isthmus, the existent possible things which God brings into existence are like shadows in relation to corporeal bodies [...]' Ibn 'Arabī goes on to explain how 'existence' is like clothing (thawb) worn by the immutable things when they come to be. Therefore, 'the reason why immutability is attributed to this Isthmus, which is the possible thing between Being and nothingness [wherein the immutable entities are located], is that it stands opposite the two things by its very essence,' SPK, pp. 204-205. For a full study of the third thing and the isthmus in Ibn 'Arabī, see Masataka Takeshita, "An Analysis of Ibn 'Arabī's Inshā' al-Dawā'ir with Particular Reference to the Doctrine of the 'Third Thing'", Journal of Near Eastern Studies 41, pp. 243–60, 1982.

things. Existence is a veritable cascade of distinct and unique theophanies (or divine manifestations) whose waters are forever renewed and replenished.

Reason *('Aql)* & the Senses *(al-ḥiss)*

For Ibn 'Arabī, no aspect of existence is ignoble, and the manner in which each and every thing *appears* to us in the sensible world is our access to the Breath or the Divine Being. Therefore, the senses (*al-ḥiss*), which give us immediate access to the things as they appear, are given high eminence (*sharaf*). The rationalist denigration of the sensible world, however, comes as a result of the denigration of the senses as an unreliable source of true knowledge, as our senses are often accused of being prone to error. But Ibn 'Arabī insists that the senses are never wrong (except, of course, when the physical organs suffer from damage or disease). Ibn 'Arabī insists that error comes from the judging faculty, which is reason: 'What the senses [*ḥiss*] perceive is true [*ḥaqq*], for it is a conveyor [*muwṣil*]; it is not a judge [*ḥākim*] but a witness [*shāhid*]. Reason [*'aql*] is the judge and any error in judgment is referred back to the judge'.[63] 'Witness' is the key word here for Ibn 'Arabī, because the testimony of the senses is never false. Our senses are the inlets of perception, the tip of the body and its point of contact with the world. It is through the senses that difference and uniqueness are perceived; they are the starting point for a plunge into the essence of things, and as such should not be denied. Reason, on the other hand, withdraws from sensible things into a universal realm beyond, free from relativity, where 'genuine knowledge is perpetually true, under all circumstances and for everyone'.[64]

Contrary to the view that reason alone gives us true knowledge of the world, Ibn 'Arabī is adamant that just as the Divine theophanies are infinite and diverse, individually unique and like no other, so the knowledge of each is likewise diverse and like no other. No two 'knowers' can possess the same knowledge of what seem to be the same thing.

---

[63] *FM*, 1 (Chap. 34), pp. 261-262.

[64] *PTS*, p. 51.

Perceiving the Breaths is not the result of a process of approximation, representation, or logic, which would yield a knowledge that is perpetually true and for everyone. For Ibn 'Arabī, reason (*'aql'*)[65] is a word that is etymologically linked to fetter (*'iqāl*) meaning 'to fetter and to bind' or 'to hobble a camel'.[66] The very nature of reason then is to bind, to limit, to fetter. Its *modus operandi* is to cognitively bind together ideas and concepts in a linear fashion to arrive at a rational or logical conclusion. It moves forward from premise to conclusion bound by the logic of its own argument. Without this binding function, reason cannot operate. But the Breaths and Divine theophanies cannot be bound in this manner. Rather than a point of view that *re-presents* the Breath, what is required is a mode of knowledge that is *part of* the Breath. If the Breath is in perpetual motion, folding and unfolding, emerging and resorbing, then only a mode of knowledge that can fluctuate with the Breath's transformations can ever actually *be with* it. The movement of the Breath never stands still long enough for thought to represent it logically. Only a process can intertwine and participate with a process. But what mode of knowledge does this prerogative belong to?

Tasting (*Dhawq*) and the Heart (*Qalb*)

Plunging into reality and experiencing things directly for oneself is the mode of knowledge called tasting (*dhawq*).[67] About a century before Ibn 'Arabī, the Muslim theologian, jurist, philosopher, and Sufi mystic known as Ghazālī[68] had distinguished between three modes of knowing something: belief, rational demonstration, and *tasting*. A person who has never experienced sexual pleasure can accept on faith the existence of sexual desire, and may accept someone's proving it, but 'all this is far removed from apprehending the reality of [sexual] desire in

---

[65] *SPK*, p. 161.

[66] In *FM*, 2 (Chap. 70), p. 207, 21-23.

[67] Eric Ormsby, 'The Taste of Truth,' *Islamic Studies Presented to Charles J. Adams*, edited by, Wael B. Hallaq, Donald Presgrave Little, 1991.

[68] Abū Ḥāmid Muḥammad ibn Muḥammad al-Ghazālī (c. 1058–1111) is known as Al-Ghazali or Algazel to the Western medieval world.

virtue of [actually] having it'.[69] Likewise, one can accept the true nature of things based on rational demonstration, or one can plunge into reality and experience it for oneself.

If the metaphor of vision, which governs the mode of knowledge called reason, presupposes possession of the object from a distance, the metaphor of taste presupposes that we can only know something by becoming it from within. But these are more than differences between metaphors, for they are two different modes of knowledge altogether. If reason holds up a universal category or concept as a mirror to reality and presupposes the distinction between a knower and the known, between subject and object, then taste involves the dissolution of the boundaries between the knower and the known, or subject and object. If reason implies that we approach the object from a distance, from the outside, then tasting approaches it from the inside. The first mediates the object to us via the concept, representation, or universal category; the second neither depends on the concept, representation, nor any universal category, but rather the unmediated thing itself in its *singular* appearance or difference. The first kind of knowledge may be said to stop at the relative, satisfied at having *re*-presented it; the second plunges into reality itself in order to *be present to* it as it appears. The first invokes logic; the second immediate experience, or direct intuitive knowledge of reality.

The sweetness of honey is only known when it dissolves within the mouth and becomes one with the body. It is a mode of knowledge that knows from within the object of knowledge itself. For the senses, no two trees are alike, no matter that they may belong to the same species. Knowing a tree, tasting it in its particular individuality as a thing both unique and as an inflection of the Divine Breath in this instant, necessitates honoring its distinct sensible appearance. Even the act of tasting what appears to be the same thing will give a different taste from instant to instant, because we recall that each and every thing is recreated at every instant, and so it is not the same thing from moment to moment.

---

[69] Ghazālī quoted in Alexander Treiger, *Inspired Knowledge in Islamic Thought: Al-Ghazali's Theory of Mystical Cognition and its Aviecennan Foundation*, Routledge, London, 2012, p. 51.

Ibn ʻArabī gives the analogy of eating an apple: ʻMan may find in himself a distinct taste in each bite of an apple he eats, a taste not found in any other bite. The apple is one, yet he finds a sensory distinction in each bite, even if he is not able to explain it'.[70]

Therefore, changefulness and transmutation must characterize the organ that can capture the fluctuating tastes of things. If the brain is often associated with the seat of reason, then the organ of tasting reality is the heart. It may at first seem odd to say that we taste with the heart, and not the tongue; however, this is not the heart that is interred in a body and bound by it. Rather, for Ibn ʻArabī, the heart is at the center of a *subtle body* which is composed of psycho-spiritual organs that are distinct from the bodily organs. In fact, etymologically speaking, Ibn ʻArabī derives the meaning of the word heart (*qalb*) from *taqallub* and *taqlīb*, which mean ʻtransformation, change, fluctuation, and variableness', and he exhorts one to turn inwards at the transformations in one's heart to find confirmation of this from one's own everyday experience.

Commenting on the Quranic verse about renewed creation, Ibn ʻArabī says: ʻIf man vigilantly observes [*rāqaba*] his heart, he will surely see that it does not remain upon a single state'.[71] This is because the Divine Being does not remain upon a single state, due to the Divine renewed creations at every instant, the continually transmuting Self-Disclosures of God with every new creation (*khalq jadīd*).[72] The internal life and movements of the heart, the internal states (*aḥwāl*), are as diverse and rich as the movements and transformations of the cosmos itself, because they are both receiving the Divine Breaths and its transmutations and renewed creations. Our internal world and the external world are but one, and the heart faces them both. ʻKnow that the heart is [essentially] a polished mirror [*mir'āt maṣqūla*]. All of it is a face [*kulluha wajh*]'[73] facing both worlds. However, the veils of ignorance

---

[70] *SPK*, p. 220.

[71] *FM*, 5 (Chap. 348), p. 229, 10-11.

[72] *SPK*, p. 264.

[73] *FM*, 1 (Chap. 2), p. 117, 12.

tarnish its surface, making it difficult to perceive these fluctuations externally. In our state of ignorance, we are not able to perceive the transmutations and renewed creation outwardly in the sensible world, but we are able to perceive them inwardly where they are closer at hand. If we could experience them externally, we would never deny them.

So vast and all-encompassing is the heart that it can contain the Divine Being itself. Commenting on the famous Sacred Tradition whereby the Divine Being says, 'Neither My earth nor My heaven contain Me, but the heart of My believing servant contains Me', Ibn 'Arabī insists that if existence is the house of all the existents, then 'the heart of the servant is the House of the Real [*Bayt al-ḥaqq*, or the Divine Being] because it contains Him'.[74] No other human faculty has this remarkable quality. Therefore, 'He who does not witness the theophanies [of God] with his heart, will deny them for reason ['*aql*] binds whereas the heart does not.' This leads Ibn 'Arabī to conclude that '[t]he heart is a faculty beyond the frontier [*ṭawr*] of reason'.[75] It is the heart, then, and not reason that is the organ that can perceive the perpetual Divine breathing in and breathing out; the transformation (*taḥawwul*) of God in the forms of the cosmos, whereby at every new instant, everything sheds its form and assumes a new form.

The Banyan Tree: Reconnecting with Reality

The banyan tree outside my office is an extraordinary thing indeed. It has its own unique energy, its own pulsating breath that differentiates it from other banyan trees, and even from itself, from instant to instant. It has a long history, one not just steeped in time, but in the depths and heights of existence itself. It has its roots in the permanent archetype that constitutes its unique essence, and is perpetually watered by the Divine Breath that replenishes its existence at every instant. One might start by paying particular attention to the manner in which it appears from a particular angle and at a particular moment of the day and, immersed in the immediacy of its appearing, lose oneself in the ocean of

---

[74] *FM*, 7 (Chap. 504), pp. 8-9.

[75] *FM*, 1 (Chap. 58), p. 348, 7-9.

being', seeing only the face or theophany of the Divine Being in that thing.

By temporarily setting aside our fixation with reason and scientific explanations, and instead plunging into this particular banyan tree by way of the heart, I am offered the extraordinary opportunity to taste reality. It is a mode of intuitive knowledge that has too often been neglected, and it is one that is needed to balance or complement the more limited type of knowledge produced by reason. We can analyze a drop of water and show its chemical makeup, but we have lost our capacity to experience the living reality of the ocean, and without that intuitive connection, we will continue to objectify nature and, therefore, to pollute and destroy it.

Like gentle waves curling upon a beach, no single wave is identical to the next, nor is the unique trace it leaves in the sand ever repeated.

References

Addas, C., Quest for the Red Sulphur: The Life of Ibn 'Arabī. Cambridge, UK: The Islamic Texts Society, 1993.

Austin, R., Sufis of Andalucía: The Rūḥ al-Quds and al-Durra al-Fākhira of Ibn 'Arabī, London: George Allen & Unwin, 1971.

---, Ibn Arabī: The Bezels of Wisdom, New Jersey: Paulist Press, 1980.

Chittick, W. C., The Sufi Path of Knowledge: Ibn al-'Arabī's Metaphysics of Imagination, Albany: State University of New York Press, 1989.

---, The Self-Disclosure of God: Principles of Ibn al-'Arabī's Cosmology, Albany: State University of New York Press, 1998.

Corbin, H. Alone with the Alone: Creative Imagination in the Sufism of Ibn 'Arabī, Ralph Manheim (trans), Princeton: Princeton University Press, 1998.

Fenton, P. & Gloton, M. 'The Book of the Description of the Encompassing Circles,' in Muhyiddin Ibn 'Arabī: A Comemorative Volume, ed. Stephen Hirtenstein and Michael Tiernan, Rockport, Mass. Element, 1993, note 12, p. 42.

Gurwitsch, A,. Phenomenology and the Theory of Science, Evanston, Illanois: Northwestern University Press, 1974, p. 51.

Ibn ʻArabī, Muḥyiddīn Muḥammad Ibn ʻAlī, Fuṣūṣ al-Ḥikam, li-Muḥyiddīn Ibn ʻArabī. Wa-l-taʻlīqāt ʻalayhi bi-qalam Abū al-ʻAlā ʻAfīfī, (critical edition), Cairo: ʻIsā al-Bābī al-Ḥalabī, 1946.

---, Fūṣūṣ al-Ḥikam, R. W. J. Austin (trans.), Ibn al-ʻArabī: The Bezels of Wisdom, Ramsey: Paulist Press, 1981.

---, al-Futūḥāt al-Makkiyya, Vols. 1–8, Beirut: Dār Ṣādir, 2008.

---Ibn ʻArabī, The Universal Tree and the Four Birds, translated Angela Jaffray, Anqa Publishing, Oxford, 2006.

Izutsu, T., Sufism and Taoism: A Comparative Study of the Key Philosophical Concepts in Taoism and Sufism, Los Angeles: University of California Press, 1983.

Mahmoud, S., 'Suhrawardī and Plotinus on Self-Knowledge as Illumination,' Selections from the Prometheus Trust Conferences, 2006-2010, edited by Linda H. Woodward, The Prometheus Trust, 2013.

Nasr, S.H., 'Intellect and Intuition in Islam: Their Relationship from the Islamic Perspective,' Studies in Comparative Religion, Vol. 13, No. 1 & 2 (Winter-Spring), World Wisdom, 1979.

Ormsby, E., 'The Taste of Truth,' Islamic Studies Presented to Charles J. Adams, edited by, Wael B. Hallaq, Donald Presgrave Little, 1991.

Rizvi, S., 'Mysticism and Philosophy: Ibn ʻArabī and Mulla Ṣadra,' The Cambridge Companion to Arabic Philosophy, ed. Peter Adamson and Richard C. Taylor, Cambridge University Press, Cambridge, 2005.

Takeshita, M. "An Analysis of Ibn ʻArabī's Inshā' al-Dawā'ir with Particular Reference to the Doctrine of the 'Third Thing'", Journal of Near Eastern Studies 41, 1982.

Treiger, A., Inspired Knowledge in Islamic Thought: Al-Ghazali's Theory of Mystical Cognition and its Aviecennan Foundation, Routledge, London, 2012.

Dr. Bruce MacLennan

Dr. MacLennan is Associate Professor in the Department of Electrical Engineering and Computer Science at the University of Tennessee, Knoxville, USA. Complementing his pioneering interdisciplinary research, from bio-inspired computation to algorithmic nano-assembly, he has also been a student of ancient Greek and Roman philosophy for over forty years. In addition to his numerous scientific publications and presentations, Dr. MacLennan is also the author of *The Wisdom of Hypatia: Ancient Spiritual Practices for a More Meaningful Life.*

Dr. Bruce MacLennan

Ancient Intuition — Modern Science

NEOPLATONISM, ARCHETYPES, THE UNCONSCIOUS

Many great scientists have acknowledged the importance of intuition in their work. Even Albert Einstein has said, "there is no logical way to the discovery of these elemental laws. There is only the way of intuition, which is helped by a feeling for the order lying behind the appearance" (Beveridge, 1957, p. 57). And Max Planck, the chief originator of quantum physics, was adamant that "imaginative vision and faith in the ultimate success are indispensable. The pure rationalist has no place here" (Beveridge, 1957, p. 55).

But the role of intuition and imagination in science should not surprise us, as it has played an indispensible guiding role in the process of many scientific discoveries, from Isaac Newton's (1642–1727) recognition of universal gravitation, to John Dalton's (1766–1844) formation of atomic theory, and Humphry Davy's (1778–1829) chemical discoveries (Beveridge, 1957, p. 58; Davy, 1858, p. 315; Spencer, 2012, chs. 2, 5). In these and many other cases, the history of science proves the importance of intuition in its major conceptual revolutions, and therefore as scientists we should be applying intuition more consciously, and as teachers we should be training future scientists to use their intuition. Fortunately we have a model of how these goals may be achieved in Platonic philosophy, especially in its later development, called *Neoplatonism*. Plotinus (c.204–270) originated this phase of Platonic thought, which understands reality as the emanation of an ineffable first principle, and which teaches psychospiritual practices for participating in this process of emanation.

Essential to Platonic philosophy are the *Platonic Ideas* or *Forms*, which are transcendental in the sense of being eternal, non-arbitrary, common to all people, and prior to individual experience. (Contrasted with them are the many ad hoc and conventional concepts we acquire by experience from the physical world and our culture, such as *computer, weed, pet, bicycle, garden*.) Many Platonic Ideas are mathematical; for example, geometrical concepts such as triangle, circle, and line, and arithmetical concepts such as number, magnitude, ratio, and continuity. Behind these, Plato identified further abstract ideas, such as unity and multiplicity, limit and the unlimited, identity and difference, stability and change. Other Platonic ideas include symmetry, harmony, beauty, life, being, and mind. Principles such as these — and more specific laws, which are mathematical in form — govern our universe, and therefore the emergence and evolution of everything in it. In Neoplatonism, the forms are not only transcendent but also immanent in the material world as formative principles. In other words, the laws of nature exist as timeless, abstract mathematical relationships (for example, the inverse square law), but they also govern specific physical processes (e.g., the orbit of the moon around the earth, and the earth around the sun). We see only the sensible effects of these principles, but we can grasp their source by our faculty of intuitive understanding (which Platonists call *nous*).

Neoplatonists distinguish several degrees of reality, and despite various esoteric and technical disagreements, they generally adhere to the basic brief distinctions I will outline here. Between the sensible world and the realm of the Platonic forms is the cosmic soul (*anima mundi*), which is necessary to bring the eternal, timeless forms into the world of time and space as causes of motion and change; it is the *animating principle*, the cause and governor of orderly natural processes. Beyond the realm of the forms is *the ineffable One*, the unifying principle of everything, the principle by which anything, including the cosmos as a whole, is what it is. In traditional terms, the degrees of reality are, in order, the One, the cosmic mind (which contains the Platonic Ideas), the cosmic soul (which brings them to life), and the cosmic body (the sensible world).

Neoplatonism in the History of Science

It is no coincidence that Neoplatonism played an important role in the development of modern science (MacLennan, 2007; Spencer, 2012, ch. 2). Since the thirteenth century, the dominant European cosmology had been Thomas Aquinas's (1225–1274) Christianization of Aristotelian cosmology and Ptolemaic astronomy. This placed a "fallen" earth in the center of the universe (with Hell at the earth's center), surrounded by progressively more heavenly spheres, with God as prime mover residing outside them (Easlea 1980, pp. 43, 57–8). Early scientific investigations challenged the Thomistic-Aristotelian cosmology. For example, Galileo's (1564–1642) observation of mountains on the moon suggested that the heavens were not so perfect as supposed. Also, the investigations of Nicolaus Copernicus (1473–1543) and Johannes Kepler (1571–1630) suggested that the earth moves around the sun, and not vice versa. By the time the weaknesses in the Thomistic-Aristotelian system had reached the breaking point, Europe had rediscovered Platonism, largely through the Latin translations of Marsilio Ficino (1433–1499), the head of the Platonic Academy in Florence.

Especially inspirational, and broadly consistent with a Neoplatonic worldview, were the *Hermetica* (also translated by Ficino), the writings attributed to Hermes Trismegistus and therefore purported to be of enormous antiquity. Hermeticism, which viewed the universe as a unified whole animated by a world soul, emerged as a possible successor to the Thomistic-Aristotelian cosmology. But it had a competitor, the emerging *mechanical philosophy* advocated by Rene Descartes (1596–1650) and Pierre Gassendi (1592–1655), and the two competed as a basis for modern science as it developed in the sixteenth and seventeenth centuries. These philosophies had in common an appeal to invisible causes to explain visible phenomena. The mechanical philosophy appealed to material properties, such as shape, position, and motion, whereas Hermeticism appealed to archetypal ideas and hidden, animating forces. As a consequence, the mechanical philosophy viewed the material world as largely inanimate and soulless, with the exception of humans and angels, thus separating humans from the rest of nature. The natural world was viewed as a resource that could be exploited by this new "masculine philosophy" (as it was called). In contrast, Hermetic philosophers viewed Nature as a divine emanation, an embodiment of the cosmic soul, more an object of veneration than of exploitation. (For more, see Easley, 1980, and Hadot, 2006.)

In the end, the mechanical philosophy won out, in that it became the de facto worldview of the emerging scientific establishment and has provided the model for most of the subsequent development of science. In part this was due to its success in practical applications and the exploitation of natural resources. Nevertheless, Hermetic, Neoplatonic, and Pythagorean insights have played a crucial role in several major discoveries. For example, in a symbolically significant structure, the traditional Thomistic-Aristotelian cosmology had earth at its center, with fiery Hell, the epicenter of evil, within; Heaven, the source of goodness was placed as far apart from earth as possible. Nicolaus Copernicus, in contrast, placed the fiery sun in the center of the universe, and attributed the idea to Pythagoras, for the Pythagoreans spoke of a central fire, not as the epicenter of evil, but as a source of vitality, and of the sun as a visible manifestation and symbol of the ineffable One. These two viewpoints have vastly different valuations of both earth and nature. Since earth and nature were traditionally feminine and were contrasted with heaven and God (traditionally masculine), the mechanical philosophy conformed to a societal devaluation of the feminine and laid the spiritual foundations of our ecological crisis (Easlea, 1980, ch. 2; Merchant, 1980).

The paradigm for mathematical physics and astronomy was established by the Pythagorean account of consonant musical intervals in terms of the ratios of small integers (measuring, for example, the lengths of strings), which thereby reduced a mysterious sensible quality to mathematical principles. In particular, the tuned string and the musical scale became exemplars for all explanations of harmony in the universe (as they are in Plato's dialogue called the *Timaeus*). These are especially prominent in the work of Robert Fludd (1574–1637), a physician and one of the principal Hermetic philosophers. He engaged Kepler (1571–1630) in a protracted argument, for Kepler objected to his concept of a harmonious universe animated by a cosmic soul (Yates, 1964, ch. 22). Nevertheless, Kepler proposed a mathematical cosmology based on the Platonic solids and inspired by the Pythagorean notion of the music of the spheres; he was also deeply influenced by the Neoplatonic philosopher Proclus (411/12 – 485) (Siorvanes, 1996; Spencer, 2012, pp. 45, 48–50, 111).

Likewise, Newton divided the spectrum, revealed by passing white light through a prism, into *seven* colors, because he was convinced there was a hidden structure common to light and the diatonic scale in music. Newton, who was also an alchemist, Hermeticist, and theologian, was unable to account for the motion of the planets and falling objects without postulating an "occult force" — gravity! — but because such forces were anathema to mechanical philosophers, who denied action at a distance in favor of direct contact, he was obliged to declare that he made no hypotheses about occult forces, and thus left his laws of motion without explanation. Moreover, he thought that Pythagoras's harmonic theory had anticipated his inverse-square law (White, 1997, pp. 348–9).

Because Hermeticists believed in hidden causes and in nonmaterial archetypal forms, they realized that they could not penetrate the mysteries of the universe with their unaided rational minds. They needed insight and intuition into the hidden sympathies and correspondences of nature to formulate hypotheses and experiments to test their hypotheses. This is why, for example, the foundations of pharmacology were laid by Paracelsus (1493–1541), a Hermeticist and alchemist (Easlea, 1980, pp. 100–3; see also Webster, 1982). Rational analysis was necessary but limited, and so if your goal was to cure patients, you had to make bold conjectures and then test them. This process of conjecture and experiment became an essential part of modern science, but many (if not most) scientists have forgotten its Hermetic, alchemical, and Platonist roots, roots which are still essential today.

One notable dissenter from the mechanical philosophy was Johann Wolfgang von Goethe (1749–1832), author and devotee of alchemy, who developed an empathetic, participatory, and holistic scientific methodology, in contrast to mechanical philosophy, which tended to be analytic, observational, and reductive (Bortoft, 1996, pp. 3–26, 49–76, 321–30; Goethe, 1996, pp. 12, 22, 28, 41, 48; Pauli, 1955, pp. 205–6). He called it a "delicate empiricism" (*zartre Empirie*, Goethe, 1996, ch. 5), and I will have more to say on this subject later.

Neoplatonism, the Unconscious, and Aesthetics

By means of our intuitive grasp of the Platonic ideas, we are better able to understand the inner life — the soul — of the universe. The techniques for this intuitive access are what future scientists need to learn and what ancient Neoplatonists taught. The approach is *phenomenological*; that is, it takes the interior world seriously and studies it objectively. Observation requires an observer and all observations manifest in consciousness; thus all external evidence is ultimately interior.

Further, because understanding is a mental activity and hence is constrained by the structure of the mind, an investigation of the psyche — that is, psychology — is fundamental to comprehending science and to training scientists. However, the changing content of consciousness is strongly affected by the unconscious mind, as shown by modern psychologists, but also well known to ancient Platonists (Schwyzer, 1960; Whyte, 1978, p. 79); for example, Plotinus (204–270 CE) has been called the first philosopher of the unconscious.

Moreover, scientists and non-scientists alike have identified the unconscious as the source of creative inspiration (Dorfman et al., 1996; Fritz, 1980; Gedo, 1997; Hadamard, 1945; Kipling, 1937/1952; Kris, 1952; Neumann, 1971; Poincaré, 1908/1952, 1929). This is because the archetypal ideas reside in the *collective unconscious*, as described by Carl Jung (1875–1961), the founder of *analytical psychology*, who inaugurated the psychological investigation of the archetypes and the collective unconscious. It is *collective* because it is common to all people and thus independent of the observer; therefore Jung also called it the *objective psyche* (Fordham, 1951; Jung, CW 7, ¶103n; Stevens 2003, p. 65). It is *unconscious* because we do not have direct access to the archetypes, but experience only their effects in consciousness. The practical result is that access to the Platonic Ideas coincides with access to the archetypal ideas in the objective psyche, but we must use specific techniques (known to both analytical psychologists and ancient Neoplatonists) to accomplish this.

The Nobel-prize-winning physicist Werner Heisenberg (1901–1976), who discovered the famous Uncertainty Principle, observes that thinkers as diverse as Kepler, Jung, and Wolfgang Pauli (1900–1958) have attributed scientific insight "to innate archetypes that bring about the recognition of forms" (Heisenberg, 1974a, pp. 177–80). For example, Pauli, one of the founders of quantum physics and a Nobel Prize laureate, argues that the archetypes, which connect sense perceptions to the world of ideas, are necessary to the formulation of any scientific theory of nature (Pauli, 1955, p. 153).

Analytical psychologists and Neoplatonists agree that symbols provide the connection between the sensible and archetypal realms. The unconscious communicates with the conscious mind by means of symbols (especially in dreams), and symbols can activate archetypes, which is why symbols may be numinous, hinting at unseen, eternal truths. Neoplatonists put the same idea in their own terms: each archetypal idea or form is the origin of a series of emanations or a line of descent, which has manifestations in each level of reality. The sensible manifestations are symbols (*symbola*) or tokens (*synthêmata*) that can be used to approach the archetypes that are their origins. Therefore, symbols have an essential role in our access to the archetypes.

It should not be surprising that Neoplatonism has much in common with contemporary analytical psychology, since Jung acknowledged drawing inspiration from Neoplatonism and from Gnosticism, which has close connections to the Platonic worldview (Jung, 1963, p. 162). Indeed, he borrowed the term "archetype" from Neoplatonic and Hermetic texts (Jung, CW 9 i, ¶5). Analytical psychology may be considered the phenomenological complement to evolutionary psychology (MacLennan, 2006; Stevens, 2003), which studies the inherited, species-wide behavioral adaptations of Homo sapiens. These behavioral adaptations are often called "instincts," and indeed Jung associated the archetypes with instincts (CW 8, ¶404), but instincts have both interior and exterior aspects. On one hand, we can observe the characteristic behavior of *Homo sapiens* from the outside, and seek to understand it in terms of the structure of the nervous system, and that in terms of more fundamental biological and physical principles. On the other, we can use phenomenological techniques to study the instinctual psyche from the inside, to discover the psychological structure of the collective unconscious (the mental aspect of human behavioral adaptations). As we probe ever deeper into the objective psyche, we discover that "the biological instinctual psyche, gradually passes over into the physiology of the organism and thus merges with its chemical and physical conditions." (Jung, CW 8, ¶420). One of Jung's colleagues, Marie-Louise von Franz (1915–1998), who explored this unity of the mental and material worlds, wrote, "The lowest collective level of our psyche is simply pure nature" (1974, p. 7). Jung emphasized that the archetypes are not static images, but dynamic forms governing the psyche: "active living dispositions, ideas in the Platonic sense" (Jung, CW 8, ¶154). When they are activated by external or internal stimuli, they can manifest externally in overt behavior, but also internally by conditioning perception, affect, and motivation toward biological ends. Their goal is life and its evolution.

Since the function of many of the archetypes is to govern specifically human behavior, they are personified (the archetypal mother, father, child, hero, seducer, trickster, clever maiden, etc.), and they are experienced as invisible personalities intervening in our lives; that is, as gods, whose complex interrelations are expressed in the myths of many nations. Zeus, Hermes, Aphrodite, Ares, Artemis, Apollo, Athena, and the rest are with us to this day (MacLennan, 2003).

As these universal archetypes are activated, they acquire personal unconscious associations, which adapt them to our individual lives. In psychological terms, they self-organize into unconscious *complexes*, which (as Jung stressed) behave as autonomous subpersonalities. Indeed, Jung and other analytical psychologists occasionally call them *daimones* (singular: *daimôn*), a term that in Neoplatonism refers to autonomous psyches mediating between our conscious selves and the archetypal gods. As such, they are located in the cosmic soul, which connects the Platonic forms to the sensible world.

It is perhaps surprising that Neoplatonic philosophical practice does not contradict contemporary science, but rather complements and completes it. To the external observation and exploration of ordinary science it adds the interior observation and experiment of analytical psychology. Further, to action in the outer world, it adds action in the interior world, as practiced in analytical psychology and Neoplatonism, to engage the archetypal ideas. As Pauli notes, it opens the way toward "a future description of nature that uniformly comprises physis and psyche" (i.e., exterior and interior reality), for which "it appears to be essential to have *recourse* to the archetypal *background of scientific terms and concepts*" (Pauli, 2001, p. 180, emphasis in original). Indeed, Pauli argues that in the future, the only acceptable scientific theory will be "the one that recognizes both sides of reality—the quantitative and the qualitative, the physical and the psychical—as compatible with each other, and can embrace them simultaneously" (1955, p. 208).

To accomplish these goals, the integrated whole person must be involved in discovery, including the unconscious as well as the conscious mind, and aesthetic as well as rational judgment. Scientific pioneers have noted the importance of aesthetics in science. For example, Heisenberg (1974b, p. 175) remarks that an aesthetic response to the whole often precedes scientific investigation of the details: "How comes it that with this shining forth of the beautiful into exact science the great connection becomes recognizable, even before it is understood in detail and before it can be rationally demonstrated?" It is not a result of conscious analysis, for "[a]mong all those who have pondered on this question, it seems to have been universally agreed that this immediate recognition is not a consequence of discursive (i.e., rational) thinking" (1974b, p. 177). He contrasts immediate, self-evident awareness (Grk. *epistêmê*) with deliberative, logical analysis (Grk. *dianoia*) (1974a, p. 137).

The coincidence of scientific truth and beauty has deep historical roots. Heisenberg (1974b, pp. 169–70) mentions Pythagoras' identification of harmonious musical intervals with simple arithmetical ratios, a discovery of immaterial form as the cause of sensible properties, "which later provided the foundation for all exact science" (p. 170). "Beauty is truth, and truth beauty," as the English Romantic poet John Keats (1795–1821) said, and therefore the cultivation of the aesthetic sense should be an essential part of the education of all scientists — indeed, part of everyone's educational experience. Similarly, aesthetic considerations should complement scientific accuracy in the presentation of scientific results and knowledge. The well known mathematical physicist, Sir Roger Penrose, also observes, "Beauty and Truth are intertwined, the beauty of a physical theory acting as a guide to its correctness in relation to the Physical World" (2004, p. 1029).

In Neoplatonism, Truth and Beauty are two fundamental aspects radiating forth from the One (the originating and governing principle of everything); the third is Goodness (Siorvanes, 1996, pp. 192–3), as Penrose also acknowledges (p. 1029). The three can and should accompany one another in our education.

Contemplative Practices

We can create a more holistic science by making appropriate contemplative practices for intuitively grasping the archetypal forms an accepted and expected part of the scientific enterprise. In the remainder of this chapter, I will describe briefly some of these practices, which can be found in the Neoplatonic tradition (see my *Wisdom of Hypatia* for more information).

Theory comes from contemplation (*theôria* in ancient Greek). By contemplating the phenomena and by experiencing the archetypal patterns of form and change that are consequently activated, a scientist can gain insight into the inner workings of nature, which can be translated into mathematics and testable theories. This is what Goethe did in his morphological contemplations, which led to his 1784 discovery of the human intermaxillary bone, an observation that supported the evolutionary continuity of humans with other animals (Goethe, 1995, pp. 111–16). Goethe's thinking was steeped in the archetypal symbolism of alchemy (e.g., *The Golden Chain of Homer*, Bacstrom, 1775/1983, and the works of Paracelsus), which also inspired Jung (CW 9 ii; CW 12–14).

We, too, can contemplate archetypal symbols to gain new insights and perspectives. Some archetypal symbols are traditional, such as mandalas, but new ones are created every day as contemporary expressions of the eternal archetypes. They are not limited to static images, but include texts and sounds, and may evolve in time according to archetypal patterns (thus echoing the deep structure of many myths). Jung emphasized that the archetypes are *dynamic* forms, and therefore dynamic, active symbols are the best way to activate them. Indeed, ritual has been defined as "symbolic behavior, consciously performed" (Johnson, 1986, p. 102), and the laboratory operations of the alchemists, for example, can be considered rituals of spiritual transformation. We, too, can enact laboratory procedures contemplatively to engage the archetypal patterns. Moreover, by experiencing the living archetypes within ourselves, we acquire an embodied, participatory understanding of the phenomena, which was Goethe's scientific method (Bortoft, 1996, pp. 22–3, Pt. III, ch. 5; Goethe, 1996, ch. 7; Heisenberg, 1974a). Through contemplative exercises, we can learn to live the inner life of the phenomena we are trying to understand. An ancient Pythagorean principle is *like knows like* (e.g., Empedocles, fr. 109; Aristotle, Met. 1000b7, De An. 404b16; Sextus Empiricus, *Adv. Math.* VII.92); in this way, we understand the archetypes by grasping them within ourselves.

One possible consequence of a scientific approach that is participatory rather than detached would be a greater reverence for Nature, which was more common among those early-modern philosophers influenced by Neoplatonism, but disparaged by the early advocates of the mechanical philosophy. Our respect for other human beings is grounded in part in our empathetic understanding of them; we can put ourselves in their place. We may have greater respect for the rest of Nature by participating in the archetypal forms that govern its life.

Dreams and reveries are also important forms of inspiration, and many relevant examples of this can be gleaned from the history of science. For example, the chemist August Kekulé (1829–1896) discovered the structure of the benzene ring after he had a vision, in a reverie, of an *ouroborus*, the familiar, archetypal image of a serpent biting its tail. He recommended such reveries as a method, saying to his fellow scientists, "Let us learn to dream, gentlemen, then perhaps we shall find the truth" (Kekulé, 1890, tr. in Benfey, 1958). Ancient philosophers also paid attention to dreams, but they couldn't always wait for a relevant dream to arise spontaneously. Therefore, they taught incubation, which is an ancient way of encouraging "big dreams," that is, dreams charged with archetypal significance, and in science such dreams can provide new insights or hypotheses. In brief, the technique begins with preparation when awake: contemplation on the problem, but also the more familiar sort of hard, rational work. The next step is to arrange an appropriate *set* (attitude) and *setting* (physical environment), such as an attitude of expectancy and anticipatory gratitude, perhaps combined with devotional activities (e.g., a petition to your scientific muse). The next step is to go to sleep with the problem in mind, but without struggling with it. As the ancients tell us, a dream might not come on the first night, and you might need to repeat the procedure. You can also cultivate the states between waking and sleeping, when you're just nodding off (*hypnagogia*) or before you have fully awakened (*hypnopompia*). Finally, it is important to keep a dream journal and to analyze significant dreams in terms of what the symbols mean to you (i.e., trusting your own archetypal intuition). (See Johnson, 1986, Pt. II, for suggestions from the perspective of analytical psychology.)

In the ancient word, dream incubation was considered a method of divination; that is, of obtaining guidance from the archetypal realm. Other methods of divination can also be useful as a means of generating new hypotheses grounded in archetypal understanding. It is well known that Jung used the *I Ching*, and Pauli also found insights in its mathematical structure (Lindorff, 2004, pp. 99–109; Miller, 2009, p. 224). Common approaches to creative problem solving use a form of *bibliomancy* (divination by books), in which a book is opened at random and the first word seen is applied to the problem. More generally, we may employ divinatory techniques that use archetypal images and mathematical structure to suggest hypotheses that can be subsequently subjected to theoretical analysis and experimental verification.

Since many of the archetypes and complexes are personified and act as independent subpersonalities (Jung, CW 8, ¶253), it is possible to communicate with them directly. In modern analytical psychology, the process is called *active imagination* (Johnson, 1986; Jung, 1997); in ancient Neoplatonism it was called *conjunction* or *alliance* (Grk. systasis), and Pauli applied it regularly as well (Lindorff, 2004, p. 101). The basic technique is to invoke an archetypal figure, activating the archetype by means of any symbols associated with it. You then remain in a state of calm expectancy until there is some (perhaps subtle) sign of quickening in the environment, indicating activation of the archetype. Then, begin the conversation with that archetype. When it is done, dismiss the archetype respectfully, and consciously involve yourself in some other activity to bring the experiment to a definite conclusion. You might worry that you are making it all up, but unless you are consciously scripting the dialogue, you will probably be surprised at the direction it takes. For inspiration in writing or hypothesis formation, one especially important archetypal figure to contact is your muse, which usually has the opposite gender from your own (in psychological terms, the *anima* in a man, the *animus* in a woman). It is also important to engage the archetype that Jung called the *shadow*, which can be helpful in clearing emotional and mental blocks and in becoming more balanced psychologically. (A complete discussion of the techniques is not possible here due to considerations of length; for more on this topic, please see the bibliography) (Johnson, 1986, Pt. III; MacLennan, 2013, ch. 12)).

The Neoplatonic perspective and practices have wider implications than in scientific method, for scientists are, after all, human beings, and the archetypal ideas are no less relevant to their lives outside science. As people, they will live better lives if they understand the archetypal forces that regulate their lives, and if they actively engage with these forces. To this end, we can all practice modern versions of Neoplatonic spiritual exercises (MacLennan, 2013) and other kinds of active imagination (Johnson, 1986; Jung, 1997). These practices can help us to pursue the lifelong process of *individuation*; that is, of becoming a psychologically integrated person. This developmental process is especially important in the second half of life, when the integration of the unconscious and its archetypes into consciousness provides a context for understanding and fulfilling the purpose of your life, but it can be useful at any age (Jacobi, 1967, pp. 7–11; Stevens, 2003, p. 173).

Conclusions

If, through these practices, science returns to its Pythagorean and Platonic roots (understood within a contemporary context), we may hope that its worldview will become more balanced, comprehensive, and integrated, encompassing the psychical as well as the physical, as Pauli urged. The result for individual scientists will be not only a deeper understanding of reality, but also better-integrated personalities. The eventual consequences for society at large, as it absorbs this new scientific worldview, will be a more balanced and harmonious culture.

References

Bacstrom, S. (Trans.) (1775/1983). *Aurea catena Homeri: The golden chain of Homer*. San Francisco: Sapere Aude, 1983. Originally published, Leipzig und Winterthur, 1775.

Benfey, O. T. (1958). August Kekulé and the birth of the structural theory of organic chemistry in 1858. *Journal of Chemical Education*, 35, 21–23.

Beveridge, W. I. B. (1957). *The art of scientific investigation* (Rev. Ed.). New York: W. W. Norton.

Bortoft, H. (1996). *The wholeness of nature: Goethe's way toward a science of conscious participation in nature*. Hudson: Lindisfarne.

Davy, J. (1858). *Fragmentary remains of Sir Humphry Davy*. London: John Churchill.

Dorfman, J., Shames, V. A., & Kihlstrom, J. F. (1996). Intuition, incubation, and insight: Implicit cognition in problem solving. In G. Underwood (Ed.), *Implicit cognition* (pp. 257–286). Oxford: Oxford University Press.

Easlea, B. (1980). *Witch hunting, magic and the new philosophy: An introduction to the debates of the scientific revolution* 1450–1750. Sussex: Humanities Press.

Fordham, M. (1951). The concept of the objective psyche. *British Journal of Medical Psychology*, 24, 4: 221–231.

Fritz, D. W. (Ed.) (1980). *Perspectives on creativity and the unconscious*. Oxford, Ohio: Miami University.

Gedo, J. E. (1997). Psychoanalytic theories of creativity. In M. A. Runco (Ed.), *The creativity research handbook, vol. I* (pp. 29–39). Cresskill, NJ: Hampton Press.

Goethe, J. W. von (1995). *Scientific studies: Goethe's collected works, volume 12* (D. Miller, Ed. & Trans.). Princeton: Princeton University Press.

Goethe, J. W. von (1996). *Goethe on science: A selection of Goethe's writings* (Jeremy Naydler, Ed. & Trans.). Edinburgh: Floris.

Hadamard, J. (1945). *An essay on the psychology of invention in the mathematical field.* Princeton: Princeton University Press.

Hadot, P. (2006). *The veil of Isis: An essay on the history of an idea* (Michael Chase, Trans.). Cambridge: Harvard University Press.

Heisenberg, W. (1974a). Goethe's view of nature and the world of science and technology. In W. Heisenberg, *Across the frontiers* (P. Heath, Trans.) (pp. 122–141). New York: Harper & Row.

Heisenberg, W. (1974b). The meaning of beauty in the exact sciences. In W. Heisenberg, *Across the frontiers* (P. Heath, Trans.) (pp. 166–183). New York: Harper & Row.

Jacobi, J. (1967). *The way of individuation* (R.F.C. Hull, Trans.). London: Hodder & Stoughton.

Johnson, R. A. (1986). *Inner work: Using dreams and active imagination for personal growth.* New York: Harper & Row.

Jung, C. G. (CW). *The collected works of C. G. Jung* (H. Read, M. Fordham, & G. Adler, Eds.). London: Routledge & Kegan Paul, 1953–78; New York: Pantheon, 1953–60, and Bollingen Foundation, 1961–67; Princeton: Princeton University Press, 1967–78.

Jung, C. G. (1963). *Memories, dreams, reflections* (Rev. ed., A. Jaffé, Ed., R. & C. Winston, Trans.). New York: Random House.

Jung, C. G. (1997). *Jung on active imagination* (J. Chodorow, Ed. & Intro.). Princeton: Princeton University Press.

Kekulé, A. (1890). Benzolfest: Rede. *Berichte der Deutschen Chemischen Gesellschaft*, 23 (1), 1302–1311.

Kipling, R. (1937/1952). Working tools. In B. Ghiselin (Ed.), *The creative process: A symposium* (pp. 157–159). Berkeley: University of California Press.

Kris, E. (1952). *Psychoanalytic explorations in art.* New York: International Universities Press.

Lindorff, D. P. (2004). *Pauli and Jung: The meeting of two great minds.* Wheaton, Il: Quest Books.

MacLennan, B. J. (2003). Evolutionary neurotheology and the varieties of religious experience. In R. Joseph (Ed.), *Neurotheology: Brain, science, spirituality, religious experience* (2nd ed., pp. 317–334). San Jose: University Press, California.

MacLennan, B. J. (2006). Evolutionary Jungian psychology. *Psychological Perspectives*, 49, 1: 9–28.

MacLennan, B. J. (2007). Neoplatonism in science: Past and future. In R. Berchman & J. Finamore (Eds.), *Metaphysical patterns in Platonism: Ancient, medieval, renaissance, and modern* (pp. 241–259). New Orleans: University Press of the South; reprinted (pp. 199–214), Somerset, UK: Prometheus Trust, 2014.

MacLennan, B. J. (2013). *The wisdom of Hypatia: Ancient spiritual practices for a more meaningful life.* Woodbury, MN: Llewellyn.

Merchant, C. (1980). *The death of nature: Women, ecology, and the scientific revolution.* San Francisco: Harper & Row.

Miller, A. I. (2009). *Deciphering the cosmic number: The strange friendship of Wolfgang Pauli and Carl Jung.* New York: Norton.

Neumann, E. (1971). *Art and the creative unconscious* (R. Manheim, Trans.). New York: Princeton University Press.

Pauli, W. (1955). The influence of archetypal ideas on the scientific theories of Kepler. In C. G. Jung & W. Pauli, *The interpretation of nature and psyche* (pp. 147–240). New York: Pantheon Books.

Pauli, W. (2001). *Atom and archetype: The Pauli/Jung letters*, 1928–1958 (C. A. Meier, Ed.). Princeton: Princeton University Press.

Penrose, R. (2004). *The road to reality: A complete guide to the laws of the universe.* New York: Alfred A. Knopf.

Poincaré, H. (1908/1952). Mathematical creation. In B. Ghiselin (Ed.), *The creative process: A symposium* (pp. 33–42). Berkeley: University of California Press.

Poincaré, H. (1929). *The foundations of science: Science and hypothesis, the value of science, science and method* (G. B. Halstead, Trans.). New York: The Science Press.

Schwyzer, H. R. (1960). "Bewusst" und "unbewusst" bei Plotin. In E. R. Dodds (Ed.), *Les sources de Plotin: Dix exposés et discussions* (pp. 341–377). Genève: Fondation Hardt.

Siorvanes, L. (1996). *Proclus: Neo-Platonic philosophy and science.* Edinburgh: Edinburgh University Press.

Spencer, J. H. (2012). *The eternal law: Ancient Greek philosophy, modern physics, and ultimate reality.* Vancouver, BC: Param Media Publishing.

Stevens, A. (2003). *Archetype revisited: An updated natural history of the self.* Toronto: Inner City Books.

von Franz, M.-L. (1974). *Number and time: Reflections leading toward a unification of depth psychology and physics.* Evanston: Northwestern University Press.

Webster, C. (1982). *From Paracelsus to Newton: Magic and the making of modern science.* Cambridge: Cambridge University Press.

White, M. (1997). *Isaac Newton: The last sorcerer.* Reading: Perseus Books.

Whyte, L. L. (1978). *The unconscious before Freud* (2nd ed.). New York: St. Martin's Press.

Yates, F. A. (1964). *Giordano Bruno and the Hermetic tradition.* Chicago: University of Chicago Press.

Dr. Brian Les Lancaster

Dr. Brian Les Lancaster is Emeritus Professor of Transpersonal Psychology, Liverpool John Moores University, and Chair of the Transpersonal Psychology Section of the British Psychological Society. He is also Adjunct Faculty at Sofia University and the California Institute of Integral Studies. His books include *Approaches to Consciousness: the Marriage of Science and Mysticism.*

Dr. Brian Les Lancaster

The Two Quests for Consciousness: Integrating Scientific and Mystical Ways of Knowing

CONSCIOUSNESS, SCIENTISM, MYSTICISM

The common ground

Despite the generally prevalent view that science and religious mysticism are incompatible, there are a number of good reasons for recognising their common ground. While *beliefs* associated with these two approaches to knowing may often highlight their differences, it is their *motivation* to understand the nature of mind and ultimate reality that unites them. Beyond this motivational aspect, the key concern is whether *data* from the two approaches may be fruitfully brought into relationship, for arguments over beliefs are largely intractable, while data drive the evolution of our thinking. In fact, data from scientific psychology and mysticism can bring mutual enrichment, informing each other's challenge to understand the mind and our potential for growth towards states of increased well-being and effectiveness.

Central to these challenges are the two quests for consciousness. The first is the endeavour to understand the nature of consciousness and its relation to the structures, most notably the human brain, which are assumed to be involved with it. It is in this sense that eminent neuroscientist Christof Koch entitled one of his books *The Quest for Consciousness* (Koch, 2004), which essentially concerns the search for the ***neural correlates of consciousness***. The term '*correlate*' is used to emphasize that the question of causation is undetermined. In other words, every time (or usually) when event A happens, then event B follows, but if we do not know that A *causes* B, we can then say that there is a *correlation* between A and B. Therefore, neural correlates of consciousness refer to a minimal set of neural mechanisms that are known to accompany, rather than cause, a specific event or state of consciousness.

The second quest is for states that are deemed more fulfilling, or more integrated, than the everyday state of mind. It is this latter quest which has largely been associated with mysticism, since the goal of union with the divine, or some form of Absolute, is viewed as the ultimately fulfilling state of consciousness. Since the nineteenth century, the mystical path has frequently been understood in terms of aspiring to some form of increased or higher consciousness—hence the epithet *quest for consciousness.*

Evelyn Underhill, one of the foremost writers on mysticism, observes that mystical consciousness is superior to normal consciousness inasmuch as the latter "is incapable of apprehending the underlying reality from which … scattered experiences proceed" (Underhill, 1980, p. 30). Similarly, the twentieth-century mystic G. I. Gurdjieff taught that the mundane state of the awake mind is relatively unconscious by comparison with the real consciousness associated with the enlightened state. Without embarking on a path of disciplined practice (referred to as the "Work"), humans are effectively 'asleep,' inhabiting a twilight consciousness; and "the object of the Work is to increase consciousness" (Nicoll, 1956, p. 1526).

Critical to my observations in this chapter is the *complementarity* between these two senses of the term quest. Science is often assumed to be the only route to identifying details of the nature of consciousness, while mysticism is supposed to be the repository of teachings for transformation. But this rigid demarcation cannot be upheld. For example, the recent upsurge of scientific interest in the state of **mindfulness** (where one's complete attention is focused on experiencing the present moment without judgement) is impacting on the ways in which meditation practices are taught. In other words, what may be considered the best way in which to approach the transformation implied by mindfulness is no longer left to the religious teachers and practitioners alone.

On the other side of this seeming demarcation, the purview of mysticism includes analysis of mental processes such as perception, thinking, and memory—all of them central to understanding the nature of consciousness. It is therefore simplistic to consider that the quest to understand the nature of consciousness is reliant on science alone, just as it is incorrect to assume that science has no role to play in specifying the detail of transformation to higher states associated with mysticism. Given the common ground between science and mysticism, we can further ask whether fresh insights might arise when we endeavour to integrate data and insights from the two areas. This challenge is where my interest lies (Lancaster, e.g. 2004, 2011a, 2013).

Contrary to what may be a common assumption, mysticism is not solely about the quest for experience of the divine or some other formulation of ultimate reality. In the first place, the emphasis on experience hardly appears as a hallmark of the majority of texts which might be classed as mystical. Steven T. Katz, Director of the Elie Wiesel Center for Judaic Studies at Boston University, rightly notes that "the literature produced by the major mystical traditions ... is not ... primarily about an independent and individual religious experience but is, rather, more often than not, composed of esoteric commentaries on canonical texts" (Katz, 2000, p. 8). Moreover, the undue emphasis on experientialism, the view that only personal experience can form the foundation of knowledge, distorts mystical teachings, encouraging a degree of spiritual narcissism which is hardly conducive of the intended aims (Ferrer, 2002).

Secondly, in cases where experience does come more to the fore, the focus may be concerned as much with cognitive processes as it is with ultimates. A good example of this tendency is the Buddhist **Abhidhamma's** treatment of thought and perceptual processes, which I shall discuss below (for an expanded treatment see Lancaster, 1997, 2004). 'Abhidhamma' means 'higher teaching,' and comprises those writings within Theravada Buddhism that systematize the Buddha's understanding of experienced reality.

On the grounds that Buddhism quintessentially entails inner meditation, Ninian Smart, a former professor of comparative religion, regards it as the "most mystical of religions" (Smart, 2000, p. 232). I would add that the Abhidhamma is mystical to the extent that its analysis of features of mind is predicated on the primacy of the transformational imperative. The student of Abhidhamma is enjoined to study his or her mind not as some kind of abstract interest but precisely to attain to greater control over mental processes that otherwise operate in habitual fashion.

Mysticism also entails a bi-directional view of the cosmos: from 'higher' to 'lower,' that all things are infused with a presence which transcends our immediate space-time continuum; and from 'lower' to 'higher,' that the primary goal in life is to transcend the space-time continuum. While cultivation of specific kinds of experience is not always a defining feature of mysticism, a readiness to enliven study of teachings by reference to experience of non-ordinary states is never far from the surface. The Hebrew term ***Kabbalah***, used to refer to the mystical strand in Judaism, serves to make this point about mysticism in general. "Kabbalah" derives from a verbal root meaning to 'receive,' which gives two connotations to the Jewish mystical tradition: to receive from a teacher (and the textual sources) and to receive inwardly by way of direct transmission or revelation. Mysticism extols the active search for both.

In addition, Abhidhamma also discusses notions like ***karma***, the universal principle of cause and effect in Buddhist thought, whereby actions have impact on the actor, both throughout the lifetime and in reincarnation. This view obviously does not fit within a **physicalist ontology**, where 'ontology' is the philosophical study of the nature of being and reality, and **physicalism** is the ontological view that there is no reality other than that which is physical. In other words, since karma implies that we somehow survive or continue beyond bodily death, then any system that accepts karma must reject any philosophical position that says reality is limited purely to the physical realm.

An ontological divide?

The above characterization of mysticism, which implicitly recognizes a dimension that transcends the space-time continuum of consensual reality, immediately introduces a conceptual chasm with science. Although, as Spencer (2012) notes, various eminent pioneering physicists have denied physicalism (also called materialism), it is axiomatic that the scientific method can address only those phenomena capable of measurement in physical terms. The general practice of science works with the ontology of physicalism. Note, however, that this is not to say that science gives a basis for denying that anything transcending physical reality *could* exist; it is simply that if such an entity is incapable of physical measurement, then it is beyond the remit of science. There is no paradox, for example, in the fact that an eminent scientist may be religious: he or she may believe that there is a realm beyond the physical, beyond the reach of science as generally understood.

The view that all things are ultimately explicable in purely physical terms is not a scientific fact; it is a belief that is a concomitant of ***scientism***, the view that the only valid way of knowing is scientific knowing. These notions are extrapolations from the fact that a physicalist paradigm has generally been successful in explaining physical phenomena, with data from scientific research in support. However, when it comes to consciousness, such explanation is lacking. There is no convincing explanation currently available as to how consciousness arises from physical matter; indeed, there is an ***explanatory gap***, which, in this case, refers to the absence of any definitive explanation of how or why consciousness is related to physical events (Levine, 1981, 2003).

As a consequence, there are three tenable positions concerning the metaphysical basis of consciousness (Lancaster, 2004). The first is the default for most working in consciousness studies, namely that the lack of explanation does not detract from the tenet that consciousness is indeed a product of physical activity, it being argued that while there is currently an explanatory gap, given more time, and with advances in instrumentation, science will furnish an explanation. The second position holds that consciousness is an irreducible component of the natural world, and therefore in its essence not generated by physical structures and processes. And the third position is that an essential aspect of consciousness transcends the natural world. The vehemence with which each of these viewpoints is held may be seen in the controversy sparked by a recent book by philosopher Thomas Nagel (*Mind and cosmos: Why the materialist neo-Darwinian conception of nature is almost certainly false*, 2012), in which he argues for the second of the above positions (Chorost, 2013).

A key question here is whether the science of mind, namely psychology, need be concerned about spiritual and mystical beliefs in the transcendent (that which is beyond the range of normal or physical human experience). Again, the contemporary interest in the effects of meditation is a case in point, since, by ignoring the metaphysical context within which meditation has been fostered in most traditions, researchers have generated a highly effective and influential research programme (Lutz, Dunne, and Davidson, 2007; Beauregard and O'Leary, 2007). However, as a complement to this approach, I have argued (Lancaster, 2002) that the branch of psychology most engaged with mysticism, namely transpersonal psychology, should at least be open to the claim that the human belief that a transcendent realm exists is well-grounded (Hick, 2000). The claim is well-grounded inasmuch as (i) a majority of the individuals making the claim are sane and generally to be trusted; (ii) the claims are not substantially contradicted by science (they may be contradicted by scientism, but not by scientific knowledge); and (iii) the claims show a significant coherence across diverse times and place.

To be sure, simply extolling the value of belief in a transcendent realm is the job of religion and not psychology, but it is also important to recognize that the transcendent is not ruled out by any incontrovertible scientific observations. The issue for transpersonal psychology in particular is whether openness to such beliefs makes a difference. The principle of ***Occam's razor*** (which prefers using a minimum number of constructs that account for the facts) would have us jettison notions of ontological transcendence if indeed there were no benefits to be gained, but I think we are indeed missing important benefits. While mindfulness practices in broadly secular contexts can bring psychological and health benefits, it seems to me that there are additional gains when we engage more fully with the spiritual and mystical traditions that developed the practices in the first place. In my experience, people develop greater insight, more profound levels of compassion, and increased harmony when they are open to teachings within these traditions about transcendent levels of being.

In the next section, I offer some examples where insights from mystical traditions can fruitfully be juxtaposed to observations from scientific psychology. The key word here is 'fruitfully,' since merely finding a degree of fit between the two approaches is trivial; my interest lies with those juxtapositions that can induce new thinking in the cognitive neuroscience of consciousness. (This is not to say that an impact in the reverse direction is not equally important —that cognitive neuroscience might change long-held ideas in mysticism; but in this short treatment that will not be my focus.) In many instances, the issues of ontology have no bearing—the emphasis on momentary consciousness in Buddhist thought, for example, may be instructive for a cognitive neuroscience of consciousness without challenging the prevailing worldview in psychological science. But in other cases, the foregoing discussion becomes relevant, and the critical questions concern the ways in which mystical knowledge of the transcendent realm intersects with scientific knowledge of the brain and with psychological models of the process of transformation.

Elements of a generative integration

The Buddhist analysis of mind presented in the Abhidhamma explores in detail the full implications of the fundamental teaching of momentariness (Banerjee, 2008; Cousins, 1981; Ratnayaka, 1981). When it comes to consciousness, the teaching insists that the notion of an enduring continuum of consciousness, an ever-flowing 'stream' of consciousness, is illusory. There are only *moments*, or *pulses*, of consciousness, each of which arises as a conditioned response to a prior moment, endures for a brief period, and decays, having triggered the next pulse. Unless prolonged through contemplative observation, each moment of consciousness is normally extremely brief, so brief, in fact, that the ancient commentators had calculated it to be 1/74,642 second per moment! (Collins, 1982). While there is, no doubt, some hyperbole in such a calculation, it was clearly the intention of the authors to stress the brevity of these moments of consciousness, which seemed to me to give a basis for viewing them as the experiential equivalents of micro-stages in neural processing (Lancaster, 1997, 2004).

This Buddhist perspective on consciousness is strikingly in accord with ideas advanced by neuroscientist Semir Zeki based on his research into the processing carried out by the many regions of the brain devoted to visual functions (Zeki, 2003; Zeki and Bartels, 1999). Zeki argues that the visual system comprises a series of functional nodes, each of which responds to specific aspects of the visual input and has a distinctive conscious correlate. Visual consciousness accordingly comprises 'many microconsciousnesses,' to use Zeki's phrase. The argument that consciousness is effectively disunified clearly corresponds to the Buddhist perspective, with microconsciousnesses paralleling the discrete moments of consciousness portrayed in the Abhidhamma.

One of the major issues in the study of consciousness concerns methodology; research into brain function can at best generate data concerning *correlates* of consciousness, but we can *know* consciousness only from the inside. The ideal must be to integrate introspective insights with the data emerging from externalized study. The convergence of Buddhist inner observation with scientific research provides an exemplary case where the value of this integration becomes apparent. The value of the insights from the Abhidhamma derives from the sophisticated power of observation underlying them. It is only as a result of extensive training through meditation and spiritual discipline that the authors of the classic texts were able to penetrate beyond the delusions of an untrained mind. It is interesting to note that Zeki specifically comments on the level of resistance to his theory, presumably on the grounds that it does not accord with simple introspection. The marriage between scientific study of the brain and the Buddhist tradition of introspection can overcome these problems attributable to scientists' inadequate training in the nuances of consciousness. Central amongst the misperceptions that tend to dominate psychology and neuroscience is the belief that during wakefulness an unbroken stream of consciousness is experienced by an enduring self.

A further feature of the Abhidhamma's treatment of consciousness is poignant when it comes to thinking about the aspiration to attain more wholesome states. For Buddhism, all the stages comprising a complete process of perception—including the very earliest—are *conscious*. This differs from the general view of cognitive scientists (notwithstanding the arguments of Zeki) who hold that the initial stages are *preconscious* (Velmans, 1999). That is to say that the stages entailed in preliminary analysis of the sensory input and activation of associations en route to establishing the meaning of the input, occur prior to an end-stage identified with consciousness. Contemporary psychology generally views the neural activity during the milliseconds that these initial stages are unfolding as having no connection with consciousness. At some point (the end-stage) the magical ingredient appears and we become conscious of the visual scene in front of our eyes. Now, leaving aside the crucial question of what exactly that magic is (dealt with at length in Lancaster, 2004), we have the terminological variance between the two ways of thinking: for the Buddhist all stages are *conscious*; for the cognitive scientist, most are *preconscious*. This is not an empty divergence of words; language is important.

By calling early stages in the process *preconscious*, we infer that they are beyond our control; they are automatic and machine-like. Buddhism identifies these same stages as conscious because the whole thrust of the Abhidhamma is towards transforming one's reactivity; the path towards *nirvana* entails ensuring that the mind remains affectively neutral to stimuli at an early stage in the perceptual process. The adept is able to assert his or her will in the early stages to bring about nonharmful consequences. In point of fact, this is not an issue of what consciousness actually is; rather, it critically concerns how one trains the mind. Unfortunately, the terminology of cognitive science distances us from the possibility of such training.

Many have argued that these kinds of Buddhist theories sit well within the physicalist ontology, but there are aspects of the Abhidhamma that are challenging, most notably the role of karma. Karma determines the way in which the final instantiations of consciousness of one life condition the next at the moment of conception. The medium through which karma operates may not be transcendent to the natural order, but it clearly stretches the paradigm dominant in psychology. Thus, at the very least, the possibility of karma challenges our understanding of memory and the medium through which causality operates. The notion that, "depending on the locations of the death and birth, there can be a physical space between the two events, but there is no mental space between them" (Ratnayaka, 1981, p. 83) challenges us to consider how mental causation intersects with physical causation in the brain, where the brain is the physical substrate of mind. Is it legitimate simply to cherry-pick those aspects of Buddhism that do not challenge us in this way, and to leave out other teachings such as that of karma, for example? I would argue that Buddhism is fundamentally about cultivating wisdom, and that engaging with an emaciated mindfulness training, and attempting to fit its teaching into a limited physicalist ontology, leaves out much that is central to that goal.

While there may be solid grounds for recognising the disunity of consciousness, our everyday experience is generally of a unified stream. How might we reconcile the difference? In neuroscientific terms, the answer concerns the '**re-entrant**' neural pathways, whereby 'higher' areas in the visual processing system re-align activity in 'lower' areas, the term 'lower' meaning closer to the beginning of the neural pathway in the brain (Clifford, 2010; Lamme, 2006; Lancaster, 2011a). Psychologically, such activity appears related to the construction of a sense of 'I' that becomes a concomitant of the meaning applied to sensory processing. As many mystical traditions aver, the 'I' which seems to be the witness to events such as those of perception and thought, etc. is not an enduring and coherent entity; rather, it is a retrospective construction, associated specifically with this illusory sense of conscious continuity. Again, detailed analysis demonstrates how integrating mystical and neurocognitive thinking along these lines enriches both areas, while framing new avenues of research (Lancaster, 2004; Varela, Thompson, & Rosch, 1991).

The operation of these neural systems, whereby a sense of the unity of consciousness is fostered through feedback loops involving re-entrant pathways, exemplifies a more overarching pattern described in kabbalistic texts dating back at least to the thirteenth century (Lancaster, 2011a, 2011b). In very simplified outline, the kabbalistic teachings portray higher realms in the macrocosmic hierarchy being stimulated from below and acting back on the lower level, bringing divine influx and harmony to the entire system. While the focus of this kabbalistic scheme is on the macrocosm, it is presented as a master plan which is recapitulated at all levels, presumably including that of the individual human brain. Again, we find an enriching degree of consonance between an ancient mystical tradition and recent research into the functioning of the brain.

As in the case of Buddhism discussed above, the Kabbalah is not simply teaching about consciousness and the macrocosm as an abstract intellectual exercise; the primary imperative is to encourage as to work on ourselves—to aspire to higher states of being. In this regard, the Kabbalah focuses on the work of *unification*. While the view from the Kabbalah is in agreement with that of Buddhism that the mundane state of mind is characterised by its *disunity*, Kabbalah holds that through contact with the ultimate unifying factor, the divine, the diverse 'sparks' of consciousness can be integrated. In fact, such unification is directed not only at individual wellbeing, but also towards the harmony of the whole cosmic system (Lancaster, 2008). Meditative practices of unification abound in the kabbalistic tradition, most involving working with the names of God in various concentrative ways. Again, constructive integration between mystical teachings and psychological science can be forged here. Striving towards greater unification in the mind is conducive of wellbeing. The kabbalistic practices encourage detaching from the ego—viewed as a limiting factor in the overall harmony of the mind—and reframing in relation to a higher integrative center.

Finally, is it possible to build bridges not only between mysticism and psychological science, but also across diverse spiritual and mystical traditions? My own view is that addressing this question is actually the most important contribution that transpersonal psychologists have to make to our culture (Lancaster, 2005). Restricting myself here to just the brief details I have drawn from Buddhist and kabbalistic systems, I should like to stress the complementarity between them, especially when viewed through the lens of psychology. Buddhism emphasises the minutiae of mind and the meditative practices that enable one to transform precise aspects of processes that most would regard as automatic. Kabbalah offers insights into paths to achieving higher levels of integration. But let me be clear: I am not suggesting that either one tradition *needs* the insights of the other; each has developed effectively in relative isolation over long periods. But in our day, scientific psychology has become a lens through which views on the nature of mind as promulgated in spiritual and mystical traditions should be viewed. Using this lens, we can clarify where and how practices passed down through the various traditions fit into a larger scheme. Indeed, it is my view that our greatest hope for understanding consciousness as thoroughly as may be possible will come through further integration between scientific and mystical ways of knowing.

References

Banerjee, R. (2007). Buddha and the bridging relations. In R. Banerjee, & B. Chakrabarti (Eds.), Progress in brain research, Models of brain and mind: Physical, computational and psychological approaches. Amsterdam: Elsevier.

Beauregard, M., & O'Leary, D. (2007). *The Spiritual Brain: A Neuroscientist's Case for the Existence of the Soul.* HarperCollins.

Chorost, M. (2013). Where Thomas Nagel went wrong. The Chronicle Review, May 13, 2013. Retrieved October 29, 2013 from https://chronicle.com/article/Where-Thomas-Nagel-Went-Wrong/139129/.

Clifford, C. W. (2010). Dynamics of visual feature binding. In R. Nijhawan and B. Khurana (Eds.), *Space & Time in Perception & Action.*(pp. 199-215). Cambridge: Cambridge University Press).

Collins, S. (1982). *Selfless Persons: Imagery and Thought in Theravada Buddhism* Cambridge: Cambridge University Press.

Cousins, L. S. (1981). The *Patthana* and the development of the Theravadin Abhidhamma. *Journal of the Pali Text Society*, 9, 22-46.

Ferrer. J. N. (2002). *Revisioning Transpersonal Theory: A Participatory Vision of Human Spirituality*. Albany, NY: State University of New York Press.

Hick, J.(1980). Mystical experience as cognition. In R. Woods (Ed.) *Understanding Mysticism*. New York: Image Books.

Katz, S. T. (2000). Mysticism and the interpretation of sacred scripture. In S. T. Katz (Ed.), *Mysticism and Sacred Scripture* (pp. 7-67). Oxford: Oxford University Press.

Koch, C. (2004). *The Quest for Consciousness: A Neuroscientific Approach*. Englewood, CO: Roberts and Company .

Lamme, V. A. F. (2006). Towards a true neural stance on consciousness. *Trends in Cognitive Sciences*, 10(11), 494–501.

Lancaster, B. L. (1997). On the stages of perception: towards a synthesis of cognitive neuroscience and the Buddhist *Abhidhamma* tradition. *Journal of Consciousness Studies*, 4, 122-42.

Lancaster, B. L. (2002). In defence of the transcendent. *Transpersonal Psychology Review*, 6 (1), 42-51.

Lancaster, B. L. (2004). *Approaches to Consciousness: The Marriage of Science and Mysticism*. Basingstoke, UK: Palgrave Macmillan.

Lancaster, B. L. (2005). The Transpersonal as a Framework for Dialogue: A Jewish Perspective. In J. Drew & D. Lorimer (eds.). *A Way through the Wall: Approaches to Citizenship in an Interconnected World*. Corpus Publishing.

Lancaster, B. L. (2011a). The hard problem revisited: from cognitive neuroscience to Kabbalah and back again. In H. Walach, S. Schmidt, & W.B. Jonas (Eds.), *Neuroscience, Consciousness, and Spirituality. Springer.*

Lancaster, B. L. (2013). Neuroscience and the Transpersonal. In H. Friedman and G. Hartelius (Eds.), *Wiley Blackwell Handbook of Transpersonal Psychology*, (pp.223-240). Chichester, UL: Wiley.

Lancaster, B.L. (2008). Engaging with the mind of God: the participatory path of Jewish mysticism. In J. Ferrer & J. Sherman (eds.), *The Participatory Turn: Spirituality, Mysticism, Religious Studies*. New York: SUNY Press.

Levine, J. (1983). Materialism and qualia: the explanatory gap. *Pacific Philosophical Review*, 64, 354-61.

Levine, J. (2001). *Purple Haze: The Puzzle of Consciousness.* Oxford: Oxford University Press.

Lutz, A., Dunne, J. D. & Davidson, R. J. (2007) Meditation and the neuroscience of consciousness: An introduction. In P. D. Zelazo, M. Moscovitch, & E. Thompson (Eds.), The Cambridge handbook of consciousness (pp. 499-551). Cambridge, UK: Cambridge University Press.

Nagel, T. (2012). *Mind and Cosmos: Why the Materialist Neo-Darwinian Conception of Nature is Almost Certainly False.* Oxford: Oxford University Press.

Nicoll, M., *Psychological Commentaries on the Teaching of Gurdjieff and Ouspensky, Shambahala* (5 vols) (first published 1955-6), 1984.

Ratnayaka, S. (1981). Metapsychology of the *Abhidharma*. The journal of the International Association of Buddhist Studies, 4(2), 76-88.

Smart, N. (2000). Mysticism and scripture in Theravāda Buddhism. In S. T. Katz (Ed.), *Mysticism and Sacred Scripture* (pp. 232-241). Oxford: Oxford University Press.

Spencer, J. H. (2012). *The Eternal Law: Ancient Greek Philosophy, Modern Physics, and Ultimate Reality.* Vancouver, BC: Param Media.

Underhill, E. (1980). The essentials of mysticism. In R. Woods (Ed..), *Understanding Mysticism* (pp. 26-41). New York: Image Books.

Varela, F. J., Thompson, E. & Rosch, E. (1991). *The Embodied Mind: Cognitive Science and Human Experience.* Cambridge, Mass: MIT Press.

Zeki, S. & Bartels, A. (1999). Toward a theory of visual consciousness. *Consciousness and Cognition.* 8, 225–259.

Zeki, S. (2003). The disunity of consciousness. Trends in Cognitive Sciences, 7, 214–218.

Glossary

Ontology. The philosophical study of the nature of being and reality.

Physicalism. Ontological view that there is no reality other than that which is physical. Hence, **physicalist ontology**.

Neural correlate of consciousness. The minimal set of neural mechanisms that accompany a specific conscious event or state. The term 'correlate' is used to emphasize that the question of causation is undetermined.

Mindfulness. A state in which one's complete attention is intentionally focused on experience in the present moment without a judgemental attitude.

Abhidhamma. The *Abhidhamma Pitaka* is one of the three sections of the Pali canon of Theravada Buddhism. 'Abhidhamma' means "higher teaching," and this scripture systematizes the Buddha's understanding of experienced reality.

Karma. The universal principle of cause and effect in Buddhist thought, whereby actions have impact on the actor, both throughout the lifetime and in reincarnation.

Kabbalah. The mystical tradition in Judaism, focused on comprehending the emanations of God and the human relationship to the divine. The Kabbalah addresses the Hebrew Bible's secret level of meaning.

Transcendent. Beyond the range of normal or physical human experience. Applied to the divine, the term means that aspect of God that is beyond the physical and therefore absolutely outside the range of human knowing. When applied to human experience, the term 'transcendence' generally means beyond the normal sense of self and need not imply a radical departure from a physicalist ontology.

Explanatory gap. The absence of any definitive explanation of how or why consciousness is related to physical events. Our inability to understand the connection between consciousness and the brain.

Occam's razor. A scientific and philosophic rule that entities should not be multiplied unnecessarily. Preferred explanations of unknown phenomena are those that use the minimum number of constructs that account for the facts.

Scientism. The view that the only valid way of knowing is scientific knowing.

Re-entrant neural pathways. Neural pathways in the brain that originate in higher areas in a processing pathway, and connect back via synapses in lower areas, 'lower' meaning closer to the beginning of the pathway.

Dr. Pierre Grimes

Dr. Pierre Grimes was professor of philosophy at Golden West College in Huntington Beach, California from 1966-2004, and has been offering five-day workshops at Esalen Institute since 1985. He is co-author of *Philosophical Midwifery: A New Paradigm for Understanding Human Problems with Its Validation.* Alan Watts wrote that Pierre is a "true jñana yogi".

Interview

DREAMS, PHILOSOPHICAL MIDWIFERY, SOUL

Param Media: How would you define reason and intuition?

Pierre Grimes: I really don't have too much interest in defining things; I much prefer to see how things function, because once you grasp the way they function, then it's secondary to define them. To explore the role between reason, understanding, insight, and knowledge—these are the big issues. But I approach it in a different way. Obviously there's a great interest in wisdom, but I'm far more interested in ignorance, because what if it turns out that the problem is really in the removal of ignorance, and not in searching for something you don't have? Suppose you already have it, but you don't know you have it? Then there's no need to search for it; what you want to do is find out why you're blocked from seeing it in the first place.

Let me give you an example. Recently, I met with a group of people, and one of them was holding to the notion that beauty is in the eye of the beholder, that everything is relative, who's to say what's right or wrong, the usual relativistic view. And so we played with this idea back and forth for awhile. We were en route to a coffee shop to explore in the way we usually do—that is, if someone has a problem, or a dream, or is into something interesting, we talk about it. Sure enough, one member of our group said he had something he wanted to talk about. He is a very creative musician, but he had found recently as he was writing a piece of music that suddenly he couldn't go any further. Everybody in the group knew that this was a beautiful definition of a problem. What is a problem? A problem is something you want to solve, and you know that if you solve it, it will benefit you in some way. If you've done a lot of work to solve something and you're stuck, then you meet the conditions of having a problem.

And so we put the problem on the table, and eventually the discussion reached a high point where the musician had to explore what he really meant when he said that he couldn't go any further with his piece of music, that he was blocked. He said something quite interesting about this: "Actually," he said, "I should do something else." You see, every problem is a problem for several reasons. One reason is that any belief you have of yourself is, in principle, inadequate, because when it comes to the true self, you can't put an image on it. A problem can also be defined as having a false image of yourself and the nature of reality. This is a problem because you've been deceived about the nature of reality, you've been deceived about the nature of yourself, and therefore you're holding a false view about it, and therefore you're ignorant. To have a false belief about yourself and the nature of reality is to believe in a lie. Why is this related to having a problem? Because we do not know the false image we have of ourselves, and we don't know that it is irreconcilable with any meaningful goal we may achieve.

If you really want to see a problem arise, go for the highest, most profound goals you have. When you throw all of your energy into trying to achieve those profound goals, your problem will surface, because the image you have of yourself is irreconcilable with the attainment of that profound goal. The two cannot coexist. The mind will not allow you to have a false view of yourself and claim a profound goal. They're irreconcilable. Suddenly you'll be hit with a block that you need to face.

Back to the conversation with the musician, I then said to him, "That's a rather interesting statement. What kind of a state were you in before you reached that block?" He said, "I was open, I was creative. I felt free, and I was enjoying it." And I said, "Is it possible that the state of mind that you just described—that you should be doing something else—has a tone, a melody, perhaps even a face or an image?" At first he said no, but after a few minutes, he said, "As a child, I was once in a really good state, and an interaction with my mother got me to give it up and do something else." He said that when she did that, she looked more beautiful, more sincere, more knowing, and more caring than she ever had in respect to him. He then said something remarkable: he said that it was a rare event for her to appear that beautiful, sincere, knowing, and caring with him. So he gave up that good state of mind, because he saw someone he loved looking so beautiful, and so interesting, and so knowing. The mere appearance of knowing and sincerity is the very mark of every single vice. Vice is a mask of virtue. His mother, and anybody that plays this game (and everybody does) presents the face of virtue, and therefore we believe that they are good and caring. Why is this important? If we have never seen this person look that way before, they are now sharing something with us; they are sharing that we count to them. So at that moment, we give up whatever it is we're doing, and we sacrifice it. We stop whatever it is we're doing in honor of that moment of sharing. And therefore, whenever my musician friend found himself in a good state like the one he had experienced in his childhood, he found he could only go so far before he had to give it up and do something else.

In the moment of seeing all this, you have to bring all of these things together into unity, to see it in a flash. That kind of seeing was far different than any kind of seeing my musician friend had done before, and he was brought to it by way of reasoning step by step using very simple questions. The same questions can be used any number of times, varied, of course, to the individual. What does this questioning do? It brings you to recognize that there is a different way of understanding, and it brings you to an insight that what you formerly thought was true is actually empty. And what does that do? It means that you can go back to the state you had given up—the state of feeling open, free, and creative—and continue it. We all give up a state of mind in our early days that was very beautiful, open, and free. When you get past your blocks, you pick up psychically that state, and you now can continue it and carry it, like someone might throw you a football that you catch on the goal line.

This state of mind of seeing past your blocks can be considerably more profound, depending upon the person who's willing to see it and the implications of it. Where that goes is a kind of understanding that brings about an insight called an intuition. It's a special kind of insight that brings the present and the past into a union, allowing you to see the blocks and the false beliefs you had about yourself. It puts you in a fresh state of mind—or rather, it allows you to recover a state of mind from the past—and now you can go into it with a sense of freedom and get on with whatever it is you want to achieve. This same approach can be used to analyze dreams. Daydreams, tangents, it's all the same. We want to know how the mind operates, how it functions, so that we can understand it and learn the language we need to free ourselves from these kinds of problems. That's the goal of humanity: to get the hell out of these problems, to come to grips with them and start directing our own lives and the future of our society, rather than be fools for all of the stupidities of our age.

Our age is empty because of this sense of relativity, this tendency of saying "who's to say who's right or wrong?" Everybody seems to agree that we are each private, separate individuals with our own points of view. And yet in the conversation with the musician and the other people in the group, we were all able to see the same thing relative to ourselves. We could all share in this experience, and that is only possible if we are not completely private, separate individuals with our own way of understanding, perceiving, and knowing. In that moment, we become in touch with something more profound through our words, which is called a shadow of the *logos*, or reason principle. The exploration of this kind of reasoning can open the mind to more profound states of knowing, the kind of knowing that brings about freedom, growth, and the ability to challenge what is.

Humankind has one destiny: to wake up, find out what's blocking us, and what would make our world better. To do this, we have to go for truth; it's there to be seen, because the very nature of reality and the nature of the self is the same. To have a false view of reality, to be deceived and ignorant about it, is what Plato called the lie which both gods and men hate. When you are deceived about what is real, from that point on anything you think of becomes a fraud. We have to purge ourselves of every false notion of the self and the nature of reality. Through these states of mind, as well as through dream work, people are able to discover states of mind that are parallel, in many respects, to some of the most profound states of mind discoverable in other meditative systems. Zen Buddhism, Chinese philosophy, Indian philosophy, all of them are after the same thing: insights into the nature of the soul.

This is the way of using the mind to discover the mind, the way of understanding, to see that you can see. If you can see that you can see, then you're free. Free of what? Every person has been taught to doubt themselves, and that's how we are controlled, so this kind of seeing can help you to get over your doubts about yourself. Then you can dedicate yourself to a better way of being, through discovering your own soul. This idea that the everyday world is empty is now shown to be false. Why? Because every problem shows that the thing that blocked you in life can be understood on a higher level, and you can break through it. Therefore, everything in life gives you the opportunity to face your own blocks, and therefore the universe, including the everyday world, is meaningful. It provides you with the conditions for your own growth, and that's what we're here for: to learn about the nature of the soul and the nature of reality.

This is a different approach to reasoning and understanding that has a different idea of causes and of the context in which learning must take place. Every problem has its own logic. You can be following logic if you make no mistakes in your reasoning as you proceed from a premise to a conclusion, but that doesn't mean your conclusion is true; it just means it's logically sound. You might be able to call this discursive reasoning, but of all the different kinds of reasoning out there, I don't see anyone doing what I've outlined here, with the style of understanding and procedure that we're using. It is a new paradigm, a new way of understanding, and it has long-range implications. It is simple, direct, effective, challenging by far, capable of awakening people to a higher and better way of living and reflecting, and ultimately, of course, of acting.

Dream work is central to this approach. You can't have a dream that you can't understand. We should be able to take the very worst in us and, if we are willing to explore, to see the roots of our problems and what brought us to the point where we now find ourselves. We should be able to see the very conditions of our problems, why we are experiencing them, and what we have to do to get out of it. It's quite simple, how the mind communicates to us through our dreams and daydreams the need to solve problems; these are all objects of the highest kind of learning of the soul. A daydream can be a route from ignorance to enlightenment. Why? When you have a daydream, you immediately identify with a figure of yourself that, in principle, is false. This is ignorance.

The drama of the daydream spins out the implications of that false image. If you allow the daydream to go to the end without intrusion, you will see that it ends in tragedy and disaster. Or, if it ends in apparent victory, the price of that victory is total chaos. What does this mean? It means that the image the daydream is showing you, that you identify with, plays itself out in tragedy, so you'd better check where you got that self-image from. Daydreams can also be predictive. How many times do we imitate the drama of the daydream (consciously or not), playing its images out in our everyday world? The relationship between daydreams and dreams is so much worthwhile seeing, including how one can play off the other. Our task is to know ourselves, and dream work is a way of approaching this self-knowledge.

PM: Which would you say is a higher use of the mind: reason or intuition? Or is this dichotomy even appropriate?

PG: Using the mind to reason is a way of understanding that invariably leads to intuition. Intuition is when you bring the scattered multiplicity of events in your life and the things that have confounded you into a unity through questioning. You're able to bring them together in an instant, and this suddenness of unification is called the intuition. Well, 'intuition' is not really the proper word; the proper word is 'intellect.' When you use understanding, it prepares the mind for the intellect to function, and the exercise of intellect—which this kind of reasoning awakens—opens the mind and encourages it to gain a greater grasp and use of the intellect to discover what is intelligible. What is the intelligible? It takes two forms, and many of the people I've worked with have reached both. In their problem solving, many have reached very clear and open states of mind akin to what is present in Zen Buddhism and Chinese Buddhism.

This way of reasoning or understanding that we are stressing here brings together the intellect to grasp in a unity the oneness of it all. This produces a state of mind that now is available to the individual not as a passing phenomenon, but that begins an opening in their everyday world and allows them to see things that before they hadn't seen. This means that both the world and ourselves are intelligible. It is entirely possible to verify for oneself that we are part of a caring and intelligible universe. The verification is a kind of proof, since it is a way of understanding that is based upon a realization that our mind constantly communicates with us for our own benefit. That's the destiny of humankind: to turn things around and save ourselves from our own madness and ignorance before it's too late.

PM: Many scholars would assume that Zen Buddhism and Platonism are incompatible. What do you think?

PG: Well, I'd rather skip the first part, because that means I'd have to pay attention to what many scholars think about Zen Buddhism and Platonism. And since I'm not known to favor most scholars in the way they deal with Plato, and equally well with Buddhism, I'll just skip that part. You could say the primary difference is in their clothes; one wears Greek clothes, and the other wears monk's robes. One shaves their head, and the other one grows a beard. They both meditate, they both contemplate, and they both reach stages of enlightenment—enlightenment with qualities, and enlightenment without qualities. Plato has the idea of the One, which is without qualities, and the Buddhists have the full brilliance of the light of being—that is, the ultimate state of mind, which has the highest qualities.

However, the predominant view in Buddhism is to go for *nirvana* or *satori*, the highest state without qualities. In the Platonic universe this equally is true, but Plato is insistent that it is important to go through the most brilliant light of being, sometimes called the idea of the Good. The idea of the Good is the same thing as the most brilliant light of being or divine luminosity. In Buddhism, it isn't that they reject that high, profound state of mind called the brilliant light of being, but they are interested in that openness, in that state without qualities. That's the primary state. Sometimes in Zen Buddhism, talk of the divine luminosity experience is dismissed. This represents a fundamental difference between Zen Buddhism and Platonism. But if anyone is thinking of disposing of these experiences from Zen Buddhism, of tossing them out the window, as it were, I assure you I'll be outside holding a bucket, capturing it, because they're pretty nice states of mind to experience.

PM: Can you talk a little bit about how the soul descends down to the self?

PG: Staying with the same twin systems that we spoke about a moment ago, we can continue it, but instead of Buddhism, we can put in Plotinus, and for Platonism we can put in the figure of Socrates. For Plotinus, he feels that a great loss has occurred as the soul drops into (or returns to) the body. This is because, fundamentally, he sees the obstacle to enlightenment in the body. And that certainly can be true; many people view the body, with its passions and desires, as their basic, fundamental block hindering their spiritual development.

What we know about Socrates from Plato and a few others is that he reached very profound states of mind. He was able to stay in a profound state of contemplation for twenty-four hours, and many people witnessed this during lulls in battle. Socrates was a skilled warrior, a philosophical midwife, and he urged dream study, but he was still human. He fathered a child at the age of seventy, so it certainly doesn't look like he separated himself from the body and his passions. Plotinus would say that the way of life, the battle, is always against the passions and the desires. Socrates was different; he could drink everybody under the table. He wasn't a pacifist; he was a warrior. He helped many people through their problems by using philosophical midwifery. And yet he also experienced a kind of yoga, a separation of the soul from the body, which is described in Plato's dialogue *Phaedo*. This separation of soul and body, this yoga, is a spiritual discipline, but that doesn't mean you're at war with the body. Platonism really looks for the fundamental ideas that block the soul's development and growth. Ignorance is the main problem. As for myself, I was in such a mess at one point in my life, and so I started studying myself to try to get out of my own problems. Combining the teachings of Platonism and Buddhism has been very helpful, enjoyable, and a lovely challenge. You get into all kinds of nice states of mind. Alan Watts used to say that the nature of ultimate reality is play, and it's true, but the best and noblest way to play is philosophical midwifery. That's the noblest game there is.

PM: Can you talk about the role of simplicity?

PG: Simplicity functions on multiple levels. Every problem, when it is properly understood, is simple. All the parts are obvious, and the solution is simple—always. There is nothing left over, no debris to gather up, and it all comes together. It simply drops, leaving no parts, and therefore it's simple. Simple means "no parts," you see. We're talking about that magnificent state of the mind, luminosity—which, by the way, Jesus experienced in the Gospel of Mark. This experience occurs all throughout history. The reason for that is simple, too. In that moment of divine luminosity, there are no distinguishable parts; it is homogeneous, and yet profoundly deep. It is the same, but nowhere is the same a bland sameness; it is an intelligible vitality, a kind of listening, a state of bliss for those who experience it. But you can't cut it up, because it doesn't have parts. If it has no parts, it's simple. When people lose or deflate many of their problems, then they can be simple—that is, they're not putting one thing higher than another, but rather allowing all things to be the way they are. That's simplicity.

Isn't it curious how dreams gather elements from our complex everyday world and put them into metaphoric languages and similes so that we can express them in terms of analogies? What does that really mean? It means that those things that are symbolized in our everyday world are there to be seen, but we can't see it; we aren't simple enough to see it. The everyday world is pregnant with meaning, and yet we don't see it. We don't see it because we believe something else is true and real. As that drops away, you can then become more simple, because you are no longer clinging to the parts that you've been taught are real. Perhaps to push it even further, we could say that that which has no parts is also the One, as Plato would call it. This is a much more profound use of the idea of simplicity. Saying that something is simple, of course, means that it couldn't really be the One, because the One is beyond all qualities. But it approaches it; you can begin to touch it with simplicity.

PM: Can you talk about symmetry, and how it is related to the One?

PG: You can play with that question on a variety of levels. You can approach it the way Damascius approaches it, or Proclus, or Plato. But first of all, what is symmetry? I accept the notion that symmetry presupposes a certain order, and there is something about that order that must reappear. For example, if I draw a line cutting myself vertically in half, one half will be like the other; the parts on one side are like the parts on the other side. That would be a single property. But I'd rather not talk about symmetry that way. Instead, I'd rather say that when we talk about people having a problem, in one way it's a problem, and in another way it's a solution, and that is also a kind of symmetry. When a family wants to make sure that its members cohere and stay together as a unity, the imposition of a problem allows all of the family members to accept the limits, the boundaries of a certain way of being, appearing, and functioning. Each one has a role; each one has an identity. If one of the family members leaves, someone else can take over that position, that role. The roles move from one generation to the next. The child then becomes the parent, and does the same thing to their children. Therefore, between any two generations there is a symmetry, just like the imaginary division of the body I mentioned earlier. Every successive generation has the property of symmetry between each successive state. That's a powerful dynamic, and it's a cohesive property that keeps the family together.

When philosophical midwifery comes along, there's a breaking of that symmetry, and a more profound order is then revealed behind it. This deeper order had been concealed, unknown, and invisible to those caught within the first order of symmetry. When the first order of symmetry is seen through, that's called symmetry breaking, and a higher, more profound order now takes its place. This deeper kind of symmetry is a symmetry of the mind; there is a symmetry between the mind and the nature of reality. This is why there is integrity in the universe. There is a meaningful correspondence between the mind, the nature of reality, and the nature of appearances. They are not divorced or at war with one another, but rather there is a property of symmetry between them. Symmetry, therefore, is a oneness. Without oneness, you couldn't have symmetry. The shadow of the oneness is symmetry. Symmetry is a oneness, and oneness comes from the One, and so the progression from the One to oneness to symmetry is the downward flow of a transcendent order. Finally it reaches the chaotic, and then it returns, and then flows back again. We're on the circle back. Humankind has been in chaos long enough, and now it's time to return to symmetry of the mind and the nature of reality and the everyday world. It's time to find a higher oneness, to come to grips with what is, after all, the nature of the One itself. That's what it's all about.

PM: What can you tell us about soul-mates?

PG: The most interesting and profound kind of soul-mate is called the *daimon* in the Ancient Greek world. A popular way of expressing it would be to say that Socrates had a voice that accompanied him from his youth. This voice would never tell him what to do, but sometimes it would say, "No." Therefore, he had this constant guide through his whole life. That's one kind of soul-mate, a very high kind.

When anybody is lucky enough to find a teacher, and they find in that particular teacher the kinds of things we all regard as eminently worthwhile having—integrity, truth, courage, sharing of knowledge—regardless of what kind of a teacher it is, whether the teacher is a swimming coach or a roshi or a yogi, that's another kind of soul-mate. This kind of soul-mate relationship happens when people recognize one another in such a way that there is that same kind of bond and kinship.

Then, of course, there's the romantic type of soul-mate. That type has its problems, because you can have a soul-mate and have a great deal of love for that person, but you may not have understanding in that same package. And that's a wicked, strange kind of symmetry. If you can find both love and understanding together in a soul-mate, then that's a high degree of soul-mate, and that is possible to find. Rare, but possible. It is also possible to cultivate that kind of soul-mate relationship. In fact, all of these kinds are possible to cultivate. In this game, you always run into soul-mates. You attract them just the way they are, whether it's through sports, music, art, philosophy—it's all the same. I suspect you can only really know the other person from such a relationship, because when that kind of understanding is not there, you never know whether the other part is freely sharing whatever it is they know. That brings a certain doubt, and therefore becomes a block to learning. Soul-mates are the very condition for learning, through combining loving and understanding.

If you were to ask me what is the purpose of all this mental functioning, or cognitive activity, I would say that all this is for the Self to come to know itself. However, it should be borne in mind that although we may discover certain things through this mental functioning, this should not be confused with knowing directly the nature of the Self; the true nature of the Self is independent of these kinds of functioning.

Bill Gladstone

Bill Gladstone, a world-renowned literary agent and author, founded Waterside Productions, Inc. in 1982 and has personally placed more than 5000 titles with dozens of publishers. He was responsible for selling the first "For Dummies" book, DOS for Dummies by Dan Gookin, which led to the phenomenal series which now has sold over 200 million copies. Mr. Gladstone personally represents spiritual teacher Eckhart Tolle, international peace advocate Dr. Ervin Laszlo, and philanthropist Shari Arison, among many others. He has also authored several books, including *Dr. and Master Sha: Miracle Soul Healer*, the best-selling novels *The Twelve* and *The Power of Twelve*, and *The Golden Motorcycle Gang* (co-authored with Jack Canfield).

Interview

BUSINESS, HEART, UNIVERSAL CREATIVE ENERGY

Param Media: How would you define intuition, and how would you define reason?

Bill Gladstone: Intuition is more of a feeling. I would define it as coming from the heart, but it's the thoughtful heart. Traditionally, intuition is thought of as having a hunch or a gut feeling. Reason, on the other hand, comes through the mind. We can train our minds; I've had lots of training, and also a natural proclivity toward certain types of reasoning. I would say I've always enjoyed using my mind more than my heart. Even as a very young child, I could multiply three-digit numbers in my head, and I always got a great deal of joy out of being able to use mathematical reason. As I went through school and attended Yale and Harvard, and then when I entered the business world, figuring things out and being able to work with numbers has always been a wonderful advantage for me, such as figuring out what is a reasonable outcome to expect from a negotiation.

At the same time, I actually use my intuition more than reason in business. I can use reason to close the deal, but there's no point in even meeting with someone if my intuition doesn't tell me, "This is a person I want to be with. This is an idea that's worth promoting." I grew up in a publishing family; my father was a book publisher, and even though he wasn't much of a reader, he could just look at a book and quickly assess it. One day, he handed me a book and said, "Tell me what you think of this." He came back ten minutes later and said, "So, what do you think?" And I said, "I barely got through the first chapter! What do you mean, what do I think?" His reply was, "I didn't ask you to read it; I asked you to tell me if you think we should publish it!" I realized then that it was not about understanding every word of a book, but rather making a very quick assessment. You do use your reason but, in fact, it's more of an intuitive decision.

If you look at the great successes in book publishing, you will see that it really comes from people who have a sense—an intuitive feeling—about a project. One of the problems with book publishing today is that the people who we call the "bean counters" have taken over the boardrooms, and everything is done based on numbers. You can analyze things and say, "This author's last book sold forty-three thousand copies, therefore we can justify a hundred and twenty-eight thousand dollar advance." All that reasoning is fine and good, but it's never going to get you the next hit. The next hit is always going to come from an intuitive feeling. One of the problems that we're experiencing in book publishing today is that big-time publishing is not set up to really honor intuitive feelings anymore. Everything has to be analyzed and subjected to reason, and it all has to be based on the probability of making money. In the past, sometimes we would say that somebody was crazy for taking a big risk on an unknown author, but we respected that decision, and we realized that none of us really knew from reason alone what was going to work.

Since we're focusing on what I do as a literary agent and book publisher, I relate reason and intuition to that part of my life primarily, although they are present in other aspects of my life, too. For example, I happen to be an avid golfer. There are two ways of playing golf: one is by reason, where you practice your swing, you perfect everything so that the angles from a physics point of view are going to produce the results you want. And then there's the way I prefer, which is when you just have a feeling that a certain club is the right one, and you feel like you should swing it a certain way. Particularly when it comes to putting, I just look at the hole, look at the green, and get a feeling; it's really much more intuitive.

Intuition and reason go together in every aspect of life. Those who fail to use both are definitely subject to greater error than those who find a way to combine both intuition and reason in their daily lives.

PM: There are many stories in the business world where the numbers say one thing, and then someone in the company gets the feeling that it should be done another way, which turns out to be right. How do you approach someone who is caught up in the numbers and can't seem to open up to intuition?

BG: I think a wonderful combination to have in a company is an intuitive CEO and a reason-based CFO. They would each represent a side of the balance and be a check for each other. Either side left to its own devices can easily result in disaster. If you only analyze by the numbers, you're going to miss out on many opportunities. On the other hand, if you trust your intuition too much without tempering it with reality checks based on reason and numbers, you may lose out in a big way.

I don't personally experience people as being strictly intuitive versus strictly reason-oriented, although I think there are very few totally balanced people. You can have the full range of personality types on each side, and there are certain personality types that don't get along or that have trouble working together, but I don't think that it's based on whether one person is reason-oriented versus being more intuitive. In my own experience, I use the numbers to make the final decision, but there's no decision to be made unless intuition initiates it. You need that balance.

PM: What role did the interplay of reason and intuition have when you were starting your company, Waterside Productions?

BG: Synchronicity played a big role in the creation of Waterside Productions. At the time, I was Senior Editor for Harcourt Brace Jovanovich, and a small publisher had come to me to ask for some assistance. The wife of the owner took me aside and said, "You know, we're making a lot of money with our production work, but we're losing it all on publishing. I think we need some help, or we're going to lose the company." I told her I'd be happy to provide some free consulting. The very next day, for reasons that are too complex to explain, I was released from Harcourt. There were no other publishers to work for in San Diego, where I was at the time. I had always wanted to have my own film company, and so I thought this was a sign that I should just do it. Within twenty minutes, I called the small publisher and told them I had suddenly become available. Then I proposed that, if they had an extra desk in their shop and a secretary who could work for me, I would come in five days a week; two of those days would be dedicated to turning around their publishing company, and three would be used to start my own company. I started the next day.

The very founding of my company was based on a combination of intuition and reason. On an intuitive basis, I simply liked the people running the smaller publishing company, and I felt like it could be a great opportunity to build something on my own. From a purely practical standpoint, using my reasoning I could see that I now had a place to go where I would have my own assistant and I could start my own company, which I had wanted to do anyway.

It's very rare for a literary agency to have "Productions" in its name, and what happened with the literary side of it was really just a matter of being in the right place at the right time. I spent most of those first six months creating a how-to film, and as I was working on it, I found out more than I should have about how difficult it is to make films, particularly when you have no capital. I was pondering how I was going to deal with this lack of capital when a couple of the authors who I had previously signed contacted me saying their contracts had been cancelled and they didn't know what to do. These were authors who hadn't previously had agents, and who were writing about new, relatively revolutionary ideas, which was not what most book publishers were looking for at the time. There were four or five good authors contacting me asking for my help. I knew a lot of people in publishing in New York, so I agreed to find them another publisher, and that's how the agenting side of Waterside Productions got started. It was an opportunity- and reason-based decision to take advantage of what was happening around me, so that I could make a little money on the side while waiting to get more capital for my film.

And then something amazing happened: as a favor for Andy Kay of Nonlinear Systems, I had hired an editorial and content expert to record the vocabulary entries for a learning device Andy had created called the Tutor Computer. At the same time, Andy also released the Kaypro computer. Nonlinear Systems soon went from being a two million dollar specialty device company to becoming the second largest computer company in the world in 1982, and they reached two hundred and fifty million dollars in sales overnight. They brought on an entire staff of technical writers to create books about how to use the technology, and when they realized I knew people in book publishing in New York, they came to me and asked if I would represent them when they began publishing commercial versions of their manuals. That's how I got into technical books, and almost overnight we became the primary source for that type of publication. There was a lot of thinking things through to be done when the situation presented itself, but the actual path was based more on intuition. Getting involved with computer books was a bit ironic for me. Even though I had always been a math whiz and had programmed computers as a child, I had no real interest in computers. I was more interested in people. While I was Senior Editor at Harcourt, I had turned down several good computer manuals simply because I didn't want to waste my time reading and editing books that bored me. But now that I was on my own, I realized that I didn't have to read these books; I just had to sell them. Within a year, I became the go-to person in the world for books about this type of technology. Reason played an important role in my analysis of the facts of the situation, and my realization that I could spend a very small amount of time and make a lot of money rather quickly. But intuition was also deeply involved, because from a rational point of view, starting your own company without any capital is not something that reason would say you should do. We became so successful with these publications and it was so much fun that I forgot all about making films for about twenty-five years. I did go back to filmmaking eventually, and Waterside has made some films since then.

In my life, intuition and reason are present all the time, and they work very happily together. I've made mistakes along the way, but I've learned to respect both the numbers and the intuitive feelings. In the long run, particularly since money is not the most important thing for me—not that I lack respect for it—I'm very happy with the way intuition and reason have danced together in my professional career.

PM: The combination of reason and intuition is so vital for business, and yet there doesn't seem to be a focus on the interplay between them in business schools today.

BG: You really can't teach it. You've either got it, or you don't. At the same time, I wouldn't choose to back a musician who had no training whatsoever, even if they truly had a gift. You need to take that gift and hone it through training. But no matter how much training certain musicians get, they're never going to have the "it" factor, and I think that holds true in so many fields. Take Bob Dylan: he's someone who has "it," and in his autobiography when he talks about the source of inspiration for his lyrics, he says, "Well, it wasn't me." This gets into some of the deeper aspects of what intuition really is. I think of the heart as being the organ in the body where intuition manifests. If we analyze what intuition is, it's really about what Dr. Ervin Laszlo would call "accessing the zero point," accessing universal knowledge which exists outside of time and space. In the case of someone like Bob Dylan, he's accessing that universal creative source when he's channeling these lyrics, and I think The Beatles did the same during their heyday. It's not something that you're going to arrive at in a traditional MBA program, or any kind of traditional program. It requires a combination of eastern and western techniques. Meditation works for many people, but it doesn't even require mastering meditation. My main source of inspiration when I'm working on a novel is walking on the beach; I walk on the beach every single day when I'm in a creative place.

We can access the universal creative energy in a number of different ways, and each one of us has to learn individually what works for us. I can access this energy in the middle of a negotiation when I start feeling the potential of what could arise out of a deal. It doesn't always work out, but at least I have a clear vision of what could be. I met Steve Jobs and had a couple of conversations with him, and I think that he was an excellent example of someone who was always in that creative space, where he would analyze things and surround himself with people who were also good analysts. Ultimately, though, he had the ability to go within and to see the possibilities, and that was what motivated him, along with the desire to show the mainstream establishment that things really could be done differently. If you look at the history of Apple, I think it's clear that his desire and commitment were probably as important as any other aspect for his business success.

PM: It's been said that Jobs apparently believed that the Macintosh computer always existed in reality.

BG: His intuition allowed him to grasp from the zero point, to access the universal creative energy. We have these different levels of knowledge that keep evolving over time, and to me, that's why intuition is always going to be more important than reason—because intuition taps into the universal, whereas reason is more closely aligned to that which has been established. That doesn't mean you should throw away reason, because it does work very well on a certain level, but intuition can take you to the next level. It was Jobs' intuition that gave him the capability of seeing the preexisting Macintosh. I think that's true for every major invention in human history.

When it comes to questions of consciousness and creation, why wouldn't it be this way? It's infinitely interesting; regardless of your level of consciousness, things are constantly evolving and changing, so no matter how evolved you may be, you should never become bored. If there is one unified consciousness, why would that one consciousness ever want to become bored? To me, the essential element of life is the unknown. A child is born, and although they share certain aspects with every other human on the planet, they are also unique. The combination of universal principles with the infinite variety of manifestation is what makes being part of the collective unfolding of consciousness an endless joy, whether it's in the bodies we have right now, or whatever we're going to evolve into next.

PM: When we have these deeper intuitive insights, how do we then go about communicating them to others, and how do you think reason is involved?

BG: I don't think that someone who just wakes up and "gets it" can necessarily communicate that insight. Going through the process of reasoning out the insight also allows you to "get it" at multiple levels and understand the insight more clearly. It's not just about having an "aha!" moment and suddenly becoming enlightened and saying to yourself, "I don't even need to be here." We're all still here, and as long as I'm here I want to have fun, and I'm going to have more fun if I can get other people to have the same "aha!" experience. That way, we can start making an actual, meaningful difference in the lives of everyone on the planet, because we are all interconnected. In Eckhart Tolle's *The Power of Now,* he talks about how the most important thing to do once you've reached this higher state is to maintain that state, and to get as many other people as possible to understand it and join you there.

PM: Can you talk about how both reason and intuition have played a role in your personal life?

BG: Reason has certainly played a role in many of the decisions I've made in my life, but I would say that intuition has always been more important. This has particularly been true with romantic relationships, which are never really reasonable. In hindsight, I would say that had I been more reason-oriented in my personal life, things would have been calmer and easier on a material level.

My intuition has led me to make some decisions that were not considered normal for most people. For example, when I was studying at private school, I was at the top of my class, and during my sophomore year I found out about a study abroad program in Barcelona, Spain. Attending private school was supposed to be all about getting prepared for college, and so from a logical point of view, it didn't make a lot of sense to leave a situation where I was captain of the baseball, football, and wrestling teams and had been valedictorian every year—all of which would look good on college applications—and take a chance on this crazy notion of going to Spain for a year. And yet, I never hesitated. I knew going abroad was what I wanted to do, and I felt good about it. In my life, I've always honored my feelings first. Once I've made a decision with my feelings, I then absolutely honor reason to get me out of the pickle that my feelings sometimes get me into, or when it goes well, to leverage my wise intuitive decision into something bigger and better.

PM: Have you ever been in a situation where both your reason and intuition are telling you not to do something, but then something else comes in that tells you to do it anyway?

BG: That's what makes life so interesting. When I got fired and decided to start my own company, it could have ended up being a total disaster. Waterside didn't have to work, and I could have been left high and dry and gone backwards in my life. But it's my life, and that's part of the joy of it. Another even more dramatic example was when I decided to marry one of my three ex-wives. At the time, I knew that I was making a mistake. The woman was just not a good fit on multiple levels. I knew I was doing the wrong thing, both in terms of reason and intuition, and it did eventually cost me millions of dollars and a lot of heartache. And yet, on another level, I would say it was my destiny to do what I did, and it got me to a different place which I might not otherwise have gotten to. There's a Spanish saying: "Lo que no mata, engorda," which means "That which doesn't kill you makes you healthy"—or rather, "makes you fatter," from the old times when fat meant healthy. And it's true; any experience that you survive will be of benefit to you in some way as a human being. Sometimes you have to overrule both intuition and reason and just do something anyway, and perhaps at a very deep level, a higher intuition—or your higher self, if you believe in higher self—is guiding you on a path and a journey that is in your ultimate best interest.

PM: Have you ever advised an author to follow their own intuition in their career? If so, why did you do that, and what were the consequences?

BG: An instance of this actually occurred just a few hours before this conversation. I have a client who has written a very innovative book combining two genres into one who just got turned down by one of the big publishing houses. Reason—which is what the big publishing houses are using to make their decisions—would dictate that you should choose one genre or the other. Instead of tailoring the book to those reason-based expectations, I told my client that in this particular case, doing something that's never been done before is the right way to proceed. They should do the book the way they want it, and I think it will be successful.

I always tell authors to write the book that they most want to write, provided that they can explain to me what their goals are. If their goal is to make money, then they had better use their reason. What's going to make money in the short term—securing a large advance and making immediate sales—is, to some extent, predictable. I am able to predict what the buyers (in this case, the book publishers) are going to do, because I know that they are relying on their reason and making decisions based on economic analysis. If making money is what you want to accomplish, you're going to have to reorganize your priority list to be more in line with what reason dictates is going to make money in the current market.

Often authors will come to me saying that there's a book that they really want to write, and they think that in order to make that book a success, they need to establish themselves as a writer and write another book first. I usually advise them to go in the opposite direction, to go straight to what they really want to do, because then their passion is going to be there. When you do something you really love, you normally do it better than if you're just doing it because you think it's a means to an end. It's not one size fits all; sometimes you should let reason dictate, but more often than not, you should start with your intuition.

On the other hand, sometimes authors will come to me saying they've had a dream or an intuitive feeling that their book is going to sell a million copies. I turn down ninety percent of proposals in those cases, because even if their book is full of incredible insights and is going to be a refinement on, for example, *The Power of Now*, no one has ever heard of this author and they're not going to be able to sell it. The conditions that existed at the time *The Power of Now* was published no longer exist, and even if Eckhart Tolle were to bring that book to me today, I still wouldn't be able to sell it. The potential may be there, but in this case reason is going to be very clear that, at least with me as your agent, it's not going to happen.

PM: We've touched on how the publishing industry is suffering from an imbalance of reason and intuition, with a tendency to lean more toward the side of reason. What do you think could or should be done to help remedy this imbalance?

BG: In the old days of book publishing, publishers were owned by individuals, and they used intuition to a large degree. Most of these companies are now owned by conglomerates, and intuition has gone out the window. The people making the decisions at the top are people who are used to running oil companies or construction companies, businesses that are based on careful analysis rather than intuition. That type of logic is being applied to book publishing, and guess what? It does not work. It can work for awhile in certain situations, but it totally kills innovation and creativity. They would almost prefer a new author make it with a smaller publisher, at which point it makes more sense for them just to buy that small publisher, and that's how they get their creativity.

There's still life in the old publishing model and in these big companies, but the real remedy is in creativity, and in the people who continue to create new companies. I don't really have a solution for the industry as a whole, because it's beyond what any logic can dictate to change a course of action that was set in motion almost sixty years ago when they started consolidating and promoting "synergy." The synergy doesn't really exist, but the conglomerates do, and conglomerates have a different mission. They're not about the wellbeing of the planet or fostering wonderful ideas; they're about money. Reducing everything to money goes against the essence of publishing, at least traditionally. Publishing was originally for the public benefit; it really wasn't about making a profit, although it was a way to have influence over society. Now, under the conglomerates, it's really about money, which is very time-limited. Money does work more with reason than with intuition. There is a book called *The Intuitive Investor* where the author, Jason Apollo Voss, talks about how intuition is, in fact, important in financial decisions. And at the very top levels of every profession—including, I suspect, the money managers—you do see intuitive people. At the very highest level, it all switches, and intuition comes back into play. But in the middle, it seems to be all about reason, and when you limit it to reason, the life and creativity is really sucked out of it.

An alternative that combined the best of the old model, with reason in its place, with a more intuitive-based way of publishing would be ideal. There is a solution out there, and it's not something that any one individual can do, but it is something that forty or fifty likeminded, experienced professionals working together with some money behind it could accomplish. The situation is not hopeless; the patient is not dead yet.

PM: What roles do intuition and reason play in your work as an author, from the inception of the idea for a book to the writing process itself? Would you advise the same sort of process to other authors?

BG: I have my own writing process that works for me, and I think there are elements of my process that are probably useful to other people. I've written both fiction and non-fiction, and particularly if you're going to write a non-fiction book, I think that you need to start with reason. You may have an intuition about which topic area or theme you want to write about, but after you've determined that—whether it's through your life choices over a thirty-year period, or by an intuitive "aha!" moment—you really need to look at reason. You need to analyze who your audience is, what other books have been written on this topic, and what specifically you can do to promote yourself as the ideal author for this book. Is this book part of a larger mission? If so, who shares this mission with you, and how can you get those people to support your book? The next step is to write an outline. When I write non-fiction, writing the outline is the very first thing I do, and then I follow that outline as much as I can. I set a minimum goal—usually five or ten pages a day—and I set aside a minimum of an hour or two a day to write. I don't really criticize my writing as I go; I just write, I know that it's not perfect, and I'm ok with that.

I don't believe in writer's block; you just have to sit down and write, period. You're not inspired; so what? You're tired; so what? You've made a commitment to write, and it's the universe writing the book through you, ultimately. Everything that you've experienced and learned plays a part; your personality, your vocabulary, everything you've previously written. Particularly when I'm working on a novel, I'll walk on the beach and think about what the next chapter's going to be. I really compose the chapter in my head while I walk. Sometimes I'll start writing and it all goes out the window. When you're writing, things just occur to you, and it's a very intuitive process. A character might say something that I didn't think they were going to say. It's like jazz, and that's the fun of it. The hard part of writing is the rewriting, which requires finding a good editor to work with. Reason plays more of a role than intuition with the rewrite, because you have to answer your editor's reasonable questions.

In terms of advice for others, I think a lot of what I've said can be applied. The more disciplined you can be, the better. It's not a hobby; it's a profession, even if you don't have a publishing contract, or if you're not certain you will get one. If you're going to do it, put everything you have into it, and do it seriously. Make it the best it can be, and don't limit yourself; let it flow, let it evolve, and know going in that the first draft is not the final draft. And most importantly, you have to love the process. If you don't love it, then you shouldn't do it. The only people who should write books are people who can't *not* write books. If you're doing it on reasonable criteria alone, then it's a very unreasonable proposition.

Dr. Ivana Gadjanski

Dr. Ivana Gadjanski is a pioneering scientist and an award winning poet. She is currently a researcher and Project Leader at Serbia's R&D Center for Bioengineering-BioIRC and Assistant Professor at Belgrade Metropolitan University. She is also the Founder of Fab Initiative, a non-profit promoting female biotech entrepreneurs in Serbia. A Fulbright Alumna of Columbia University, she was handpicked as one of TED's Global Fellows in 2012.

Dr. Ivana Gadjanski

Poetry and Science, Reason and Intuition: A Personal View

BIOLOGY, POETRY, EDUCATION

1. Can you offer brief definitions for both intuition and reason?

Intuition is for me an umbrella term for the cognitive processes happening at the subconscious level, while reason is the process of reaching conclusions based on clear logic—by "clear logic" I mean that we are aware of the logical principles we are using and can express them verbally. When I say subconscious, I do not simply mean something subliminal, which would be information processing in response to rather weak stimuli that do not reach the threshold of sensation or consciousness [1]. By subconscious or even unconscious I refer to the mental processes that are occurring without the awareness of the individual, while the stimuli could still be observed with awareness. Such stimuli that cause intuitive processes are not weak; on the contrary, they might be very strong and perhaps even too strong to be logically analyzed.

If we venture briefly into the field of artificial intelligence (on which I am by no means an expert, but in which I am very interested), we could say that intuition occurs when categorizing information based on similarity, but with decision borders too complex to be reduced to logical rules. Intuition can also be described as a process based on partial observations, where neural network activity selects only those paths that may lead to a solution, excluding all the bad moves [2]. This is an interesting concept. Intuition described in this way might be understood as a faster and even more reliable way of reaching conclusions that are beneficial to the person's well-being than reason is capable of offering.

In my personal view, intuition is something that cannot completely be explained verbally, while reason has its internal decipherable clockwork mechanism that can be put to words and even into mathematical symbols.

2. (a) What roles do intuition, creativity, and emotion play in your scientific work?

Scientific work has always been very creative for me, especially in the early stages of a project when you are starting from scratch. You have to work out a hypothesis, to set up the experiments, and you should already be able to envisage potential applications. This demands quite a lot of intuition and ability to see the bigger picture. It can get rather emotional as well, when that hypothesis becomes so important to you that it is not only a matter of scientific curiosity, but also a genuine wish to get to the bottom of the problem, because you feel like that knowledge can change the way you and others see the world. If you work on a problem that is very closely related to you personally, like when you work on a neurodegenerative disease that someone you love suffers from, it can become highly emotional. This can be both a driving force and a blinding mechanism, which is why I believe it is necessary for scientists to embrace the existence of the emotional side of science and learn how to use it in a positive way. Scientists are not machines, we are human beings, and human beings have such a wide spectrum of feelings that it would be very unscientific to ignore all those empirically detectable phenomena.

b) Also, what roles do reason and logical thinking play in your poetry?

In my poetry I like to use words in a way they are not ordinarily used. I would say that there is logical thinking at play there, just that the logic used is not the regular, everyday logic, which is to say that there is, for certain, reason underlying my poems, but that it takes some intuition to get to it, both for me when writing the poem and for the reader when grasping the meaning of these words. Perhaps it is best to let our readers make their own conclusions—here are two of my poems:

Centrifuge

Like music
Like claws
Like narrow canyon
It grabs you
It holds you
It takes the best of you
To press you to pellet
To dust and pebbles
To sounds of crickets
In starry night
Unpublished

Associations

It is hilarious
Hilarious indeed

Can you guess what I am reminded of
When I look at the hand
With all those fingers
Movements
It is fast no doubt
And skillful

And it reminds me of crystals
Motionless
And mystical
And transparent
And so thoroughly
Complicated

From my book "Cuneiform script" ("Klinasto pismo"), published in Serbian and awarded literary award "Strazilovo", 2008 [3]. Own translation.

c) How can science help you develop as a poet, and how can poetry help you develop as a scientist?

Science has been helping me immensely to develop as a human being, which of course has implications on my work as a poet.

What do I mean by developing as a human being? I mean that by learning and doing science (biology in particular), I keep becoming more and more aware of the complexity of the world we live in. When you start thinking of the multiple ways in which different types of cells in the body work and connect, how many extremely complicated mechanisms are constantly at play inside your very own cells, tissues, and organs, how invasive the fetal development is to the mother's body, how bones heal after fractures, how intricate the regulation is of what cell type stem cells will turn into, these things can shock you, move your axis. And our potential to discover knowledge as well as the knowledge itself seem indefinite. There is always something new to learn, to find out, to define more precisely, to verify, to see in a different context.

This is what I am searching for in poetry, as well. New ways to look below the surface of the words, searching for the hidden meanings, new ways of combining the building blocks of language and thought. In this way, for me, science and poetry are almost interchangeable; both are on the quest to identify true existence; it's just that in poetry the existence spans beyond the material world and into the immaterial world of imagination. Immaterial is perhaps not the best adjective to use here, because, as I think any book lover would agree, something fictitious can be very real, almost as if a new 'real-life' entity is created. By immaterial, I am referring to the thoughts and feelings that fiction can cause and stir.

On the other hand, my poetry has taught me that not everything is the way it seems at first glance. Just as I use words in a poem with the second or third or whichever meaning in mind, the empirical phenomena we detect and measure in science can also be of multiple origins. Poetry prompts me to keep an open mind in science, to look at the same phenomenon from different angles. It helps.

Interestingly, I have a poem with the title **Building blocks**, where I mix the words with organic structures.

Building blocks

Sharp words
And soft tissues
Pointy teeth
And tender loins
Deep down
Self-replicating
Always dividing
Mixing and crossing
Selfish and ruthless
Simply existing
Surviving.

Unpublished

3. (a) Why do you think it is important for scientists to be able to consciously integrate their intuitive capacities with their rational abilities?

I think this is not only important; it is crucial, if we want any fundamentally new ideas and discoveries. Rational thinking is great for deduction and analysis, but for induction and synthesis you need to also include intuition.

An interesting example of how human intuition can be very helpful in science concerns the process of protein design. In the design of new enzymes and binding proteins, human intuition is often used to modify computationally designed amino acid sequences prior to experimental characterization. The software initially designs proteins with new structures or functions, starting from a set of naturally occurring protein scaffolds of known structure. The software then proceeds with optimizations for the placements of the ligands and other residues. Human researchers then inspect the resulting products using their intuition about protein stability, aggregation, and binding interactions to modify the computer-generated model. In fact, new algorithms are being developed that attempt to recapitulate the modifications made to computer-generated models by human designers [4].

(b) Have you encountered much resistance to the idea of this integration, and if so, why do you think that is, and how can we change that situation?

I wasn't always very eager to let my co-workers know that I write poetry. I was not certain what reactions that could cause. Over time, I became more comfortable, especially after seeing very positive reactions from some scientist colleagues. In general, I see a positive change happening in the direction of embracing more of the arts and humanities within the scientific community. It can, no doubt, become even better, and one of the ways is to improve how science and the humanities are taught in schools. It all starts from an early age.

(c) How do you envision the arts and humanities being successfully integrated into the STEM [science, technology, engineering, and mathematics] education program?

This is a very good question. I just recently submitted a grant proposal about new ways of teaching STEAM in primary and secondary schools in South East Europe. STEAM is a new iteration of STEM, with arts (the A in STEAM) and humanities included.

STEAM infuses both the creative process and design thinking into the teaching of STEM subjects [5]. This is especially important at a time when the boundaries between science and business are diminished and scientists need to obtain at least some of the business skills necessary to be successful in running a laboratory, obtaining grants, etc.

Why do I mention business now? Because I think we need to show interested young people how both science and the arts/humanities can help them achieve success in a lucrative way. As unromantic as it may sound, in order to have a sustainable system for doing and teaching STEAM we need to motivate young people and point out to them the options STEAM can provide for gaining various satisfactions—including financial satisfaction.

In every serious endeavor, whether scientific or artistic, one needs concrete funding. It is probably fair to say that most young people (millennials) do not wish to invest a lot of their energy into something that cannot be funded or cannot bring any revenue. This would seem to be true especially because this generation Y has been forced to face the most uncertain economic future of perhaps any generation since the Great Depression [6].

This is why it is very important to show to young people the financial advantages to be found at the intersections of science, arts and innovation, and entrepreneurship—which is a very natural combination, in fact. Science, arts, and entrepreneurship are all in their essence very disruptive, each capable of bringing new solutions and interpretations to existing problems, as well as identifying new problems in the process, and their merging can be very synergistic.

On the other hand, there is an ever-present challenge of job creation for scientists—what is needed in the labor market today is not only more technical scientific expertise; scientists also require an increasing number of soft skills, like the ability to think imaginatively, develop creative solutions to complex challenges, and adapt to changing circumstances and new constraints [7].

This is where the arts and humanities can play a crucial role. Exposure to literature, philosophy, and history can inspire scientists to be more creative, innovative, and more aware of the need for a multidisciplinary approach in research. In addition, arts integration—the use of the arts as a teaching methodology throughout the STEM curriculum—may improve long-term retention of content [8]. Furthermore, visual arts in particular have been documented to be effective for students to hone in on a concept, taking it from the abstract to the concrete, making students really able to understand it [9].

4. In an OZY article, you mention that "Science is mainly dealing with facts".

(a) Can you define what you mean by the word "fact"?

By the term "fact" I was referring to characteristics that can be empirically tested, verified, and quantified and which are independent of the observer—e.g. distance, speed, mass, and biological processes. However, I am not claiming that everything in science can be quantified unambiguously, or empirically verified, especially if we start thinking about quantum physics in general, Heisenberg's uncertainty principle, the theory of relativity, or a number of other scientific theories. Nevertheless, science is basically always testing if the "old" facts still stand and if the new, more precise theories and measurements can be applied, or the new facts identified. Everything is open to scrutiny in science, even the well-known "facts" (and sometimes they are the most open to scrutiny).

(b) Can the arts also lead to factual discoveries about reality independent of science, or do they merely have instrumental value in helping scientists use their creativity to discover facts?

Well, that is a hard question to answer. I do not think that art can replace science or vice versa, either in the factual discoveries or in any other way. They could and should complement each other. Visual arts in particular can help a lot in identifying new facts. For example, making a visual model of DNA was crucial in understanding how the helical structure of the molecule takes form, and there is a whole new discipline of molecular animation that is based purely on scientific facts about molecules and their interactions. This also brings in a lot of completely artistic values, and these together make for an amazing combination, showing something that we cannot actually see in any other way: how single molecules interact.

(c) Do the arts have their own intrinsic value?

Yes, without a doubt. I believe we can all find different ways of how the arts influence us. In my case, the arts can inspire me, change my point of view, and give me another perspective. The arts can ease the anxiety that is quite frequently present while working on a particularly challenging scientific problem, and they can help me to see possible connections between seemingly unrelated fields; they can also help me to remember, i.e. to memorize better certain scientific principles. I am a visual thinker and I always prefer visual presentation of data, both scientific and artistic.

5. (a) How is inspiration different from (or the same as) intuition?

In my view, inspiration and intuition are somewhat similar, in the way that both are more or less subconscious, occurring without the person's full awareness, and you cannot really evoke them on purpose. However, there are differences.

Oxford Dictionaries define inspiration as "the process of being mentally stimulated to do or feel something, especially to do something creative". [http://www.oxforddictionaries.com/definition/english/inspiration] While I find this definition rather good, I believe it could be expanded as well. To do something creative would generally seem to imply the performance of a work of art, I suppose. However, I would argue that inspiration is at play also in athletes when they get "in the zone, in the flow." In fact, the way I perceive inspiration is very similar to the concept of flow, which is defined as "The mental state of operation in which a person performing an activity is fully immersed in a feeling of energized focus, full involvement, and enjoyment in the process of the activity. In essence, flow is characterized by complete absorption in what one does" [10].

Inspiration is what I feel when I get the urge to write down a poem. Writing it feels completely like being in the flow – the words just follow one another, without difficulty, without even much rational thinking. This is why I said inspiration and intuition have similarities for me.

(b) From where do you believe your inspiration and intuition arise: are they purely biological functions, or do they in some way ultimately come from somewhere outside you?

I adored reading about ancient Greek gods when I was very young and, as a result, I am inclined to say that the Greek pantheon, in my opinion, offers the most concrete descriptions of where inspiration/intuition might arise from – from the Muses [11]. Personally, however, the concept of a higher power somewhere on the outside is quite ambiguous to me – the closest I can get to accepting it is if I relate it to Nature, in its broadest sense, as the whole of the known (and unknown, yet to be discovered) universe filled with physical and living entities. Nature does inspire me. I remember once when I flew over the Andes, in the midst of extreme turbulence, I looked through the airplane window and felt inspired very strongly to write a poem, to try to put into words the power of the elements and those impressive mountains I was observing. Then again, I also like the quote by Picasso: "Inspiration exists, but it has to find you working".

From these two points I will try to extrapolate something like advice, although it is hard to advise anyone on how to get inspired; it is quite a personal experience. Nevertheless, I would say that you could increase the likelihood of getting inspired when you combine several factors. For example, working in a very focused way on a problem while letting your thoughts wander, preferably while in a new environment, be it in the physical sense or in situations like meeting new people. Further on, it helps immensely to be reading books about topics you do not usually spend much time thinking about…figuring out what makes you tick, what moves you emotionally, and doing it in between the times when you work very hard on what really moves you rationally, be it a mathematical problem, an experiment in the lab, your PhD thesis or a novel you are writing or whatever it is that causes your thoughts to "work" in a clear logical stream. The mix is a very potent idea generator, I find. This can be another definition of inspiration – a process of generating ideas.

As for intuition, I cannot say I know where it comes from. In terms of artificial intelligence (AI), it is worth mentioning what Herbert Simon said in 1995: "Al has already reached the stage of human simulation where it can model such "ineffable" phenomena as intuition, insight and inspiration". [12] His theories of expertise and intuition include the "chunking theory", which postulates that experts' knowledge that supports their intuition is composed of information chunks. [13]

Perhaps this is where intuition comes from: pieces of data we gather throughout life, and then in the moments when we need to solve a particular problem our brain picks them out, probably sorting out the most useful ones and using them to make a rapid conclusion. Obviously, if we accept this at least as a working hypothesis, the advice on how to develop your intuition would be to keep learning more, to gather experience and knowledge, and let your brain use those chunks when needed. Another suggestion would be to accept that the intuitive "gut feeling" conclusions are worthy of taking into consideration and can be very useful.

Finally, I would like to point out that both of my interests, for science and poetry, stem from my own family. My father Ivan Gadjanski was a much translated poet who instilled in me a great appreciation of Nature and a love for the use of scientific views in poetry, and my mother Ksenija Maricki Gadjanski holds a PhD in Philosophy and is a university professor of Classical Studies. They both taught me to look for multiple meanings, in the words themselves, in natural phenomena, in other people, in the whole of life.

This is another important aspect that I would like to touch on: family values are crucial in teaching young people how to embrace their own creativity and curiosity, how to put them into practice, and how not to ignore the gut feeling signals. In fact, I consulted my mother for her expertise in linguistics and comparative etymology for the last part of this chapter.

If one looks at the references I have cited so far, one can observe that most of them are quite recent publications. This is a paradox on its own, since the terms in question here, like 'poetry', 'science', 'intuition', 'inspiration', etc. are very old, and did not originate in English (which has become the language of science in the 20th century). Furthermore, these words do not have one single meaning in all contexts.

I will give some examples. The first mention of the Latin noun *intuitio* (intuition) was most likely an invention of Chalcidius (2/3 century AD), translator of Plato's dialogue *Timaeus.* [14] His rendering of Plato's Greek expression for the "image reflected in the mirror" was used. Three centuries earlier, Roman author and statesman Cicero used the verb *intueor* with the meaning "to reflect upon, consider, contemplate", and long before that the term had a wide range of usage, to denote, for instance, "to look at, to watch, to examine visually, to inspect". [14]

As for *scientia* (science), the term developed in a similar way. Two thousand years ago it simply meant "knowledge" (of a fact or a situation), implying certainty in opposition to mere beliefs. For Cicero, it signified "theoretical and practical understanding of things", and later "learning" and "education". [14]

As is widely known, Latin was the language of science in Western Europe throughout two millennia, and these notions of the terms mentioned above slowly developed through that time to the meanings they hold today. It is interesting to note that a century ago the comparative etymology established that not a single language in the group of Indo-European languages had a corresponding root to the Latin verb *scio* "to know", from which the noun *scientia* was derived. [15]

The same situation arises in the word *spiro*, "to breathe," "to respire," which is found in the word inspiration. There are no corresponding roots of the word to be found outside of Latin! As *scientia* was a translation from the Greek *επιστήμη*(epistími, "science"), *inspiratio* is translation for the Greek word *ενθουσιασμός* (enthousiasmós, "enthusiasm"), found in the same translation of Chalcidius. The meaning was "supernatural inspiration," infusion of a feeling or an idea into a person. [16] In ancient theory, inspiration was compared to or identified with religious process. In different contemporary languages, the word "inspiration" has many equivalents—*Einhauchen, Eingebung* in German, *nadahnuće* in Serbian, etc. Generally, it denotes the preceding influence on the creative process and a sort of a prerequisite for creating poetry.

All of these different meanings should be kept in mind when thinking about the links between these mentioned phenomena.

As for the origin of the word poetry, it is quite well known. In Greek it meant "creation, production, fabrication," as opposed to *πραξις* (*prâksis*, "action, activity, practice"). [17]

I would like to finish with another poem, which tries to show what it is like to be without inspiration, so let us all—scientists, artists, entrepreneurs, and everybody else—remember the importance of intuition and inspiration:

No inspiration

I squeeze the words
Taking them
Out of somewhere
Throw them to a pile
Naked as bones
And they keep silent
Unappreciative
Of all my efforts

They are mute
They are deaf
Each for itself
And all against me

From my book "Demons" (Serbian "Demoni"), published in Serbian, 2003[18]. Own translation.

References:

1. Bargh, J.A. and E. Morsella, *The Unconscious Mind. Perspect Psychol Sci*, 2008. 3(1): p. 73-79.
2. Duch, W., *Intuition, insight, imagination and creativity.* Computational Intelligence Magazine, IEEE, 2007. 2(3): p. 40-52.

3. Gadjanski, I., *Klinasto pismo*. 2008, Sremski Karlovci Brankovo Kolo. 129.
4. Nivón, L.G., et al., *Automating human intuition for protein design*. Proteins: Structure, Function, and Bioinformatics, 2014. 82(5): p. 858-866.
5. Bequette, J.W. and M.B. Bequette, *A Place for Art and Design Education in the STEM Conversation*. Art Education, 2012. 65(2): p. 40-47 %@ 0004-3125.
6. Mark P. Cussen. *Money Habits Of The Millennials*. Available from: http://www.investopedia.com/articles/personal-finance/021914/money-habits-millennials.asp.
7. Phelps, E.S. *Why teaching humanities improves innovation*. 2014; Available from: http://forumblog.org/2014/09/stem-education-humanities-creativity-innovation/.
8. Rinne, L., et al., *Why Arts Integration Improves Long-Term Retention of Content*. Mind, Brain, and Education, 2011. 5(2): p. 89-96 %@ 1751-228X.
9. Robelen, E.W., *STEAM: Experts make case for adding arts to STEM*. Education Week, 2011. 31(13): p. 8.
10. Nakamura, J. and M. Csikszentmihalyi, *The concept of flow*. Handbook of positive psychology, 2002: p. 89-105.
11. Dodds, E.R., *The Greeks and The Irrational*. Sather Classical Lectures 1964, 2004: University of California Press.
12. Simon, H.A. *Explaining the ineffable: AI on the topics of intuition, insight and inspiration*. in IJCAI (1). 1995.
13. Frantz, R., Herbert Simon. *Artificial intelligence as a framework for understanding intuition*. Journal of Economic Psychology, 2003. 24(2): p. 265-277.
14. Gaffiot, F., *Dictionnaire latin-français*. 1934, 2000: Hachette.
15. Ernout, A.M.A., *Dictionnaire étymologique de la langue latine*. 1959, 2001: Les Belles Lettres.
16. Bailly, A., *Dictionnaire Grec-Français*. 1950, 2000: Hachette.
17. H. G. Liddell, R.S., *Greek-English Lexicon*. 1968, 1996, Oxford: Clarendon Press.

18. Gadjanski, I., *Demoni.* 2003, Vrsac: KOV-Knjizevna Opstina Vrsac. 84.

Karen Elkins

Karen Elkins' entrepreneurial spirit started at the age of 22 when she launched her ad agency of 23 years. Today Karen is still in the business of communicating ideas as she produces, designs and themes *Science to Sage* e-Magazine, which advances progressive ideas while featuring best-selling authors and innovative thinkers like Bruce H. Lipton and Rupert Sheldrake. Through *Science to Sage*, Karen has collaborated with such renowned publishing houses as Hay House and Namaste Publishing, in addition to hosting a bi-weekly radio show, a live version of the e-Magazine.

Interview

INFINITE POSSIBILITY, MAGNETIZATION, VIBRATION

Param Media: How do you define the terms intuition and reason, and how do you view the relationship between them?

Karen Elkins: We reason along an axis of past, present, and future. What you consider to be reasonable can depend on how you have grown up or the cultural environment you are in. Looking around the world, there are extreme differences in what people view as reasonable. A particular culture's reasoning can nurture your evolution, or it can limit your growth.

We live in an electric-magnetically charged universe, where our brain functions like a computer. We analyze information based on stimuli, and then a charge is sent through our network, akin to a computer with its gateways and switches. This might be considered the automated "machine aspect" of our being, the mechanics of living. It is based on judgments found on some point of the axis, usually in the past. This is also a survival mechanism.

The intuitive self resides in the realm of infinite possibilities, and also at the heart of each of us. It is tapped into in those "aha" moments when you get a chill running through your spine. Where does this feeling come from?

When we look at the way our universe is physically constructed, it would seem on the surface that everything is separate and fragmented, even reason and intuition. Yet we are each a fraction of a greater whole, all intertwining parts dancing together.

The ancients described our universe as a liquid crystal ether, a virtual "water world." The "living waters" have been shown to be the medium which transports and holds information. Water carries the charge, the light of life. It informs with form. Water's prism structure is like the prism of light; it is also fractal in nature. Like a kaleidoscope, this matrix is a "mind field" of infinite possibilities. Intuition, to me, is tapping into the infinite, living holographic field where we can see into our true selves. We are light beings, and we are part of the living waters.

As Walter Russell states, "Nothing can be without the desire to be." Your breath is your spirit, your fire is your desire, and water is your means. We are an electric light show in this electromagnetic universe, where everything is about charge and impulse.

PM: Is this electromagnetic charge something akin to intention? As in, you have to charge up your intention and then direct it forward in order to make change happen in your life?

KE: Yes. Living in an electromagnetically-charged universe, what we bring charge to—whether based on good or bad, love or hate—we magnetize into our life.

In modern medicine, your pulse and brainwaves can be measured along the electromagnetic spectrum; it's a waveform. All of your senses are electric in nature. Consider these little dancing electrons as pixels in a television screen. Imagine your body is like a TV set, and ask yourself: what are you dialed into? Drama? Romance? Comedy? The buttons you push and where you choose to be dialed into is a state, a bond. We have our reasons to plug into a certain channel. Your intention is your "inner tension" that drives people (other electromagnetically-charged particles) toward you. Your body on a molecular level is composed of mainly water. Water stores memory and transmits information. We are dancing in a vibrational sea of consciousness.

PM: When we get an intuitive feeling or an intuitive knowing, where does this feeling or knowing come from?

KE: Most of the greats in human history had inspired "aha" moments, like Mozart when he was composing his music. For some, it is like transcribing, and for others the intuition comes in dreams, or like Archimedes' "eureka moment" while relaxing in his bathtub. Inspiration and insight are available twenty-four hours a day, seven days a week; they are our ability to tap into to the cosmic web.

As for me, when I'm working on my magazine, Science to Sage, I often receive information through dreams, images, or what I call "downloads." Each edition of the magazine is themed, and every time I switch topics, it's like switching the channel on a TV set. The right people seem to be attracted to my field; often, the right pixels, or people, seem to just appear!

PM: How does logical thinking integrate with these moments of inspiration, or downloads? If one part of the process is to actually receive the download—which requires being open to receiving it in the first place—then how you put that information into action?

KE: The key is to ask yourself the right questions. Then all the pieces of the puzzle start clicking into place. I start seeing visual patterns connecting in my mind's eye. The way I see the world, and the way I synthesize meaning, is mainly through images.

PM: Are these patterns arising from some kind of underlying order?

KE: When I put together an issue of the magazine, I look across disciplines to see how they weave together. Seeing how the patterns connect is key for me. The magazine is heavy on visuals, because my aim is always to graphically convey the wisdom behind the creative force that manifests our universe.

What happens all too often in our education system is that we put a lot of emphasis on math and sciences, and forget that often, what we are experiencing is more akin to art. You can reason out or intellectualize something to death, but to get to the real core of anything, we have to use our hearts, our intuition. Ask the right questions, and the door will be opened.

PM: How have these intuitive capacities played a part in your previous work in marketing?

KE: When I ran my ad agency, I could walk into a client's place of business, look around, and immediately get a flavor—a feeling or an essence—of the client and their work. If I'm going to create something for someone, I'm going to mirror their aesthetics and their creative vision. If you are really good at what you do in that realm, then it isn't about you; it's about the creative vision of the client's product or service.

When I put together the magazine and I'm creating visuals for each piece, what the contributors appreciate is that I first seek to deeply understand what they are saying, and then create a visual design to complement that. My aim is to allow the audience to intuitively grasp in a flash the theme of each piece, and of the issue of the magazine as a whole.

PM: Does aligning with your own purpose play a strong role in your work? And does this alignment then result in more information and ideas being able to flow through you?

KE: To me, purpose is akin to passion, so yes, aligning with my purpose does play an important role in my work. My passion and quest as a child was to understand how the creator of the universe had brought everything into being. I wanted to access the cosmic "designer's studio" and see where it all came from. At first I thought this would only be possible after death, but what I have since discovered is that we don't have to check out of this plane of existence in order to access some understanding of this.

Throughout the journey of my life, I have been dialed into the channel of discovery. This has been my reason for being, and has kept me alert to the present moment, to the choices I am making, to the "aha" moments that beckon me into new directions of exploration. This passion for discovery also allows me to let go of things and ideas with more grace when it is time to do so.

We are each like a drop in the sea; we are all aspects of the greater ocean. We are like an instrument through which that greater universal force can express and explore itself, but first we have to be aligned with it. Otherwise, it's a struggle, which is where our ego comes into play.

PM: How would you describe this universal force?

KE: The way I understand it is that the universe is like a vast ocean containing everything. I call it "the Living Water of Light."

We are all explorers playing with our kaleidoscope, arranging and rearranging the matter in our lives. Each of us is a player in the game who gets to arrange their own "patterned world." Source is pure geometry in motion. We are all pattern makers in life.

The sense of wonder is something that I watched in action every day when I was running a school. Some kids wanted to be scientists, some wanted to actors. All we're doing in this life is exploring different aspects of a desire to see and be.

One of the problems comes in, I think, when people judge too narrowly from their own individual perspective. Our perspective is only one frame of reference, one angle, and all too often it is a very narrow lens.

PM: It seems that many people stop exploring because they have become too comfortable, and they think there is some safety in that.

KE: When we stop exploring, asking, and creating, the "charge" or "spark" is gone from our lives. A light goes out. When we tap into our intuition, we turn that light back on.

Most people desire predictability and certainty. What is considered reasonable is to stay within the norm, and to conform to certain customs.

The brain is programed to replay and react to certain predictable patterns, yet the artist can change what is presented on their canvas in whatever way they choose. As the wisdom keepers of our world have said, the art of living is in the heart. The way is not "out there" in the world, but within ourselves.

PM: As you've followed your passion in life and received certain intuitive downloads, have you noticed that this translates into an ability to attract people to your magazine?

KE: Yes, I have. Again, it is like arranging and rearranging pixels on the screen. The contributors I have attracted to the magazine are some of the best in their respective fields, as well as being truly innovative, out-of-the-box thinkers. The artwork I feature is conscious art, created by inspired artists and photographers. This collaborative adventure allows me, via Science to Sage magazine, to meet people who show me that the creative force of our universe is science and spirit. We are made up of both mind and heart, science and soul, reason and intuition.

My connection to these inspired and talented people reflects back to me the interconnectedness of people in the world at large. It inspires me to remind my readers that we are all creators. Our school systems tend to value rote memorization, while art is considered fringe. Brilliance is not made up of memorized facts, but is a creative expression of intuition and inspiration.

As the artist and philosopher Walter Russell says, "The inspired genius of great imagination has great intelligence. He is able to use his intelligence creatively."

Too many of us are living in a trance with all of our gadgets and advanced technology, abdicating our life to our TVs and computers. We seem to be living someone else's story, rather than creating our own.

PM: How would you characterize the relationship between science and spirituality?

KE: How can we separate them? Our bodies are like a science kit, designed for us to have a sensory experience, and all of our senses are electrical in nature. We are experiencing the vibration of our thoughts and words in action. We have been gifted with an amazing vehicle—the body—and garden of life to play in. We need both science and spirit in order to feel this experience fully.

Remember that atoms are nothing but particles being attracted or repelled by a field, being acted upon by strong and weak force. We can consider the whole matrix of the universe to be a "mind field" of creation, where particles are like the pixels that make up the world we see and experience around us.

As quantum physics pioneer Max Planck said, "I regard consciousness as fundamental. I regard matter as derivative from consciousness. We cannot get behind consciousness. Everything that we talk about, everything that we regard as existing, postulates consciousness."

PM: Can you offer any advice about how to move towards a greater balance between reason and intuition?

KE: Your reason and intuition, or your brain and your heart, can work as a great team. When using your reasoning capabilities, make sure to ask yourself which coordinate points of understanding you are referencing. From which starting points are you making your arguments? Our reasoning capabilities can allow us to reach intellectual conclusions, yet they can also hinder us from experiencing the present moment. For me, when I am working I try to stay in the flow and be spontaneous, to remain open to the gifts of the present moment. This is a pure joy for me, as it allows me to live from a place of wonder and surprise.

Our reason also tells us that we are all born with certain innate talents and gifts—so why not use them? In my case, whether through advertising, designing a publication, or creating an educational curriculum, I have created vehicles for people to express and expand themselves. I created these pathways in order to evolve myself, yet I never thought of it that way at the time. What has been critical for me along my journey has been to follow my hunches, to do what lights me up, and to keep a sense of humor. I also stay focused on my gifts, and as I am also dyslexic, focusing on the visual aspect of communication is essential to me.

We did not come into this world with our canvas already painted; we are always creating and evolving. When it comes to combining our reason and intuition, I look at it this way: once we have an intuition of what we want to accomplish or be, we can use our reason to figure out why and how to bring that desire into being.

Terry Dee and Roy Husada

Terry Dee has over 10 years of experience as a designer and art director in an agency environment. He has led teams of creatives and strategists as well as seeing projects through independently. Strategic and objective communication is the foundation for all of his clients' relationships.

Roy Husada is a Creative Development professional with 12+ years of leadership experience. He has developed solutions for world-leading consumer and corporate brands such as Motorola, Puma, and Unirac, with a focus on combining UX and digital content strategies to produce award-winning and metrics-driven work.

Roy and Terry's team at Rival Schools designed Param Media's Beacon of Mind conference branding.

Interview

DIGITAL DESIGN, USER EXPERIENCE, RETHINKING CORPORATE CULTURE

Param Media: How would you define digital design solutions for the layperson?

Roy Husada: Digital design is something that we as a company at Rival Schools work around. People are generally more familiar with terms like "website," "app," or "animations," and digital design encompasses those things. There are quite a number of things that we do as a design studio, and the way that we explain it to our clients is that we don't necessarily focus on executing different types of projects; what we do is look at design problems and then solve them, and then figure out which technology or platforms we can implement to help solve those problems.

PM: What kind of a technical background do you need to do this kind of work?

RH: It depends on what role you want to specialize in. I actually didn't have any technical education when I started Rival Schools, although I do have a habit of staying curious and learning new skills as required. My education was originally in traditional art, graphic design, and illustration. I learned about typography, desktop publishing, and how to paint and take photos as part of my college education, and most of my education in digital design happened after I graduated, out of necessity as well as curiosity. This included learning things like HTML, ActionScript, CSS, and PHP, and I started to learn them just because I thought they were interesting and because I wanted to try something new. Right from the beginning, I always looked at these things from the perspective of how they can be used to solve the design problems that we were facing at the time, but I also wanted to use them artistically. I immediately wanted to integrate some kind of beauty into technology, and I was always fascinated with that merger.

And for me, beauty is not about the flourishes. Everyone has different definitions of what beauty means to them; for me, I find something to be beautiful when a product or tool has been designed in a way that creates a joyful emotional reaction. It is not just visually attractive, but it is also extremely functional. It's using the limitations of the available technology to push a medium even further. For example, when websites first came out there were many technical limitations in place, and those limitations allowed you, as a digital designer, to start thinking about how you could arrange things to effectively draw people's attention and make something usable at the same time.

Traditionally, there's the designer, and then there's the developer. Those have always been the two main sides of modern digital technology. At Rival Schools, we blur the lines between the two, as we believe that cross-disciplinary collaboration is the only way to innovate. And the key here is collaboration, an idea which is often said by many and not actually done. Our approach to design stems from an understanding that the products we build are used by people, not machines. People are emotional. People process information in different ways. We appreciate creativity and art. Can you imagine machines standing around in an art gallery discussing the colors used a painting? Art and beauty are things that are special to humans. Our culture and lives are made richer by our deep connection to the spiritual and emotional power behind art.

PM: It seems that you're talking about beauty in a way that is not limited to visual aesthetics. Would you say that beauty transcends what we can see?

RH: Beauty, simplicity, and usability can overlap a lot of times. To me, beauty is partly visual, but of course it does transcend beyond that, such as the beauty of something that works really well. At Rival Schools, we're trying to solve design problems; we're not making something look visually appealing just for the sake of visual appeal. We have an opportunity to design something and add functionality to it, and if we do our jobs really well, then an incredibly beautiful project emerges.

PM: Before you start a design project, do you already have an intuition of how to make something beautiful? And is that beauty relative, or is it something more objective?

Terry Dee: To me, beauty is such an abstract term. One person can say, "Isn't this flower beautiful?" and I might say yes, but somebody else might say they hate flowers, so they're not going to find it beautiful at all. We can define beauty, in the abstract sense, as a collective experience, whereas aesthetics are very subjective. When we're working out a process with our clients, we will use visuals to help shape their message, and hopefully that will evoke some sort of emotion in the user. If the app or the website that we're building serves its purpose and we meet all of the client's criteria, then there is something beautiful in that, too. The end product may not be aesthetically beautiful for one person because it doesn't relate to them, but for the audience with which it resonates, it can be a beautiful experience.

RH: We need to understand the context of what we are designing. We know that beauty is abstract, but there can be common ground in which a certain type of beauty can be appreciated. In terms of making something look more appealing, budget can sometimes make a difference. We try to always formulate these factors into our processes, because we have all different types of people working together with different ways of thinking. Having these processes in place helps us to keep our projects on track, and allows us to collectively create something that works for everyone.

PM: Where does talent come from, and is it an intuitive process?

TD: Intuition is a wonderful thing, but I think that the term can be used a little lazily sometimes. We are all shaped by our experiences, and we all have wisdom and knowledge that helps make us who we are. If you grew up in a vacuum, like a small town, and you never tried to expand your horizons beyond that vacuum—whether by traveling or by reading about different experiences and ideas—then your intuition is going to be really lacking. When it comes to talent, a lot of repetition is involved. If you're an amazing illustrator, designer, or composer, that means you've probably done it over and over again. Even if you're a savant, you need to have some sort of repetition to really develop your craft. When you talk about intuition, even if you're incredibly talented, there is a gut feeling involved, but it's based on everything that you've experienced and everything that you've learned. The deeper that experience is, the more you can trust it, and you will probably put yourself in better situations because of that experience.

It's sort of like muscle memory. The more experience and wisdom you have, the more you can draw on it and rely on your intuition. It doesn't mean you're always going to be right, but you have a better chance of being successful.

RH: There are a lot of factors at play when it comes to talent. Physical prowess is one example. I see it in my kids; my son has more physical agility than my daughter, while she's more intellectually focused and interested in language. People can differ physically and mentally, and some people just have the ability to do certain things physically or mentally better than other people.

Some people are naturally more dedicated to learning, which I saw first-hand when I was teaching design. There are people who may be a lot more talented, but who have less desire to hone that talent. Some of the people who are less talented but put in ten times more effort will eventually see their work improve, maybe even past the level of their more talented peers.

PM: Can you describe a moment when you used your gut feeling while working on a project?

RH: With a lot of the projects that we do, there is some element involved that we haven't done before. Rival Schools is not a shop that does one thing in a cookie cutter way over and over again. Whenever I talk to clients, I stress that what we're doing is solving design problems, and that our perspective involves thinking about the way that people use these certain products and how to integrate a brand message into different mediums. If we're doing a certain type of effect in a video shoot, then prior to actually creating the video we have a brainstorming session about what we should do, how we can bring the message together, and what that will look like. At that stage of the project, we still don't know one hundred percent whether or not we can do it, because we've never done it before. Through our gut feeling—part of which is emotion, and part of which is experience— we look at it collectively and decide whether or not this is something that we can move forward with. To a certain degree, sometimes you can't actually know until you do it, and in those cases you put backup plans in place; there's a Plan A, a Plan B, and a Plan C. We give ourselves different milestones; if we reach a certain milestone, then it means that part of the project is possible, and then we continue building on it.

From beginning to end, we do have to use a lot of intuition and gut feeling in our projects. Working in technology is inherently like that; there are so many digital companies these days because it's such a new industry, and technology changes so quickly that people are always trying new things to adapt. It's not like working as a shoemaker who has been making shoes for fifty years; the styles may change, but peoples' feet never change. With technology, it just changes so fast that you're always using your intuition and gut feelings, every step of the way. But that intuition has to be combined with logical planning and the technical aspects of the work.

TD: There's always a certain element of the unknown in any project. For example, with a project I'm working on right now, I've got about five different components that involve things we've done before, and now we're looking at what the next iteration looks like and how we can combine them all. We have a discussion as a team and we formulate a process, but we still don't entirely know what's going to happen. We end up discovering new ways of doing things, and really interesting by-products can come out of that. I've had to use my intuition to decide whether the people we've assembled and the knowledge we have at our disposal can be used to move this innovation forward.

Expectations play a huge part, too. If we exceed expectations on the first go-around of a project, now we want to push the envelope even further. With another client, the expectation might be that they could actually fail, but if they succeed then it will be a groundbreaking, life-altering achievement for everybody involved. The perception of the expectations at play can really differ, and that changes how reason and intuition come into play in those projects.

RH: It's really interesting, because the type of people who can actually work and stay in this industry are different from pretty much everyone else out there. You're not going in to work and doing the same thing over and over again; you're being thrown into an unknown land with every new project, and you're trying to navigate through it. But that's what makes it exciting and fun, because it's never the same. It's a very dynamic industry, and it's not for everyone, but for a certain type of person it can work really well and be very fulfilling.

TD: However, there are other digital design shops out there that are a lot more process-driven. What I really like about our approach at Rival Schools is that we do have a process and there are fundamentals that we make sure to hit—a checklist, so to speak—but we still also understand that to be innovative and achieve great things means that you sometimes have to do things on the fly and rely more on intuition.

RH: We do have a process, but to stick with one process forever would mean that your process was perfect with no room for improvement. But no process is perfect, and there is always room for improvement.

TD: When we were first getting into a recent project, the client said to us, "We are putting a certain amount of risk into you figuring an innovative solution," and I said, "Well, yes, that's because we're trying to be innovative." At some point, you need to take a leap of faith and trust us. While we can't define everything to the letter before the project begins, we can tell the client what to expect, give them our technical analysis and the things that we know we can achieve, but then they have to let us follow our path. And the byproducts that can come out of following that path can be amazing.

You look at the client's needs, and then you need to listen to your intuition to figure out whether or not they can handle the innovation. Sometimes you can even play off their ego. We had a client who we knew were the underdog in their industry, and so we offered them a way to rise to the top of their field. Of course, that appealed to them, and now the potential payoff for their investment was exponentially greater than what they initially had imagined. They had started out by saying they wanted to just get on the same playing field as their competitors, and we told them, "No, you're going to rise up to the top." Other clients may say, "We're just focused on this one goal, and we don't care what anyone else is doing." And that's fine, if that's what they are capable of handling.

I come from a design background, but I took a lot of art history as well. Of course, there is a very important business element to this job, and if you can't talk to people and understand both sides of the story, then you're not going to be able to sell anything. You have to see the interconnections between business, art, and technology, and a lot of designers don't fully appreciate that. They'll often just stick to being a designer, or maybe an art director, or they might go into freelance because they just want to focus on the aesthetic portion of it, but then they're missing out on a certain rational and intuitive aspect that's involved in the business side of it.

Roy and I are breaking the mold in that regard. Usually, copywriters go on to become creative directors and take on the business side of things, and art directors usually stick to the other side of the fence. Roy and I embrace both sides.

PM: Intuition obviously plays an important role in your work. How would you define intuition itself?

TD: Intuition is the collection of your experiences and your wisdom, and it gives you the ability to react and make a decision. Reason, on the other hand, is more logic-driven.

RH: Intuition is a combination of emotion, experiences, and your gut feeling. All of that influences what your intuition tells you, and how you use that intuition.

TD: When people say, "Trust your gut," it doesn't mean that it's going to work for everybody.

RH: Listening to your gut is like listening to the advice of one person on a committee, and it can be an emotionally unstable person at times. If you listen to your gut on a day when you're not feeling your best, then it might not be steering you in the right direction. That's why you have to use your experience, logic, and other factors to counterbalance everything. Maybe it is partially a manufactured thing, but that doesn't mean that it's any less important to listen to it.

TD: I like the idea that we're all part of one big collective consciousness. There's a macro and a micro level though, and so we're still playing various little games at this level, as individuals and as a society. There are a lot of people out there making tons of money, and they may not necessarily be the best people in the world, but they know how to read a situation and play it to their own advantage. They know how to use their intuition and knowledge to exploit or control business power. It seems like a grand idea to think that we could all live in harmony and in sync with one another in some kind of utopia. It's almost too difficult of an idea to grasp, because we all still have to lead our individual lives, and survive them, in some primitive sense.

PM: Does the blending of rational, logical thinking with intuition have an effect on the harmony of your team at Rival Schools?

TD: Absolutely. We encourage each other to discover and to think. When you know that everybody on the team is supporting a decision, then it's easier to go back to the client and convince them of your vision, because you know that everybody on your team is backing it up. It's part of our company culture. At a bigger agency, a more traditional model is usually followed, and generally that works for them. For us, we have to sell a little harder, and having unity in our team is crucial to that.

PM: With the rapid advance of technology in your industry, how do you remain a pioneering agency? How do you keep driving innovation forward, and will blending reason and intuition play an important role?

RH: Reason and intuition are important in this industry, because it's about balancing different factors. When you start focusing on one particular area, your business changes, which is why a lot of bigger agencies have to buy smaller agencies to gain back creative innovation. With bigger agencies, their focus is primarily on being profitable, and you can tell that by the company structure; there are a lot more people working in accounts and sales versus people who actually produce creative work. That's not necessarily a good thing or a bad thing; that's just one piece of this industry that makes the whole work.

PM: Is there a more beautiful way to run an agency and still be successful? Does this success involve giving back to society in some way?

TD: You have the option as a company to make socially responsible decisions. We have the opportunity as an agency to say we choose not to work with companies who do harm. Corporate culture is what you make of it.

RH: There are definitely bigger companies out there that have the reputation of being good employers and doing good in the world. That means they have a good company culture, there's a balance of work, pay, and the physical and mental health of the workers.

PM: To address the complexities of the problems we're facing at a local and global scale, do you think it will be necessary to start embracing a more balanced way of thinking, incorporating both rational thinking and intuition?

RH: We do have to balance these things, because we're human, we're not machines. In today's society, we're always trying to put ourselves into boxes; you're this kind of person, or you've got to do this to be successful, but no one has a clear definition of what "success" is. You can talk about it in monetary terms, but what about happiness and health? Money is only one type of currency.

I don't look at Rival Schools as just a building with a logo on it with money flowing through it. To me, Rival Schools is the deep working relationship I have with the people who are part of this team, people who are incredibly talented and who I enjoy working with, and we're using Rival Schools as the umbrella brand to go out and do things that we like. But of course, we wouldn't be able to operate the company without the logo and all that material stuff, because that's the vehicle of how you work with other people.

Everyone has different ways of measuring success, and for me, Rival Schools has been a personal trial of mine. I've learned so much from starting this company and meeting the people that I've met through it. To be honest, I didn't really know much about how to create a business before I started, and I'm still learning. You have to have the desire to take something on if you're going to actually accomplish it.

PM: Why did you choose to be part of this publication, and what value do you think it can bring?

RH: I always feel like there's something to learn from everyone. A lot of what we do at Rival Schools is really about taking into account how people act based on their emotions and experiences. We have to deal with this ever-changing landscape of technology, and it's always interesting to hear different peoples' perspectives. Being part of this anthology is a great opportunity, partly because I get to learn a lot about other peoples' experiences and insights as well.

TD: In my current life, I've started to accept a lot of the things that I used to try to shut down. I'm not religious and I'm not particularly spiritual, but there are things that I've read and things that I've experienced that have had a deeper influence on me. There's a philosophical link between what I'm doing and what you guys are doing at Param Media, and there's an openness that I now have in my own head, and that can translate down to the tangible level of how we operate at Rival Schools.

I would hope that people who are more fixed in their point of view will be encouraged after reading this book to look at things a little bit differently, and see that this different perspective can have very positive outcomes. Self-awareness is a really great thing, and it often feels like it's lacking in our society. I don't know if that's due to ignorance, or a lack of open-mindedness to experience new perspectives. Even though I'm not religious, I picked up a book about the Dao at a certain point in my life, and it helped me find a different way to think, to get through certain things and put things in a new perspective. Books like that can be one part of your personal arsenal, part of the collection of tools you have at your disposal.

RH: I've been thinking a lot recently about an article I read about the top regrets people have on their deathbeds. It talks about how we've allowed society to define what our lives should be, and it made me realize that we're basically letting society decide what happiness is. But it's not even real happiness; it's more of a routine or a comfort zone. One of the regrets that really stuck with me was, "I wish I had the courage to let myself be happy." The fact that this was one of the top regrets says a lot about how people aren't taking the time to look into themselves, to really know who they are and what they want. Why would you do something that doesn't make you happy? It sounds ridiculous! But most people do that, if you think about it. It's not a question of superficial happiness; you have to take away the consumerism that surrounds us and ask what we're left with. If you think about happiness as something that's important to have, and if it's not about the money or material things, then why aren't we pursuing it more? Tapping into our deeper intuition and coupling that with strong reasoning ability can help us know ourselves better, and to pursue happiness in our lives.

Shaherose Charania

Shaherose Charania is the President and CEO of Women 2.0, a San Francisco-based media company at the intersection of women, entrepreneurship, and technology. They have hosted nearly 10,000 attendees at their Founder Friday events, which attract entrepreneurs and investors in 20 cities around the globe (and growing), and their biannual conferences feature pioneers in tech and media such as U.S. Chief Technology Officer Megan Smith and USA Network and Syfy Channel founder Kay Koplovitz. Shaherose has also led new consumer products at Ribbit (BT), and was Director of Product Management at Talenthouse and JAJAH (sold to Telefonica/O2).

Interview

ENTREPRENEURSHIP, GENDER IN TECH, DIVERSITY

Param Media: How do you define intuition, and how do you define reason?

Shaherose Charania: Intuition comes from an internal frame of mind that we already have, which we can reference in order to make sense of new information or to help us make a decision. It is something very personal that's based on your own experiences, assumptions, and worldview. Reason, however, seems to have some sort of grounding that's outside the personal frame of mind, which is somewhat objective, based on data and known facts. When we use reason, we often intermix intuition with hard, fast data and we don't always know where intuition ends and reason begins. I see it as a wide continuum or spectrum, reaching all the way from reason to intuition with lots of steps in between, but all of the steps are connected.

PM: Do you feel there's a difference between insight, a gut feeling, an emotional reaction, and inspiration, as opposed to just branding them all as intuition?

SC: During the process by which we make a decision or process information, we often have a gut feeling, and then perhaps some sort of insight or intuition. They are all part of a process we go through when analyzing information or making a decision.

A gut feeling is something that's speaking to you without very much reflection, which seems to be closer to intuition along the spectrum. It may even be the first step, or the first thing that comes to mind, which may or may not turn out to be right once you have further information. Insight, however, is a little further along the spectrum towards reason; it's an "a-ha moment." I feel insight comes from some reflection and maybe even with some data (reason) sprinkled in.

An emotional reaction seems closer to a gut feeling, whereas inspiration is on the other end of the spectrum, closer to reason; it's something that gives you the drive or motivation to make a decision or to do something in the first place. This motivation or inspiration can be a result of analyzing information or making a decision, and it leads to action. Thus, while inspiration can lead to an outcome or action, intuition seems to be more like the guiding light by which you make decisions or process information.

PM: It's very interesting how you put these interdependent concepts along a spectrum. How do you discern whether or not a gut feeling is actually based on your own excitement or fear, or some other emotion? How can you tell from where it's arising?

SC: Being able to discern the source of the gut feeling very much depends on one's level of self-awareness. Self-awareness is something people can work on actively and then tap into actively. It can be built through reflection, meditation, and enlightenment. When fully expressed and fully developed, self-awareness can allow you to determine the finer details of a given situation, as well as tap into the source of your gut reaction.

Let's take an example of evaluating someone as a potential hire. When you first meet that person, you are walking into the room with your own worldview, and your gut feeling can help you to quickly assess the various important factors you are looking for in the person: Can you trust them? Do they have the type of smarts you're looking for? Will they fit within your corporate culture? I let my gut feeling play itself out, but then I pause and say, "Okay, now that I have more data [maybe from references or from the conversation I had with the person], I feel like I can then step back and process where those gut feelings came from. Did they come from my own excitement at meeting this person, or from my own fear, or from any other personal issues I may have? Or did they come from evaluating the person themselves?" It's good to be aware of the process of adding data to your gut feeling, allowing yourself to pause and ask yourself what the source of your gut feeling is. Active reflection, introspection, and meditation can be the channels to help you determine the source of your gut feeling.

I also ask myself, "Where am I coming from today? What position or frame of mind am I in today? What needs do I have? What am I looking for? What does this person bring to the table, and why am I seeing it this way?" It's a very active process that can be tailored from moment to moment, from day to day. First, it's important to know where you are. Are you already in a state of fear, panic, confusion, or stress? That can entirely influence where those initial gut feelings may be coming from. Or are you evaluating your gut based solely on that person's input?

PM: That's a good example of using reason to help us evaluate our gut feelings. Would you be able to expand on your views a bit further regarding the relationship between intuition and logical thinking from within the perspective of an entrepreneur?

SC: I see both reason and intuition as vitally important. As an entrepreneur, you don't always have the information you need to move forward with or commit to an idea or decision. You want to see the world change or move in certain ways, and therefore you create things to reach that outcome. And that process should always remain, but it is not always based on known facts or hard data. You have to ask yourself, "Do I know if my customers will actually like this product? Will they actually pay for this product?" But you do not *really* know until you begin, especially in the case of disruptive products and businesses, and so tapping into your intuition and gut feelings is how you sustain the wild ride, and it's also how you make a first decision and begin your entrepreneurial journey. In parallel, you need to use reasoning and logical thinking to help you make these decisions, because your gut feeling could be wrong or slightly off, and you could end up destroying your business. You need to use data to help ensure sustainability. It's very easy to say, "Oh my god, I want to see this change in the world!" and then forget all about the business model, and whether or not people actually want to pay for what you think is beneficial to the world. And then, before you know it, you're broke.

As an entrepreneur, I think it's important to have a balance at all times, as much as you can, to really sustain yourself in times of chaos and to make the right business decisions as best as you can. You will never make perfect decisions, and that's okay, but that's why you need to bring data, logical thinking, and reasoning together with your intuition and gut feeling.

PM: It's a very tricky balance. Could you give us an example of when this process of combining your intuition and reason has worked for you in business, and when it didn't work out quite the way you had planned?

SC: We ran Women 2.0 as a side project for five years, where we were only (or mostly) using our intuition. We said to ourselves, "We need to see change in the world, and therefore we're going to do this work." For a very long time we didn't think that we could build a business out of it, because we didn't pause and use our logical thinking to help us answer some key questions, such as, "Will people pay for this? What is our business model? Will it achieve sustainability and scale?" We simply assumed people wouldn't be willing to pay for anything we were offering; after all, this was a passion-project. Then, after a few years of operating Women 2.0 as a side/passion-project, we paused and said, "Wait a second. If we approach this more logically and we do an analysis of the existing media landscape, is there room for a brand like ours: yes or no? Is there a possibility that people will begin to pay for the products and services we offer: yes or no?" The change we wanted to see in the world suddenly began coming together after we started asking the right questions, where the answers were driven by demographics, a budget, and all the relevant data. It's been working out and we're doing well as a company, but our growing success would not have been possible without pausing to add the right kind of data and applying more logical thinking to our original intuition.

Sometimes it hasn't worked for me in hiring situations when, for example, I didn't pause and add reasoning to my initial gut reaction. My gut feelings are sometimes coming from my own state of mind or my needs in that moment, and those feelings can more easily lead to the wrong understanding of the person I just hired. Instead of seeing how I truly felt about them as a person and as a hire, I was seeing how they made me feel in that particular situation.

PM: What recommendations do you have for optimizing one's ability to pause and blend reason and intuition in that way?

SC: One thing that definitely helps is to bring relevant data to whatever the situation is, whether it's to process the information at hand, make a decision, or arrive at a new framework. Every entrepreneur does this, in one way or another. The other thing is to actually pause and reflect on your gut feelings and take time to step away from the situation, so that you can see more clearly what your intuition is telling you. This pause can be in the form of active reflection and introspection, or a deeper reflection through meditation, where you are choosing to clear your mind to create space. Whatever form you choose, taking a pause will help you bring clarity.

After looking inward, I often then look outward. I do this by reaching out to my advisors, but I don't tell them right away what I am thinking about the situation. I take in their input and then go away and make sure I'm listening to my own intuition, because at the end of the day, I understand my business the best. Advisors are great, but they're more like a gut check to make sure I'm not forgetting anything or not seeing the situation from different angles. Advisors bring their own personal experiences to the table, which gives me a new way of seeing the situation. They also bring years of experience, meaning that over time, they have been able to see patterns that I have not yet noticed or put together. Too many people get caught up in pleasing their advisors, and then they forget about their own intuition. Time and time again, my way of running Women 2.0 as a business—positioning it a certain way, pricing it a certain way—has been based on my intuition. My advisors have access to certain data, they have access to their own experiences, but they do not have access to my intuition.

I would say you should take objective advice, but at the end of the day you need to make sure you pause, reflect, and understand what your guiding light is, because then you are more likely to make better decisions. And don't forget the data. That being said, you also have to stop and step away from the objective input, from the data, and even from your own intuition. To help achieve this difficult part of the process of stepping back, I like to practice walking meditation, sitting meditation, and yoga. Of course, there are many other ways to help you remove yourself, and this part of the process is very important.

We first subconsciously process what's going on, then we process it consciously, and then we find a way to explain our decision. If the data is talking to you more loudly, don't ignore it; if trends or patterns are speaking to you more loudly, don't ignore them. It can be easy to ignore what is most important, so you have to be very aware of what's speaking to you in the moment.

PM: Do you think that women in the tech industry, or in business in general, are more likely to have better intuitive abilities than their male peers, and so have an advantage in this respect? Or is this view a false stereotype?

SC: We often need to find ways to quickly categorize things, and that is where stereotypes can come in. We tend to say, "Women do things like this," and, "Men do things like that," but I don't see the world that way. That is too black and white. Rather, I see the world and the people in it on various spectrums. I'd like to reframe the question and consider the words "masculine" and "feminine" rather than "men" and "women". Using these terms can allow us to sort typical behaviors more effectively. I like to think of the world as generally being masculine and feminine, but not male and female. It is commonly said that data-driven decisions are very masculine/male, but I prefer to say they are masculine, not male. Intuition is said to be more feminine/female, but I would want to say feminine, not female. Entrepreneurs, whether male or female, need to have a balance of both masculine and feminine traits. Do women have more feminine traits? Yes, obviously, because they're female. Does that mean they're more intuitive? Maybe. Some women do possess more masculine traits. Masculinity and femininity are sort of like a continuum blend, similar to the continuum from reason to intuition. I don't want to say that every woman does this, or every man does that; I just want to say that individuals—regardless of gender—who possess more feminine than masculine traits may be more likely to be better attuned to their intuitive abilities.

PM: Do you think that, in general, the tech industry needs a better balance between masculine and feminine traits?

SC: I think that most successful entrepreneurs, both men and women, are the ones who tend to have a balance—whether it's between masculine and feminine traits, or reason and intuition—so I don't think that the industry needs to change much in this respect. On the other hand, in terms of leadership or the ways we create culture, we do need to work harder to increase the feminine perspective to achieve a better balance. As we increase diversity, such as having more female role models in business leadership positions, then we move closer to a greater overall balance in the industry, from employees to founders to investors.

We are fighting now with this gender imbalance in the technology industry, which at this point is the most important industry of our time. The industrial revolution was also driven by technology, by a certain set of companies, which were generally driven by men. Their dominant masculine approach set the standard for the way we think about and run businesses, and even for what types of businesses are more likely to be pursued.

As the tech industry gives rise to the most prolific set of companies of our time, having diversity is key to ensuring that these companies are sustainable, that they're addressing the right problems, designing products the right way, and that they're not carrying around hubris about themselves and their products.

PM: How is the growing impact of Women 2.0 affecting the high-tech startup culture in terms of diversity?

SC: Women 2.0, while a business, is truly also a social impact movement; we are a community, we are a force for change. We have achieved and continue to drive impact in the technology industry by having women speak, write, and be visible. This has allowed for people to look at our platform and notice the influencers that represent our brand, and say, "Oh! I can do that too. There are people that look and act like me who are doing this; that means it's legitimate, it's attainable, it's possible, and it's not a gated community." The results we have been seeing are amazing. More and more women, every year, take the leap and become founders of their own technology companies. Diversifying the founder base has a direct impact on the culture. It builds companies that have an intentionally balanced, inclusive, and diverse culture.

For existing technology company cultures, our work is focused on increasing the number of women in the founding and leading roles of technology companies and startups. At the core, we provide a networking platform to build relationships with smart, achieving women who have the opportunity to hire or be hired into this sector.

Our work has inspired technology companies both small and large to pay attention to diversity at the hiring level. More companies are now filling the "Head of Diversity" position. This role can vary from company to company, but generally it is someone who works specifically on recruiting from a diverse pool of candidates and building and maintaining an inclusive and supportive company culture. This change is a significant step in the technology industry and will, over time, truly change the culture of these companies by bringing about the masculine and feminine balance it needs. It will be a slow process of cultural change, but it starts with this level of awareness and these intentional roles within technology companies.

PM: From where do you draw your inspiration for your projects and business?

SC: I remember when I first arrived in Silicon Valley, my inspiration was to look for anyone doing something where they combined social impact with technology and were still able to build a thriving business. When I meet people who have started companies that have a positive impact on the world to markets that need help, I am inspired. I am also inspired by the work that we do at Women 2.0, especially when people who were not thinking about entrepreneurship come to us and say, "Now I'm thinking about it, now I'm running my business, now I've joined a tech startup, now I'm an entrepreneur, now I'm an investor." These people made a change in their lives by entering the technology industry, and that is inspiring.

I used to be more inspired by others running social ventures that were sustainable financially and leveraging tech, and now I am also very inspired by our own people at Women 2.0. It's awesome to see them take that risk, be adventurous, think in a new way, start a company, fund a company, join a company, whatever it is, because there are so many important challenges they are facing, and I am inspired by them every day.

PM: What inspired you to contribute to *The Beacon of Mind*?

SC: I like the basis of it, and I think we need to talk about these ideas more. When I found out about the anthology, I remember thinking, "This is interesting, because this is real." Unless you write about these topics, unless you codify this idea of intuition and reason being a genuine part of our information and decision-making process, then it doesn't feel like it exists. If we don't acknowledge the reality of this interplay between reason and intuition, and how the spectrum is so important for entrepreneurship, then we can't give it the importance it deserves.

People ask me how I got to where I am today, and I can't always articulate it, but there is something about us entrepreneurs leveraging intuition to achieve our goals. The more people follow their intuition, the more they will change the world on their own terms, and feel fulfilled with a purpose in life. That makes for a happier world, really. It may sound cliché, but people living their highest purpose—once they find out what it is by listening to their intuition—can make a better world. Business is a sustainable means to realize a positive passion, if you want it to be.

Dr. Mario Beauregard

Dr. Mario Beauregard is a neuroscientist currently affiliated with the Department of Psychology at the University of Arizona. His groundbreaking work on the neurobiology of emotion and mystical experience has received international media coverage, and his publications include *Brain Wars: The Scientific Battle Over the Existence of the Mind and the Proof That Will Change the Way We Live Our Lives.* Mario is also a co-founder of the Campaign for Open Sciences, as well as a co-editor and contributor to a forthcoming Param Media anthology on Post-Materialism.

Dr. Mario Beauregard

Brain, Mind, and Reality[1]

NEUROSCIENCE, PERCEPTION, POST-MATERIALISM

1. Introduction

Does the brain create mind and reality[2]? This brief essay revolves around this central question, which has been pondered by philosophers and scientists for centuries. To address this paramount question, I examine recent findings of cognitive neuroscience and research on near-death experiences (NDEs).

In the second section of this essay, I explore the relationship between brain, perception, and the physical world. In the third section, I present the dominant view from mainstream neuroscience regarding the mind-brain relation, and in the fourth section I examine findings about NDEs in cardiac arrest. Lastly, in the concluding section, I defend the hypothesis that the brain does not produce mind, consciousness[3], and the various levels of reality (physical and non-physical). I also propose that this organ acts as an interface and as a filter for the mind.

2. Brain, perception, and the physical world

Most of us tacitly believe that the physical world we experience is real. But because appearances can be deceiving, it seems legitimate to ask ourselves whether the world around us is the real world or a construction generated by the senses and the brain.

To explore this issue, let's examine the case of visual perception. Nearly half of the brain's cortex is engaged in this function; billions of neurons and trillions of synapses are activated when we open our eyes

---

[1] Correspondence: Mario Beauregard Ph.D., Laboratory for Advances in Consciousness and Health, Department of Psychology, The University of Arizona, PO Box 210068, Tucson, AZ 85721-0068, USA. Email: mariobeauregard@email.arizona.edu

[2] In this essay, the term "mind" refers to mental functions and events, whereas the term "reality" refers to the state of things as they actually exist.

[3] Here, "consciousness" means awareness and subjective experience.

and look around. The common assumption people make about visual perception is that this is a simple process comparable to taking a picture. Some have called this common sense view the camera theory of vision.[I] What we have learned from decades of research in cognitive neuroscience is that visual perception is a complex, reconstructive process. When we open our eyes, our visual system reconstructs very quickly (in milliseconds) all the shapes, textures, depths, motions, and colors of the objects that we see. This construction is done so rapidly that we are fooled into believing that we are simply taking a snapshot of the world as it is.

Although visual perception is based on a reconstructive process, most cognitive neuroscientists agree that there is an objective physical world, and that visual percepts[4] are normally fairly accurate representations of the true physical properties of objects. With respect to this question, it has been proposed that the reason that visual percepts are usually accurate reconstructions is due to evolution by natural selection. Specifically, the more accurately an organism's visual system matches the objective physical properties of its environment, the better are its chances of surviving long enough to reproduce.[I]

The generation of our mental representations of the world is to a large extent determined by our sensory organs and brain. However, these sensory organs only offer us a small window on reality, which means that much of the information in physical reality is not processed, leaving us with a very limited set of data with which to construct our picture of the world. In other words, the world contains a multitude of features of which we are not conscious. For instance, we humans cannot perceive ultraviolet rays, but many insects and birds can see the ultraviolet light.

Cognitive neuroscience research has also shown that visual reconstructions of physical objects are never totally "objective," since mental states play a pivotal role in how perceptual information is processed. For example, our hopes, expectations, and fears influence what we perceive.[II]

---

[4] Percepts are mental impressions of something perceived by the senses.

To summarize, we do not experience the physical world directly; all we ever know is the image of the physical world generated in our awareness. But the fact that our experience of the physical world is based on a reconstructive process does not imply that reality is an illusion.

3. A central dogma of neuroscience

Contemporary neuroscience is a reductive materialist enterprise. For example, one of its central dogmas is that higher mental functions, consciousness, free will, and self are produced by—or can be reduced to—electrical-chemical processes in the brain.[III-IV] That is, mainstream neuroscientists believe that all mental events and experiences (e.g. intentions, emotions, spiritual epiphanies) are equivalent to brain activity. These scientists also believe that the physical world is the only reality, which makes them *materialists* in the philosophical sense.

Various neuroscience methods (e.g. recording, stimulation, lesion, pharmacology) have allowed researchers to make strides toward the identification of the neural correlates of mental processes and events. The results of studies conducted using these experimental methods support the view that mental activity is closely associated with neuroelectrical and neurochemical activity. For instance, electrical stimulation of the fusiform gyrus (FG) in epileptic patients can lead to selective distortion during the visual perception of human faces.[V] This finding provides evidence for a key role of the FG in face perception. But it does not entail that conscious visual perception of faces can be reduced to neural activity in the FG. Indeed, neuroscience studies do not demonstrate that neural correlates directly produce mental phenomena, and they do not establish that mental states and conscious experiences are identical to brain processes, such as the propagation of nerve impulses across synapses or the release of neurotransmitters via exocytosis. As a matter of fact, there is a huge gap between conscious experiences (the first-person perspective) and the electrochemical activity of the brain (the third-person perspective).

If the standard view of neuroscience regarding mind-brain relationship is valid, i.e. if mind is nothing more than what the brain does, then the mind cannot operate independently of the brain. However, as we shall see in the next section, research on near-death experiences (NDEs) shows that the mind can operate when the brain is non-functional.

4. Near-death experiences in cardiac arrest

NDEs are vivid, realistic, and often deeply life-changing experiences occurring to people who have been physiologically or psychologically close to death.[VI] Enhanced mental activity, a clear memory of the experience, and a conviction that the experience is more real than ordinary waking consciousness are core features of NDEs.[VII] Other common features include: an out-of-body experience (OBE), i.e. a sense of having left one's body and watching events going on around one's body and, occasionally, at some distant physical location; feelings of peace and joy; passage through a region of darkness or a dark tunnel; seeing an otherworldly realm of great beauty; encountering deceased relatives and friends; seeing an unusually bright light, sometimes experienced as a "Being of Light" that radiates complete acceptance and unconditional love and may communicate telepathically with the near-death experiencer (NDEr); seeing and reliving major and incidental events of one's life, sometimes from the perspective of the other people involved; and returning to the physical body, often unwillingly.[VII]

Unsurprisingly, a number of materialist interpretations have attempted to explain away the subjective experience of NDEs. Some researchers have speculated that NDEs are hallucinations produced by lowered levels of oxygen, i.e. hypoxia or anoxia.[VIII, 5] However, NDEs can occur in the absence of hypoxia or anoxia (as in non-life-threatening illnesses and near-accidents), and the subjective effects of hypoxia do not have much in common with NDEs.[VI] Furthermore, when oxygen levels decrease markedly, individuals whose lungs or hearts do not work properly experience an "acute confusional state," during which they are highly confused and agitated, and have little or no memory

[5] Hypoxia refers to an inadequate oxygen supply to the cells and tissues of the body, whereas anoxia is a condition characterized by an absence of oxygen supply to the brain.

recall. In stark contrast, during NDEs people experience lucid consciousness, well-structured thought processes, and clear reasoning.[IX] In addition, if anoxia played a central role in the production of NDEs, most cardiac arrest patients would report an NDE; however, studies show that this is clearly not the case.[X]

Other researchers have hypothesized that increased levels of carbon dioxide—hypercarbia—may be implicated in NDEs.[XI] However, NDE-like features are rarely reported in hypercarbia. Moreover, there have been instances in which arterial blood gases in NDErs did not reflect elevated carbon dioxide levels.[IX]

It has also been speculated that temporal lobe epilepsy (TLE) can produce all the main features of NDEs.[XII] A review of the literature on epilepsy, however, indicates that the typical features of NDEs are not associated with epileptic seizures located in the temporal lobes.[XIII] Experiential symptoms of such seizures include mental confusion, hallucinations, illusions, and negative emotional states.

Nearly half of NDErs report an OBE. Reports of OBE perception of events (e.g. attempts by medical personnel to resuscitate the NDErs) are quite important because they can be corroborated, i.e. proven to coincide with reality, and several reports of OBE perception have been corroborated by independent witnesses.[VI] Such veridical OBE perceptions constitute a serious hurdle for materialist theories of the mind, since there is no adequate purely physical explanation. Nevertheless, some proponents of these materialist based theories[XII], [XIV] argue that OBE perception of events happening around the NDEr's body is simply a retrospective imaginative reconstruction based on the memory of events that the NDEr might have witnessed just before losing consciousness, or while regaining consciousness. However, this hypothesis is incorrect since, generally, memory of events occurring just before or after loss of consciousness is either confused or totally absent.[VI X] Importantly, confusional experiences remembered by individuals as they lose or regain consciousness generally do not have a life-transforming impact.[7]

NDEs occurring in cardiac arrest pose another major problem for materialist theories of the mind. During cardiac arrest, breathing stops, and blood flow and oxygen uptake in the brain are rapidly interrupted. When this happens, the electroencephalogram (EEG) becomes isoelectric (flat-lines) within 10-20 seconds and brainstem reflexes disappear.15 The individual undergoing cardiac arrest is then considered to be clinically dead. Because the brain structures mediating conscious experience and higher mental functions are severely impaired, such patients are expected to have no clear and lucid mental experiences that will be remembered. Nonetheless, studies conducted in the Netherlands,[X] United Kingdom,[IX] and United States[XVI-XVII] have revealed that approximately 15 percent of cardiac arrest survivors do report some recollection from the time when they were clinically dead. In those studies, more than 100 cases of full-blown NDEs were reported. In some of these cases, NDErs provide evidence for veridical OBE perception.

Materialist scientists frequently argue that even if the EEG is isoelectric, there may be some residual brain activity that goes undetected because of the limitations of scalp-EEG technology. This is possible given that current scalp-EEG technology measures mainly the activity of large populations of cortical neurons. However, Bruce Greyson, a Professor of Psychiatric Medicine, correctly notes that the crucial "issue is not whether there is brain activity of *any* kind whatsoever, but whether there is brain activity of the specific form agreed upon by contemporary neuroscientists as the necessary condition of conscious experience".[18] This form of neuroelectrical activity, which is well detected via current EEG technology, is clearly abolished by cardiac arrest.

5. Conclusion: The brain as an interface and as a filter

The fact that enhanced mental experiences and accurate OBE perception can occur at a time when brain activity is greatly impaired or absent (during clinical death) strongly suggests that the prevalent neuroscientific view about mind-brain relationship is erroneous; that is, mind and consciousness are not produced by brain activity. Furthermore, NDEs occurring in cardiac arrest patients indicate that there are other levels of reality that are non-physical, which is to say that since not all of reality can be reduced to physicality, then reductive materialist assumptions are clearly false.

NDEs also imply that the brain does not create reality (whether physical or non-physical). In fact, such experiences during cardiac arrest provide support to the hypothesis that the brain acts as an interface for the mind, an idea that was first proposed more than a century ago by William James, one of the most influential founders of psychology in America.[XIX] James also speculated that the brain acts as a filter (or a reducing valve), normally restricting our access to extended forms of consciousness. In allowing registration and expression of only a narrow band of perceivable reality, this organ serves to block much that we would otherwise potentially be able to experience. Philosophers Ferdinand Schiller and Henri Bergson,[XX-XXI] as well as writer Aldous Huxley,[XXII] have expressed similar views. In particular, Bergson and Huxley believed that over the course of evolution, the brain has been trained to eliminate most of those perceptions that do not directly aid our everyday survival.

The filter hypothesis suggests that the brain normally limits the human capacity to have transcendent experiences (TEs). These experiences, which extend or lie beyond the limits of ordinary experience, are characterized by altered or expanded consciousness. A significant alteration of neuroelectrical and neurochemical activity seems necessary to incapacitate the filter function of the brain and occasion TEs. It is noteworthy that this filtering function of the brain can be lessened in a variety of ways (e.g. through meditation, spiritual practices, psychedelics, shamanic practices, sensory deprivation, and so forth).

In line with the idea that the brain is an interface for the mind, this organ may be compared to a television, which receives broadcast signals (electromagnetic waves) and converts them into image and sound. If we damage the electronic components within the television, we may induce a loss or distortion of the image on the screen and the sound produced, because the capacity of the television to receive and decode the broadcast signals is impaired. But this does not mean that the broadcast signals (and the program) are actually produced by the television. Likewise, damage to a specific region of the brain may disrupt the mental processes mediated by this particular cerebral structure, but such disruption does not entail that these mental processes are totally reducible to neural activity in this area of the brain. Our brains do not create reality, but they do impose limits on what aspects of reality we are able to perceive.

REFERENCES

I. Hoffman, D.D. (2012) The Construction of Visual Reality, in Blom, J.D. & Sommer, I.E.C. (eds.) *Hallucinations: Research and Practice*, pp. 7-15, New York: Springer.

II. Dror, I.E. (2005) Perception is far from perfection: The role of the brain and mind in constructing realities, *Behavioral and Brain Sciences*, 28 (6), p. 768.

III. Beauregard, M. & O'Leary, D. (2007) *The Spiritual Brain*, New York: Harper Collins.

IV. Beauregard, M. (2012) *Brain Wars*, New York: Harper Collins.

V. Parvizi, J., Jacques, C., Foster, B.L., Witthoft, N., Rangarajan, V., Weiner, K.S. & Grill-Spector, K. (2012) Electrical stimulation of human fusiform face-selective regions distorts face perception, *J Neuroscience*, 32 (43), pp. 14915-14920.

VI. Holden, J. M. (2009) Veridical Perception in Near-Death Experiences, in Holden, J.M., Greyson, B. & James, D. (eds.) *The Handbook of Near-Death Experiences: Thirty Years of Investigation*, pp. 185-211, Santa Barbara, CA: Praeger/ABC-CLIO.

VII. Greyson, B. (2011) Cosmological implications of near-death experiences, *Journal of Cosmology*, 14, pp. 4684-4696.

VIII. Blackmore, S.J. (1993) *Dying to Live: Science and the Near-Death Experience*, London: Grafton.

IX. Parnia, S., Waller, D.G., Yeates, R. & Fenwick, P. (2001) A qualitative and quantitative study of the incidence, features, and aetiology of near death experiences in cardiac arrest survivors, *Resuscitation*, 48 (2), pp. 149–156.

X. Van Lommel, P., Van Wees, R., Meyers, V. & Elfferich, I. (2001). Near-death experience in survivors of cardiac arrest: A prospective study in the Netherlands, *Lancet*, 358 (9298), pp. 2039–2045.

XI. Morse, M.L., Venecia, D. & Milstein, J. (1989) Near-death experiences: a neurophysiological explanatory model. *Journal of Near-Death Studies*, 8 (1), pp. 45-53.

XII. Saavedra-Aguilar, J.C. & Goimez-Jeria, J.S. (1989) A neurobiological model for near-death experiences, *Journal of Near-Death Studies*, 7 (4), pp. 205-222.

XIII. Rodin E. (1989) Comments on "a neurobiological model for near-death experiences, *Journal of Near-Death Studies*, 7 (4), pp. 255–259.

XIV. Woerlee, G.M. (2004) Cardiac arrest and near-death experiences, *Journal of Near-Death Studies*, 22, pp. 235-249.

XV. Clute, H.L. & Levy, W.J. (1990) Electroencephalographic changes during brief cardiac arrest in humans, *Anesthesiology*, 73 (5), pp. 821–825.

XVI. Schwaninger, J., Eisenberg, P.R., Schechtman, K.B. & Weiss, A.N. (2002) A prospective analysis of near-death experiences in cardiac arrest patients, *Journal of Near-Death Studies*, 20 (4), pp. 215–232.

XVII. Greyson, B. (2003) Incidence and correlates of near-death experiences in a cardiac care unit, *General Hospital Psychiatry*, 25 (4), pp. 269-276.

XVIII. Greyson, B. (2011) Cosmological implications of near-death experiences, *Journal of Cosmology*, 14, p. 4688.

XIX. James, W. (1900) *Human Immortality: Two Supposed Objections to the Doctrine* (2nd ed.), Boston: Houghton Mifflin. (Original work published 1898)

XX. Schiller, F(1891) *Riddles of the Sphinx*, London: Swan Sonnenschein.

XXI. Bergson, H. (1914) Presidential address, *Proceedings of the Society for Psychical Research* 27, pp. 157–175.

XXII. Huxley, A. (1954) *The Doors of Perception*. New York: Harper & Row.

Dr. Debashish Banerji

Dr. Debashish Banerji is Dean of Academic Affairs, University of Philosophical Research, Los Angeles; Adjunct Faculty, Department of Asian and Comparative Studies, California Institute of Integral Studies, San Francisco; and Executive Director, Nalanda International. Dr. Banerji is the author *of Seven Quartets of Becoming: A Transformative Yoga Psychology Based on the Diaries of Sri Aurobindo.*

Dr. Debashish Banerji

Building an Intuitive Consciousness: Sri Aurobindo and the Supermind

CRITIQUING THE ENLIGHTENMENT, EPISTEMOLOGY, THE SUPERMIND

This chapter will serve as a brief introduction to the extraordinary depth of understanding and subtlety of thought of Sri Aurobindo (1872-1950), an Indian nationalist, philosopher, and spiritual teacher.

Sri Aurobindo spent most of his school and college years in England, before returning to India to participate in India's anticolonial struggle and later become the philosopher-sage of Pondicherry (now known as Puducherry). Schooled in London and at the University of Cambridge, he understood very well the interconnections between the knowledge and power structures making up the fabric of modernity and originating in the intellectual revolution of the European Enlightenment. It is this grasp of the systemic and totalistic nature of the Enlightenment project that informed the anticolonial politics of Sri Aurobindo and several other educated Indians of his time, and that make their resistant gestures and projects continue to resonate with a postcolonial and postmodern potency.

The Enlightenment project, though with its variant strands and tensions, can be reduced to a few salient principles, which developed consistency by the end of the eighteenth century. These can be summarized as:

1) A faith in the reasonableness of the cosmos—i.e. the power of Reason (*logos*) as an organizing principle of the cosmos; with its corollary, the hierarchical and systemic nature of knowledge, reducible to a single or very few "grand theories."
2) A faith in human mind to comprehend the reason or logic of the cosmos by the power of human rationality, qualitatively identical to cosmic Reason.
3) The need to focus human effort in a systematic bid to uncover the reason of the cosmos—i.e. all its laws forming the grand systems theory of total knowledge.

4) The development of a systematic method and archival standards (the scientific method) to universalize the knowledge acquired as part of the ongoing worldwide academic research enterprise.

These principles constitute what is today called the *logocentrism* of the Enlightenment project, where its central faith is that the logic or reason will provide us with the complete knowledge of reality. The all-round systemic nature of this turning in human history should not be underestimated. As one of its consequences, the faith of the Enlightenment project is based on the assumption of a single correct knowledge structure inclusive of everything, (i.e. an absolute epistemology). But since human beings are bound in space and limited in life span, such an assumption can only be validated by piecing together the contributions of many beings globally through history. This has made it necessary to establish a systematic method universalized through space and time, which we generally refer to as the *scientific method.*

Human beings thus find themselves yoked to the Enlightenment as a universal condition of our times. Moreover, such an accumulation of knowledge must, of necessity, develop increasingly finer resolutions, leading to ever-increasing specialization, which fragments knowledge endlessly and creates increasingly narrow domains and languages of expertise shut off from each other in prisons of incommunicability. Aurobindo offered a critique of the Enlightenment project, which we can think of as not only correcting, but also completing it.

Critiquing the Enlightenment

A number of critiques of the Enlightenment project have existed through its history, increasing in clarity and intensity in our times. For example, the goal of an absolute epistemology and the scientific method utilized to arrive at it may be more suited to gaining knowledge of objective material reality than knowledge of the subjective world. The former is generally approached through the "hard sciences" (e.g. physics), whereas the latter is generally studied through the "human sciences" (e.g. psychology), "social sciences" (e.g. sociology), and the "humanities" (e.g. philosophy). The study of objective material reality (the outer, or the "what") has been the main focus of the Enlightenment project, whereas it has generally neglected or attempted to explain away our subjective experiences (the inner, or the "who").

The human sciences, social sciences, and humanities do not easily fit within the restricted goals and methods of the Enlightenment project (with the exception of those theorists who try to reduce all of our inner experiences to nothing more than chemical interactions in the brain). Indeed, the impossibility of objectification of the self, the fuzziness of definable categories of experience, and the inherent complexity or multiplicity of relevant relationships between various categories, render absolute classification suspect. This allegiance to the objectifying method of the Enlightenment has led to a number of detrimental results, prominent among which is an unevenness in the progress of modern knowledge, slanted towards a privileging of the hard sciences and resultant technologies. As a corollary, this also implies a privileging of cognitive knowledge over other forms of knowledge, such as emotional, instinctive, and intuitive forms of knowledge.

Related to such a resultant bias of the Enlightenment project is the complicity of power designs. The philosopher Martin Heidegger has referred to the abstract accumulation of knowledge and the "knowledge workers" involved in generating this as "standing reserve," the world and its inhabitants reduced to resources in an omni-database (an all-inclusive store of knowledge), that lends itself to exploitation by those who gain advantage over it. Since the Enlightenment was initiated in Europe, these designs of power, in the context of Sri Aurobindo's critique, reveal the intimate complicity of western knowledge production with colonialism. But the postcolonial and postmodern implications of the Enlightenment project are no less destructive.

The Enlightenment assumption that an additive epistemology will lead to complete knowledge has also increasingly been questioned for various reasons. For example, physicists have been confronted with weird phenomena that do not fit the assumptions of the Enlightenment project when investigating the extreme edges of macro and micro levels of matter, (such as in relativity theory and quantum mechanics). In other words, physics, the foundational science of the so-called hard sciences, has forced us to question some key assumptions of the Enlightenment project.

Critiques of Enlightenment epistemology may be summarized as follows:

1) The faith in piecing together a single logical "systems theory of everything" is impossible and misplaced.
2) The Enlightenment project has increasingly deferred its promise of total knowledge, while continuing to generate endless specialization, and forcing all of humanity to accept its assumptions, universalized through the knowledge academy and the world market.
3) The Enlightenment project privileges having over being and becoming, where the human being is merely a static knowledge worker, increasingly dwarfed by the gigantism of the continually generated volume of knowledge.
4) The abstract production of knowledge alienates it from the life world (the world of human interaction with their environment that brings its immediate needs of knowledge), rendering it vulnerable to exploitation, analogous to colonization.
5) The Enlightenment project privileges cognitive knowledge over other forms of knowledge, such as emotional, instinctive, and intuitive knowledge, inferiorizing, subjugating, and obsoleting them.

Sri Aurobindo and the Supermind

While anticolonial thought in India responded in a variety of ways, it was also clear that such responses could not simply reject everything related to the Enlightenment project. Indeed, despite their critiques and further developments of the Enlightenment project, various spiritual teachers, such as Vivekananda (1863 – 1902), Rabindranath Tagore (1861 – 1941), and Sri Aurobindo maintained an interest in the scientific method, total (or integral) knowledge, and epistemology. For our purpose, we are particularly interested in one of these thinkers, Sri Aurobindo, who advanced the idea of what he called the *Supermind*, which transcends the distinction between subject and object but is available subjectively and individually through processes of creative becoming.

In order to understand his basis for the Supermind, we need to first understand the two key intuitions Sri Aurobindo received soon after his return from England when he studied the Upanishads, which are a collection of ancient philosophical/religious texts in India. These two intuitions come from the *Mundaka Upanishad*, which Sri Aurobindo had translated by 1909. This Upanishad begins with the question "By knowing what does all this that is become known?" (MU I:1:3, trans. Sri Aurobindo 2001: 131). It then points to two kinds of knowing, "the higher and the lower" (MU I;1:4, trans. Sri Aurobindo 2001: 131). The lower is constituted by all forms of exteriorized knowledge, while the higher is the self-knowledge of Reality (*Brahman*), from which all manifestation proceeds as expression and self-presentation. Knowledge of this *Logos* (divine ordering principle, not to be confused with the finite logic of reason) is to be arrived at through self-knowledge, since it is the "Light of lights" and the "Self of selves". (MU II:2:10, trans. Sri Aurobindo 2001: 141).

Thus, the first intuition is of subjective identification with the original Logos, knowing which all may be known, while the second intuition is the distinction between a higher and a lower knowledge. These two forms of knowledge are further refined and specified in other Upanishads as Knowledge (*Vidya*) and Ignorance (*Avidya*) respectively (note that the capitalization of these terms is necessary when being used as principles or forms of divine consciousness). The distinction between Knowledge and Ignorance is a pervasive one that runs through the Upanishads. The *Isha Upanishad*, for example, which came to form a foundation for Sri Aurobindo's philosophy, poses this distinction as that between the knowledge of the One and the knowledge of the Many, but does so in a way that he considered to be methodological and cutting to the root of the Enlightenment project (Sri Aurobindo 2003). According to this view of the Upanishads, all forms of indirect knowledge arrived at by use of logic, analogy, and experimental verification are actually forms of Ignorance, whereas today we have been conditioned to believe that they alone produce knowledge. However, the term Knowledge can only be strictly applied to a direct knowing by identity of being (to know something by being it)—"I know because I am."

To these one may add a third intuition, that of the *modes* of knowing. Sri Aurobindo intuited that human knowledge was of a variety of kinds, due to differences and discontinuities in modes of experience. In the *Brahmananda Valli* of the *Taittiriya Upanishad,* he found confirmation in terms of a number of bodies with their independent beings and qualitative natures in the human system (Sri Aurobindo 2001: 216-220). Of these, the first three belonged to the Ignorance, and were normal to human beings, while the last two were transcendental and belonged to the Knowledge, hence they are presently rare for human beings. The bodies of Ignorance are the physical (*annamaya*), vital (*pranamaya*) and mental (*manomaya shariras*) bodies. Each of these could be said to have its own modalities and forms of knowledge, where the mental relates to cognitive function, the vital relates to emotional and volitional functions, and the physical relates to volitional and is also based in skill or dexterity. The intuition of discontinuities between these modes of existence may be arrived at existentially through one's own self-reflective experience, but Sri Aurobindo also related these three bodies to evolutionary emergence in successive discontinuous steps – non-living matter (physical), life-in-matter (vital), and rationality in living matter (mental).

The fourth body is known as the causative body (*karana sharira*), which Sri Aurobindo equated with the Supermind (*vijnana*), a comprehensive, qualitative knowledge-consciousness. He found further confirmation for this in Chapter 7 of the *Bhagavad Gita* (another primary text of ancient Indian wisdom) where Knowledge is related to the self-awareness of Reality in its two modes: essential and comprehensive. In the first case, there must be an essential self-awareness of Reality, a self-evident consciousness of Being that can energize itself as ideation and comprehend its possibilities ideationally. This essence of ideation (the forming of ideas or concepts) is known as *jnana*, while its consciousness of itself with its parts and proportions as a whole is called *vijnana*, which Sri Aurobindo translated as Supermind. Thus Supermind could be seen as the ordered self-perception of the Infinite One. This is a logical paradox in the finite realm, but possible to a self-conscious Infinite that grasps its wholeness ideationally in terms of related gradations and variations. Thus this self-knowledge of God could be equated to the Divine Logos. Such a Logos, however, is not primarily cognitive in the mental sense and not an arrangement of finite knowledge, but an ideational principle that maintains its essence in an infinite self-presentation (Sri Aurobindo 1997: 266). This is the nature of knowledge by identity.

At our level of inferential knowledge, however (which, as discussed earlier, the Upanishads refer to as Ignorance), such a grasp of the wholeness of infinity is lacking and all knowledge is fragmented. Yet we can see how our knowledge is a partial appearance of the truth of Supermind, an appearance in which the wholeness is suppressed and we are left to piece together the fragments. Putting Knowledge and Ignorance side by side, one can see their relations, the dependence of Ignorance (Avidya) on Knowledge (Vidya). On one side is the appearance, on the other side is the truth which gives meaning to the appearance. In other words, Knowledge implies the self-consciousness of the One in all its parts (unity consciousness), whereas Ignorance is the loss of the self-consciousness of the One, hence a separative consciousness. The latter is the "appearance," the former is the "truth."

One also sees here that the transition from the one to the other is mediated by the solar light, the Knowledge principle. However, this is not the principle of mental cognition, but includes this principle and transcends it. The knowledge project of transitioning from Ignorance to Knowledge then becomes one of finding relations in knowledge between the two, essentially relations between separative consciousness and unity consciousness. If one can characterize the knowledge of the Ignorance in terms of the three modalities of mental, vital, and physical knowledge or the four attributes of cognitive, emotional, volitional and skilful knowledge, may one find corresponding modalities in Supermind from which these derive. Are there processes of transforming the above modes of knowledge in the Ignorance to their corresponding modalities in the Knowledge? This became the alternative Enlightenment project of Sri Aurobindo.

The Differentiations of Knowledge

Sri Aurobindo was to find the key to this problem in the *Aiteraya Upanishad.* (It should be noted that, while this section may be more challenging than the others, it is nevertheless vital in order to attain a fuller understanding of the Supermind) Here the modalities of knowledge in Supermind are enumerated as *Vijnana*, *Prajnana*, *Samjnana* and *Aajnana* (which are clarified below). Sri Aurobindo interprets these four as the primary modes of *supramental knowing* (knowledge belonging to Supermind), of which two (*Vijnana* and *Aajnana*) are comprehensive and two (*Prajnana* and *Samjnana*) apprehensive. Of these, the originary comprehensive knowledge is *Vijnana*, which may thus be called the Divine Logos, Supramental ideation, or integral knowledge. We can see from this why Sri Aurobindo translates *Vijnana* as Supermind. The other three may be thought of as specialized operations of *Vijnana—prajnana* as cognitive, *samjnana* as sensate, and *aajnana* as volitional. In the Knowledge, *Vijnana* is the knowledge by identity of the One (*Jnana*) exercised in a comprehensive awareness of its totality and its infinite ideational proportionalities (the relative qualities of parts to whole in keeping with the idea).

Sri Aurobindo refers to these ideas as Real-Idea or reality as idea, self-presentations of reality rather than representations. *Prajnana* (cognitive) objectifies these ideational parts according to their proportions, taking a position as of witness to its cosmic possibilities. *Samjnana* (sensate) pervades these cosmic possibilities sensing qualitative distinctions as differentiations of the integral Wholeness; and *Aajnana* (volitional) enters into each discrete possibility as a point of prospection of the Whole controlling it by immanence of Will.

In each of the specialized operations of *Prajnana*, *Samjnana*, and *Aajnana*, *Vijnana* acts and is experienced as the direct Knowledge of the Whole in the parts. In the Ignorance, this presence of *Vijnana* becomes obscured and each of the specialized operations seems to act independently and discontinuously. The objectifying cognitive property of *Prajnana* becomes active in the mind as the relation of knowing between the subject and the object; the sensate property of *Samjnana* becomes active in the feelings as subjective sensation and emotion; and the volitional property of *Aajnana* becomes active in creative execution as will and skill. We can thus see how these map to the modes of mental, vital and physical knowledge in the Ignorance. Still, a further reflection will clarify how each of the human modes of knowing imply all the other modes, with one predominating and the others latent. For example, physical skill is primarily a volitional mode of knowledge with sensate and cognitive modes latent and co-existing; vital instinct proceeds from a primary sensing but carries a volitional and cognitive knowledge implicit in it; and mental cognition primarily uses a conceptual intelligence while also including an imaginative sensing and a mental will (intentionality) implicit in its operations.

However, by remaining solely within these lower modes of knowing (the Ignorance), we live in ignorance of the genuine knowledge, accessible to the fourth body or Supermind This is because the constitution of the Ignorance is obtained through the maintenance of an objectified operation of knowledge imposed upon the faculties of all creatures. The *Katha Upanishad* draws attention to this important point: "The Self-born has set the doors of the body to face outwards, therefore the soul of a man gazes outward and not at the Self within: hardly a wise man here and there, desiring immortality, turns his eyes inward and sees the Self within him" (KU II:1:1, trans. Sri Aurobindo 2001: 117).

Turning Inward

But how does one achieve this turning inward, which is necessary to attain the intuitive knowledge available to the Supermind? To help us with this important goal, we need to understand the following three distinctions offered by Sri Aurobindo: knowledge by outer contact (*adhibhautika*), knowledge by inner contact (*adhidaivika*), and knowledge by identity (*adhidaivika*) (2005:Ch. X, 543-572). Normal human knowledge is acquired through outer contact, and comes through our senses (or technological extension of the senses) coupled with processing of sense knowledge by use of our reasoning capabilities (or technological extension of logical and computational operations). The knowledge gained through outer contact is of material reality, and it is this type of knowledge that is considered supreme (or the only real knowledge) by the Enlightenment project. Unfortunately, it is this very process of rational scientific knowledge accumulation that keeps us in Ignorance.

At the other end of the spectrum, knowledge by identity is achieved through identification with *jnana* and *vijnana* of Supermind or the Divine Logos. This knowledge by identity is the knowledge of the *atma* or Self of all selves (*adhyatmika*). In between knowledge by identity and knowledge by outer contact is what is characterized as the knowledge of the gods (*devas*) or knowledge by inner contact, which forms a bridge between the two extremes. As a bridge, this knowledge by inner contact (*adhidaivika*) is our genuine intuition, or what Sri Aurobindo referred to as our "intuitive mentality", and he believed this power needed to be normalized in the human being, if we are to move out of the troubled ignorance of our separative consciousness and achieve the Self-Knowledge of unitive Being.

Around 1912, Sri Aurobindo developed seven lines of yoga practice, each with four principal goals, to which he gave the name *sapta chatusthaya* or seven quartets. Within this framework, he recorded his experiments in consciousness in diary notes, mainly over the period from 1912-1920, which have presently been compiled in two volumes as *The Record of Yoga* (2001 b). Within these quartets, Sri Aurobindo outlined four goals related to the development of an intuitive mentality. These were a set of spatial intuitions involving cognition, sense and volition (*prajnana, samjnana* and *aajnana* respectively as discussed above), a set of temporal intuitions dealing with prediction and direct perception of temporal events in past and present, eight paranormal powers dealing with cognition, sensation, volition and experience and an access to integral supramental knowledge (*Vijnana*) through transcendence (*samadhi*) (Banerji 2012: 157-215)). Sri Aurobindo's development of these ideas involves many important distinctions, clarifications, and complex analysis, which we need not explore here (see Banerji 2012: 157-215).

We can, however, benefit from even a basic understanding of these ideas, leading us towards building an intuitive self.

From Cognition to Intuition

Cognition (*prajnana*) generally refers to ways of knowing through mental processes, as opposed to feeling, will, intuition, and so forth. In describing the transformation of cognition into an intuitive mentality, Sri Aurobindo points to the extension of this activity to the feelings (*samjnana*), will (*aajnana*), and psychic activities (1999: 808). Further, Sri Aurobindo distinguishes four forms of cognitive knowledge, known as sight (*drishti*), hearing (*shruti*), memory (*smriti*), and discrimination (*viveka*). Together they form a hierarchy, a higher and lower pair, moving from knowledge by outer contact (such as science) to knowledge by inner contact (intuition) to knowledge by identity. The higher pair consists of sight and hearing, and the lower of memory and discrimination.

Sight and hearing, which are aspects of knowledge by identity (in their highest expression), are translated by Sri Aurobindo as Truth-seeing or "revelation" and Truth-hearing or "inspiration", and they are related to direct and divine knowledge. In contrast, remembering is a form of knowledge by inner contact, an intuition, which can arise because we carry within ourselves the hidden root of Oneness that has been veiled by Ignorance. This form of remembering is really an intuition, a psychic memory of our Origin, of the One Self in all selves, and it is what we often think of as *faith*. Often mistaken for indoctrinated sectarian belief, this form of faith is completely different. In Sri Aurobindo's words, "Faith is an intuition not only waiting for experience to justify it, but leading towards experience" (Sri Aurobindo 1972: Vol. 22, 166).

The other form of knowledge in this lower pair is discrimination, which refers to the distinction between right and wrong, what is to be chosen and what rejected. This is a cognitive skill, a spontaneous improvised selection from a variety of possibilities, a practical knowledge of choice, proportion, priority, and emphasis. Discrimination arises in the rational intelligence as judgment, and yet it is really an intuitive discrimination that lies in a spontaneous certitude based in a knowledge by identity with the One Conscious Being, known in the Upanishads as *Brahman*.

In this context, memory comes to us from the depths of the heart, and discrimination comes from above, as the mind becomes more silent and is prepared to receive self-evident cosmic intuitions or the knowledge by identity of Supermind. The heart and the mind thus become channels for these intuitions. We see as in a flash what is preexistent and how things are to be done. These intuitions prepare the consciousness for the operations of the higher pair of revelation and inspiration, which are properties of knowledge by identity. In other words, by developing our intuitive capacities in this way, we are then able to move into the higher faculties of revelation and inspiration, or truth-seeing and truth-hearing. However, to achieve this goal the preparatory intuitions of memory (*smriti*) and discrimination (*viveka*) must replace rational thought, allowing us to ascend to the consciousness of Supermind where truth presents itself in visionary and vibratory modes.

But how is this process possible? How can our senses lead us beyond not only their normal operations but also beyond rational thought? When the divine, the One, becomes manifest to itself in varied sensible form, it must do so to varying degrees under the cloak of Ignorance, appearing to our senses in fragments. It is through a combination of using our normal senses and rational functions that we have the ability to achieve indirect knowledge of reality, and it is this indirect, slow, and perpetually limited form of knowledge progression that has come to be known as the scientific method, the glory of the Enlightenment project. But if our seeing and hearing, our eyes and ears, were to resist nature's outward pull and open to their inner potential, this could initiate a progression where, tuned to a cosmic key, these visionary and auditory capacities could rise beyond regular thought to realms of revelation and inspiration. Through such achievement, we would be far better prepared for attaining the extraordinary powers of supramental knowledge.

Many of us may be satisfied with achieving greater intuitive abilities to help us achieve practical goals, from creating a successful marketing campaign or developing a new product to intuitively knowing how to beat one's opponent in a sporting match. However, developing our intuitive capacities is really a necessary step for even higher states of Knowledge. Unfortunately, because such Knowledge is so far beyond the reach of mainstream scientific assumptions rooted in the Enlightenment project, it is dismissed as impossible, hindering the evolution of humanity. Sri Aurobindo acknowledged the systemic rational drive of the Enlightenment project, propelled by science, but also recognized that reality cannot be reduced to or enclosed by finite human rationality. His teachings and experiments with consciousness are an invitation beyond rational parochialism, into the realm of intuition leading to the Supermind.

Some examples of the powers of knowledge he discusses include the powers of prophecy, cosmic memory, clairvoyance, clairaudience, and telepathy. These are intuitive powers derived from and leading to Supermind, which can be developed by us. For example, attuning to cosmic memory (both backward and forward in time), implies the directly experienced knowledge of the past, not an imagined or remembered knowledge, as in a mental memory-image. Other powers of intuition include invoking a response from a greater cosmic or divine Will, and achieving an inner control over the natures of things so that when one speaks to them, they obey. The former example is essentially the power of prayer, which Sri Aurobindo believed that all human beings utilize consciously or unconsciously to some extent. The latter example, though it may seem extreme, involves becoming so perfectly identified with the inner nature of an object or living being that the control over it is automatic. It obeys, not because there is an external will dominating it, but because it is a will that understands it and is identified with it. Sri Aurobindo's diaries are replete with many interesting examples of his development of such powers, with and without the use of divinatory means. To develop and test these means, he conducted many experiments involving such things as the flight of crows, the flitting of butterflies, and the movement of ants. For example, he observed butterflies moving from plant to plant, and attempted to have his consciousness enter the mind of a butterfly. He recorded his intuition and the result. These experiments were conducted with the impersonality of a scientist - he recorded faithfully instances of success, failure, and partial success.

Sri Aurobindo held that it is possible to transit from Ignorance to Knowledge by building an intuitive mentality by such means. Today, many scientific studies indicate the possibility of attaining some of these powers, and the continued suppression of such knowledge is becoming increasingly more difficult to maintain.

Summary

The main purpose of this chapter has been to provide a brief yet beneficial introduction to ways of attaining greater intuitive powers, with the help of the extraordinary insights and abilities of Sri Aurobindo.

Unfortunately, the Enlightenment project has tried to reduce all of reality to human reason and our basic sense capacities, leaving aside many other parts of our being, such as emotional, instinctive, and intuitive forms of knowledge. As a result, those who adhere strictly (and often unconsciously) to the precepts of the Enlightenment project also tend to ignore the many other aspects of reality that are only clearly experienced and understood through our higher faculties, beyond the familiar functioning of our senses and reasoning capacities.

One the one hand, therefore, we must transcend the parochialism of the Enlightenment project if we are to have any hope of attaining a deeper understanding of reality and of ourselves. On the other, we must not lose sight of the importance of following certain assumptions of the Enlightenment project that have proven to hold great power for gaining scientific knowledge of certain aspects of the material realm of existence.

Indeed, one may draw attention to the importance given by Sri Aurobindo to the development of a mental impersonality befitting a scientist and the need to test each step of the way in these experiments leading to an intuitive mentality. For this, the primary power necessary to develop among all those discussed above is given by him as discrimination.

In a world that has grown so accustomed to such a fast paced mode of living, demanding instant knowledge and gratification, we would be wise to heed Sri Aurobindo's advice: "Knowledge is not for the hasty mind but only for the *dhira* [the patient], who can sit long, accumulating and arranging his store and does not rush away with fragments like a crow darting off with the first morsel of food on which it can feed" (2001b: 17-18).

ABBREVIATIONS

AU: Aitareya Upanishad
IU: Isha Upanishad
KU: Katha Upanishad
KeU: Kena Upanishad
MU: Mundaka Upanishad
CWSA: Complete Works of Sri Aurobindo

WORKS CITED

Banerji, Debashish 2012. Seven Quartets of Becoming: A Transformative Yoga Psychology Based on the Diaries of Sri Aurobindo. (Los Angeles: Nalanda Interna-tional and New Delhi: DK Printworld).

Aurobindo, Sri 1972 Sri Aurobindo Birth Centenary Library. 30 vols. Pon-dichery: Sri Aurobindo Ashram Trust.

---1997 Essays on the Gita. CWSA:19 (Pondicherry: Sri Au-robindo Ashram Trust).

---1998 The Secret of the Veda. CWSA:15 (Pondicherry: Sri Aurobindo Ashram Trust).

---1999 The Synthesis of Yoga. CWSA:23&24 (Pondicherry: Sri Aurobindo Ashram Trust).

---2001 Kena and Other Upanishads. CWSA: 18 (Pondicher-ry: Sri Aurobindo Ashram Trust).

---2001b Record of Yoga. CWSA: 10&11. (Pondicherry: Sri Aurobindo AshramTrust).

---2003 Isha Upanishad. CWSA: 17 (Pondicherry: Sri Auro-bindo AshramTrust).

---2005 The Life Divine. CWSA: 21&22 (Pondicherry: Sri Au-robindo AshramTrust).

Dr. Sara Ahbel-Rappe

Dr. Sara Ahbel-Rappe is Professor of Greek and Latin at the University of Michigan. Her research focuses on the history of Platonism, including study of the Christian, Jewish, and Islamic interpreters of Platonism. She is the author of several books, beginning with *Reading Neoplatonism: Non-discursive Thinking in the Texts of Plotinus, Proclus, and Damascius.*

Dr. Sara Ahbel-Rappe

Intuition in Ancient Greek Philosophy: A Developmental Approach

ANCIENT PHILOSOPHY, CONTEMPLATION, SELF-REALIZATION

A common assumption about ancient philosophy is that it is a rather arcane discipline, concerned mainly with dry logical arguments that few people understand. Sometimes that assumption is correct, but that is not the whole story.

Modern day analytic philosophers (who are generally the dominant group of philosophers in academia) might wish to claim the Greeks as the inventors of their own techniques, of their ability to analyze the arguments that work for or against a given argument. Ideally, the analytic philosopher is able to use reason to explain various aspects of reality, and this rationality in service of explanation itself is usually understood as an inheritance from the Greeks. However, I would like to highlight aspects of the Greco-Roman philosophical legacy that explore dimensions of the mind that are not analytic, that are not concerned with explanation, rational or otherwise. What I am about to suggest is that one of the important concerns of ancient philosophy is the awakening of the *intuitive* dimension of the mind.

As with other contemplative traditions (i.e. certain forms of yoga or of Buddhist meditation), in the Greco-Roman world, the raw ingredients of the practices for developing intuitive wisdom were furnished by the mind itself, and these raw ingredients were themselves considered as a field of study and exploration. In this chapter, I will draw attention to a number of ancient texts that teach the student how to investigate the mind and its objects directly, without analysis.

On the one hand, the texts we are about to explore aim to point out the ground of awareness, what one might call *pure attention* or the *unity of awareness*. On the other hand, these texts study the nature of the objects of awareness, insofar as they are impermanent, ungraspable, and insubstantial in themselves. In other words, these texts help the reader study, notice, and eventually discipline or expand certain features or aspects of the mind that are not approached by means of conceptual content per se.

I will consider in particular the intuitive mind, its disciplines, and the results of those disciplines in the ancient philosophical traditions. Before undertaking this study, however, some caveats must be set in place, and these concern the very meaning of the words *reason* and *intuition*, as they appear in Greek and Roman texts.

In ancient Greek, there is one word for intellect, *nous*, but many words that denote one or another aspect of mind: *dianoia* ("discursive thought"), *logos* ("reason," "argument," "account," but also, "divine mind"), *psyche* ("the mind," "seat of mental capacities"), *sophia* ("wisdom," a very ancient word), *episteme* ("knowledge," often "scientific knowledge"), and *theoria* (a word whose meaning can vary widely, as "contemplative activity" or "theoretical, systematic knowledge"). There are also words that denote specific aspects or capacities of the mind, but in some periods, it seems as if the technical meaning associated with these words is absent or not yet fully developed. For example, the Hellenistic (ancient Greek) philosophers who took their name from the Painted Stoa in Athens, the Stoics, had a word, *prosoche*, which meant exactly, "attention, awareness directed toward the self," whereas in Classical Greek this noun does not appear. At a later stage, the Platonic philosopher known as Plotinus (204/5 – 270 CE) used the word *sunaisthanomai* to convey the idea of what we might call consciousness, or even self-awareness. So the Greek psychological and contemplative vocabulary develops over time.

Yet another problem is the range of meanings that can attend a single word, as, for example, with *logos*, which can mean "argument" or "reason," but can be associated with a "universal or divine mind." For example, consider the text at the beginning of the *Gospel of John*: "In the beginning was the *Logos*,"[1] or the "*logos theou* ("word of God"), as the first century Jewish philosopher Philo of Alexandria uses it when

[1] *John* Prologue: ἐν ἄρχῃ ἦν ὁ λόγος

he discusses the creation of the world.[2] In these cases, it seems clear that "reason" will not suffice to translate *logos*.

Similarly, the word *nous* can cause considerable confusion, precisely because we have ready access to the words "intellect" or "intellectual," and by these, the modern person might understand simply "intelligence," or "intellectual culture" more generally. By contrast, in the classical period, *nous* ("intellect") was associated with certain kinds of knowledge not available through forms of what we might today think of as "mental" activity. Indeed, as I will make clear, *nous* most closely approximates to what we would call "intuition" rather than "intellect."

Again, there are some concepts that are prominent in Eastern (i.e. Buddhist) contemplative traditions, for which there seem to be no appropriate Greek words. Do the Greek spiritual disciplines simply lack the corresponding function if they somehow lack a word? For example, there is no Greek word for concentration, in the precise sense that we might think of the Sanskrit word *Samadhi* ("concentrated absorption") or the Pali word *Jhana* ("trance," "absorption"). Yet the Greeks do have the word "unity," and there are numerous Greek texts that prescribe techniques for training thought, for cultivating tranquility and detachment. One might think that the Greek words *ataraxia*, (freedom from care), *hesuche* (peaceful calm), or the Latin word, *tranquilitas* (tranquility) connote analogous states of mind. For example, the Roman philosopher Cicero (106 - 43 BCE) recommends an exercise involving anticipating possible adverse outcomes, such as *Praemeditatio* or anticipatory visioning, in order to avert grief. (*Tusculan Disputations*, III.20) In fact, on the Latin side, the word *Meditatio* is used in numerous texts, from the Stoics to the Christians, to denote the exercise of sustained attention directed inward.

Perhaps a final word with respect to the context in which these texts arise is appropriate. Without question, training (*askesis*) or practice is at the center of several ancient Greek spiritual and philosophical traditions. The Cynic philosopher Diogenes (412/404 - 323 BCE) reportedly

---

[2] *De Opificio Mundi* I.20

practiced soliciting donations from statues in order to cultivate self-reliance. (Diogenes Laertius, *Lives* VI) But the orientation of any contemplative path lies in its aspiration: for Platonic philosophers, this would be assimilation to God; for Evagrius, the fourth century Christian ascetic, this would be divine knowledge. In some cases, the goal or end of a given *hairesis*, or school, is "well being," though this school is shaped by a doctrinal and experiential account, with prescriptive force, of how "well being" might be structured. The prescriptive formulae proffered by different Hellenistic schools might remind us of certain Eastern concepts. For example, compare the Epicurean *ataraxia* ("absence of pain"), the Stoic and Christian *apatheia* ("freedom from suffering or passion"), and the Skeptic *epoche* ("suspension of judgment") to the Buddhist concept of *Nirvana* ("extinction"), the Vedic concept of *Moksha* ("liberation"), or the Yogic concept of *Nirodha* ("elimination of the modifications of the mind").

The goal of this chapter is to show that what Plotinus calls "footholds in the intelligible world," (*Enn.* VI, 7 [38] 36. 26) or points of access to insight, are one of the great legacies of the ancient contemplative traditions. These hints for the development of intuition are also loosely comparable to the "Pointing Out" instructions of the Tibetan Dzogchen lineage, which show the aspirant how to recognize the nature of the mind. By looking for traces of these instructions in contemplation in ancient texts, we realize that even today the Greeks can speak powerfully and directly to anyone curious about the human mind and its hidden dimensions. In other words, if you really want to set out on the path to know yourself at the deepest levels, then you would do well to learn from many of the ancient Greek pioneers in studying the mind.

To facilitate this approach, I divide my work into two main sections, viz., mind and its objects.

Section One: The Objects of Awareness

In this section, we explore texts from ancient philosophy that approach the objects of awareness, taken simply as a field comprised either of sensory perceptions or of mental ideation (thoughts, concepts, viewpoints, and so forth). These texts, focusing as they do on the fleetingness of objects that we contact by means of sense perception, purport to show that all such sensory phenomena are inherently unstable, subject to dissolution, void of essence, and unsatisfactory.

Already, the Pre-Socratic philosopher Heraclitus (c. 535 – c. 475 BCE) famously characterized the sensory world as flowing or constantly changing. While his colleagues from Ionia developed the study of nature (Ionian physics) and described the order (*cosmos*) of the world, Heraclitus instead offered a radically volatile representation of reality. He uses phenomena from the natural world as well as metaphors to powerful effect to illustrate his insight into the nature of reality as effervescent, self-renewing, and radically impermanent: "Upon those who are stepping into the same rivers different and again different waters flow." (12a) "The sun is new every day" (6) "War is father of all." These pithy adages attempt to penetrate to the heart of experience and break apart stable conceptions, thus seeking to elicit an intuition. Heraclitus relies on complex structure, paradoxical turn, and brevity to bring the reader to the insight that change is just the way things are. At the same time, Heraclitus came to inspire an entire tradition of philosophy, especially as developed by the philosopher Plato (fourth century BCE).

One way to describe the metaphysics of Plato is to say that it is rooted in the changeless, eternal world of divine essence, but grounded in the fluctuating, impermanent world of phenomenal appearances. Absolute truth, beauty, and the good are examples from the eternal world, while everything that is bound in time—from the physical universe to every living creature and all sense experiences—are impermanent. In other words, everything is really in motion, except for the timeless eternal world.

For Plato, self and other co-arise in a mutual interpenetration of quality and awareness. For example, Plato would argue roughly along the lines of saying that the experience of color arises within us from a combination of the relevant quality of an object and the physiological functioning of our eyes.

At *Timaeus* 28a1, Plato draws this crucial distinction between the eternal and the transient: "What is that which always is and has no becoming, and what is that which becomes but never is?" This realm of becoming is a place where, as Plato says, "the verb 'to be' must be totally abolished." (*Theaetetus* 157b2) "This is wrong" Plato goes on to say in that same passage, "nor should we allow the use of such words as 'something,' 'of something' or 'mine,' 'this' or 'that' or any other name that makes things stand still." (*Theaetetus* 157b 5-6) According to this way of looking at things, which Plato hints is inspired by Heraclitus, everything is really motion.

Speaking of sense perception, Plato says, "the eye and some other things—one of the things commensurable with the eye—which has come into its neighborhood, generate both whiteness and the perception which is by nature united with it. In this event, motions arise in the intervening space, sight from the side of the eye and whiteness from the side of that which cooperates in the production of the color." Seer and seen arise together in one field that is purely a play of motion. As mentioned above, self and other co-arise in a mutual interpenetration of quality and awareness.

But Plato extends this analysis to every form of sense perception: "We must understand this account as applying in the same way to hard and hot and everything else; nothing, as we were saying before is in itself any of these. All of them, of all kinds whatsoever, are what things become through association with one another, as the result of motion." (*Theaetetus* 182) Here, under the banner of Heraclitus, Plato allows us to dissolve the sensible world; the sense fields and the experiencer of those fields only arise by virtue of contact. In Buddhist parlance, we could say that Plato explores the emptiness of the "*skandhas*," (a Sanskrit word, meaning aggregates, or heaps, and denoting the factors that comprise conscious experience) wherein sense perception, consciousness, and phenomena all mutually condition each other.

Beyond the discursive description of how the sense fields function, there are texts that reflect the practice-oriented approach that teaches mind training. Often these texts take the form of short notes or reminders (*hypomnemata*) that assume frequent repetition and display a recursive structure that can be referenced in the course of daily life. Of the Hellenistic schools of philosophy, the Stoics both emphasized their allegiance to Heraclitus and also gave rise to an extensive meditative literature. Although much writing from the early Greek Stoics has disappeared, we are fortunate to have the teachings of the Roman Stoic, Emperor Marcus Aurelius (d. 176 CE), who penned a series of notes entitled literally, *Book to Himself* (translated as *Meditations*) while out on campaign against the enemies of Rome. These meditations combine Marcus' record of his own flow of thoughts with active attention to the stream of experience to create a reminder, not so much for the reader, but for Marcus himself, of how impermanence penetrates and infuses the entire world with radical instability and non-identity.

We begin with meditations on death, with Marcus employing some standard techniques that we find in Roman literature, working with exemplary individuals and then moving on to ordinary people, in keeping with typically Roman social logic.

(III.3) "Hippocrates," Marcus writes, "after curing many sicknesses, himself fell sick and died. The Chaldean astrologers foretold the death of many persons then the hour of fate overtook them also." We further see the emphasis on universal impermanence; not just the flow of time and the decomposition of all things, but the sheer repulsiveness of the physical form. Marcus recommends seeing through the façade of social symbols as well as fundamental desires when he compiles a list of repugnancies: "My purple robe is sheep's wool stained with a little gore from a shellfish; copulation is friction of the members and an ejaculatory discharge." Marcus' practice of envisioning the allure of sensory experience under the category of the repulsive might remind us of similar instructions in the Theravada meditation manual, the *Visuddhimagga*, as it is written in the Pali language, or *Path of Purification* (ca. 430 CE).

Marcus works most frequently with the aspect of impermanence that attends all phenomena, alluding to Heraclitus' famous river fragment, but visualizing the flow of experience as a current of impermanence: "There is a kind of river of things passing into not being, and time is a violent torrent. For no sooner is each seen, then it has been carried away, and another is being carried by, and that, too will be carried away.“ Looking at the stream of phenomenal appearances, Marcus brandishes the weapon of contempt for the world as a method of guarding his senses, exclaiming, "how cheap, contemptible, soiled, corruptible, and mortal."

The ancient Stoics and Platonists concerned themselves with the inner dimension of experience as well, including thoughts, feelings, attachment and aversion, states of cognition, certainty, doubt, and opinion, all of which they recognized as essentially volatile. The Stoic essayist Seneca (c. 4 BC – AD 65), whose employment at the court of Nero was terminated in a forced suicide, writes in his essay, *On Anger* [I.7.4], about the mind's invasion and defeat under the advance of its own self-generated thoughts: "There are certain things which at the start are under our control, but later hurry us away by their violence and leave us no retreat. ...So with the mind -- if it plunges into anger, love, or the other passions, it has no power to check its impetus." Yet this initial observation does not yet develop insight. The cultivation of the mind must additionally include access to inner calm, stability, even joy and freedom. Thus, just as is the case with Buddhist traditions, in the Stoic schools and its extensions, the practitioner progresses from the observation of phenomena to concentration, which helps foster tranquility.

To see how this tranquility blossoms, we can turn to another Roman Stoic, the philosopher Epictetus (c. 55 – 135 CE), a one-time slave who inspired Marcus Aurelius. Epictetus, whose *Discourses* were recorded by the Greek essayist Arrian, developed a practice of self-dialogue designed to remind us that much of what we think of as true is merely the unreflecting habit of assenting to our own thoughts. According to the Stoics, one aspect of the mind—*phantasia*, the appearance, the given, how things seem,—needs to be guarded against by another aspect of the mind,—*katathesis*, assent, the commitment that "this is so; things really are this way!" In a meditation Epictetus describes (3.12.150), the practitioner addresses each appearance: "wait a minute, appearance! Let me examine you." Scanning the thought flow and recognizing the habit energy that keeps it fueled, the Stoic does not have to believe everything she thinks. Stoics call this practice "withholding assent" from the surface presentation, from the way it seems. Epictetus recognized that caution must be exercised in the realm of thoughts, and this caution is one of the most important ways we can take care of ourselves.

What would it be like to be free from passions, to see things as they are without the clouds of attachment that condition how we experience whatever is occurring? This state of natural openness is the foundation of the ability to discern reality in itself. One name that the Stoics gave to this openness is *apatheia*, freedom from passion, or tranquility, inner calm. The Stoic meditative tradition focuses on visualizing chance events to practice detachment, the capacity to undergo experience without emotional investment. Epictetus asks, "When someone becomes Caesar's friend, has he ceased to be impeded or constrained? Is he serene and flourishing?" 4.1.45-6 (Long: 85) The social position that everyone longs for, being the friend of an emperor, offers no advantages in this regard. Instead, that very desire matches such a person with a fickle friend, ties him to an unstable social rank, and worst of all, deludes him with the false belief that this friendship somehow improves his lot.

Later, Evagrius Ponticus (345-399 CE), the Christian ascetic who lived in the solitary cells of the Nitrian desert outside of Alexandria, merged Stoic theory with the power of mindfulness. For Evagrius, mental disturbance (*pathos*) is fueled by erroneous thoughts that quickly become habits coloring the mind, infusing it with compulsive tendencies. Tranquility is the result of working through eight negative dispositions (lust, gluttony, anger, sorrow, torpor, avarice, pride, and vainglory). The work consists in using a mantra to see through the deluded thoughts that arise when the mind is clouded by these grasping, painful states, to let these thoughts subside.

Intuition, or direct insight into the nature of reality, is primarily obscured by passion. Evagrius warns that "a man in chains cannot run. Nor can the mind that is enslaved to passion see the place of spiritual prayer. It is dragged along and tossed by these passion-filled thoughts and cannot stand firm and tranquil." (Harmless 348) Evagrius links the capacity to discern the heart, to distill the mind of wisdom beneath the veil of delusion, to the great work of ceaseless prayer. The monks of the Egyptian desert recited as a mantra the Jesus Prayer ("Lord Jesus Christ, Son of God, have mercy on me"), perhaps offering a tradition that corresponds to the devotional *Japa* ("recitation") of the Hindu path of *Bhakti* ("loving devotion to God"). Even so, for Evagrius, freedom from passion (*apatheia*) and loving awareness of God (*agape*) develop side by side.

In this section, we have discussed a number of meditations that focus on the objects of consciousness, some very crude indeed (the succession of sense appearances or the birth and death of living beings) and some quite refined (divine love, meditational states). Although the student might gain some peace and detachment from engaging in such practices, the mind is nevertheless bound up in conditions; therefore, we must study the mind as it is in itself.

Section Two: Meditations on the Subject of Awareness

Whether conceived as outside the subject (as, for example, belonging to the sensory world) or as within the subject (as, for example, in the domain of the mental), the objects of the mind are not yet pointed in the direction of the knower (i.e. you). The knower of these objects, whom we can conceive as the very light that illuminates the field of the mind, is worthy of exploration in its own right. But how are we to study this subject? How can we gain access to pure awareness? Does the Ancient Greco-Roman world recognize this intuitive aspiration? The answer is a resounding yes; especially within Platonism, *nous* ("intuitive wisdom") appears only when the person opens and sees by means of what one ancient text called "the sacred backward turning eye." (*Chaldean Oracle*, 1.10)

The first order of business is the insight that the knower is not any of the things known. So Socrates asks, "is there a sight that is not of anything visible, but of sight itself? Is there a sound that is not of anything audible but of sound itself? Is there a thought that is not of anything conceivable but of thinking itself?" (Plato, *Charmides* 168d) Socrates leaves this question unanswered, but it is just in this question that intuition can be awakened, leaving us with the inquiry, what or who is the knower, apart from anything it knows? By what do we know this knower?

To turn back from the sense fields is to undertake what Plato once calls "turning around:" to awaken intuition is not to put knowledge in someone but to help her become oriented correctly. (*Republic* VI) The third century Egyptian philosopher Plotinus, who taught in Rome and left a record of his teachings (*The Enneads*) edited by his pupil, Porphyry, often resorts to visual meditations to help the student to clarify the distinction that we are trying to develop between the field of awareness and that awareness itself. Here we see Plotinus, as it were, provoking an intuition: "So far as possible, try to conceive of this world as one unified whole" (*Ennead* V.8.9.1-3). Already Plotinus points to the intuitive capacity; by what do we know the whole? All of the sense fields are present as a whole, and yet what is the nature of the whole? Intuitive thought, *nous*, Plotinus always insists, sees things "all at once (*athroon*)" (V.8.6.9). To develop this intuition, he suggests "if you were to make a small luminous mass a kind of center and then to place a spherical body around it so that the light inside illuminated the entire container, there being no other source of light for the outer mass" (VI.4.7.22). The ground of awareness, represented by the center, is described as pervading the entire sphere. Then where is the knower? She will not find herself as one of the things illuminated within the sphere. She must be the light itself.

To extract, so to say, the knower from the teeming morass of all possible objects, to abide as that very center of awareness or luminous ground, as Plotinus suggests in these meditations, is also, as he puts it elsewhere, to await the "inner sunrise". "Let it imagine soul as if flowing in from outside, pouring in and entering it everywhere and illuminating it: as the rays of the sun light up a dark cloud, and make it shine and give it a golden look" (V.1.2.18-20).

The soul, or in other words, our very mind, the one that belongs to each one of us, is thus ripe for the intuitive mode of knowing; all we need do is to take hints from the ordinary way that the mind encounters the world and study this encounter, looking for clues as to our true nature, our true source. The very fact that our minds encounter the world as whole, the very fact that no matter how hard we look, we cannot find the knower "out there" on the surface of the sphere—for Plotinus, these facts of awareness can become the spurs for intuition.

Now it is time for a deeper look into this intuitive mode of knowing, intellect (*nous*); it is time to study it, not in relationship to its contents, and not only in terms of glimpsing a fleeting intuition, but rather more closely, more as it is in itself. Astonishingly, Plotinus tells us that in its highest phase, intuitive mind or intellect does not think at all. (VI.7[38].35.30) There is a side to intellect that remains without thought. Moreover, this side of intellect always belongs to it: "Intellect always has intellection and always non-intellection" (VI.7[38].35.30). In its most interior mode, intuition becomes a seeing that has no object: "while the vision fills his eyes with light it does not make him see something else by it, rather the light itself is what is seen" (VI.7[38].36.20). This is the "hyper-noetic" phase of intellect, its "pre-thinking" phase, which encounters its very own nature (self-luminosity) as the culmination of its intuition.

To encounter the light of intuition as it is in itself is, after all, not to encounter it, strictly speaking. Later on in the Platonist tradition, the last head of the post-Platonic Academy, Damascius (who along with his fellow philosophers went into exile when Emperor Justinian closed the Academy in 529 CE), wrote an abstruse guide to Neoplatonist metaphysics, entitled *Problems and Solutions Concerning First Principles.* In this work, he studies the formulations of his predecessors concerning the meaning of divine reality and the capacity for the intuitive mind to know that same reality. To know reality is to arrive at the perspective in which there is no longer an intuition that appears to come or go, to be, of something else. Furthermore, it is unclear that "intuitive knowing" can actually be knowledge, if knowledge implies the separation of knower and known or implies the objective apprehension of an external reality. Of the intuitive mind that awakens to the implications of its own unity, Damascius states that knowledge demands differentiation, "but differentiation as it approaches the One collapses into unity, so that knowledge disappears into unknowing." But this is not an unknowing in the sense that we are ignorant; rather, it is the unknowing of our own selves through identification with the One (the Divine). Damascius continues: "We attempt to look at the sun for the first time and when we are far away, at least, we succeed. But the closer we approach the less we see it. And at last we see neither [sun] nor other things, since we have completely become the light itself, instead of an enlightened eye." (*Problems and Solutions* I.85)

Intuitive wisdom, the direct self-realization of the nature of the mind's own unity, the very ground of one's own intellect, is fundamentally free from any objective determinations. As Plotinus writes, paradoxically, in releasing all the objective conditions, intellect, intuitive mind, no longer exercises intellection! We learn further from Plotinus that intellect takes a backward step from its identity as intellect: "the intellect must return, so to speak, backwards, and give itself up" (III.8[30].9.29). The nature of intuitive wisdom is to be empty; as Plotinus tells us, that kind of intellection is non-intellection.

But how to unify the mind? How to develop that concentrated attention and focus (the Buddhists call it "*Samadhi*," literally "unified mind") that becomes the support for this realization, the fundamental emptiness that is the essence of pristine wisdom? Plotinus puts the matter simply when he says, "Cut away everything!" (V.3) Perhaps that is too huge an assignment for the ordinary mind. Damascius, over two hundred years later, but still writing in the tradition of ancient Platonism, uses the visualizations that Plotinus employs together with a meditation on the nature of the vastness of water to indicate the expansiveness of the intuitive mind, its innate spaciousness, its merging of all distinctions: "Then taking all the forms that are distinct at once and dissolving their circumference, as if making many bodies of water into one unbounded body of water." Next, he directly applies this meditation to the ground of mind, teaching us how to realize our own connection to ultimate reality, our own original nature: "this is therefore the way that we simplify ourselves back to the One, first by concentrating [our thoughts] and then by letting go of what has been concentrated, into what is beyond simplicity, the transcendence of that One"

(*Doubts and Solutions* I 84). Knowledge might be understood as grasping the real; unknowing, then, is always in the direction of letting go of any attempt to grasp the real.

Conclusion: Wisdom and Love, Two Sides of the Ancient Greek Tradition

I hope this brief chapter has given the reader some space to question the tendency to reduce the ancient Greek philosophical tradition to nothing more than rationality, or the rules of logic and reason. Indeed, the meditative and contemplative practices described here identify the intuitive mind as most truly the light of awareness, the knower that is not any of the things known, and this approach is tremendously evident in ancient Greek texts. And yet, there are also aspects of this broad tradition that emphasize the "yoga" of devotion. Certainly, Greek meditative traditions when fused with Christianity exploded in a powerful form of devotional meditation, such as the fourth century mystics in the Hesychast movements of Nitria and then Palestine. We glimpsed the work of one representative of this tradition in the person of Evagrius, whose instructions to monks span the whole course of development for the intuitive mind, from the devoted invocation of God's name all the way to that open or empty mind that is transparent to the divine, what Evagrius calls "the Sapphire light of the mind." (*Skemmata*)

But long before this fusion, Plato expressed the path to perfection as a synthesis of love and knowledge. Plato tells us that love is the surest way to regrow the wings of the soul, to regain the vision of the divine forms.

In the coda to this chapter, I sketch some of the devotional meditations of the Platonic tradition, starting with Plotinus and ending with Proclus' hymns. Inspired by the language of Plato's dialogues *Phaedrus* and *Symposium*, Plotinus asks how we can awaken intuition: "But how shall we find the way? How can one see the 'inconceivable beauty,' (*Symp.* 218E2) which stays within in the holy sanctuary and does not come out where the profane may see it?" (I.6.8.27-9). Plotinus does not pretend that such higher intuitive abilities come easily; we must work hard to awaken them within us: "Let him who can, follow and come within, and leave outside the sight of his eyes ... Let all these things go and do not look. Shut your eyes and change to and wake another way of seeing, which everyone has but few use" (I.6.8.27-9). The ancients urge us to fall in love with the interior vision, casting aside the lure of appearances. Proclus, the fifth century head of the post-Platonic Academy in Athens, urges us to hasten on this path: "Let us run to the hot, let us escape from the cold. Let us become fire, let us travel through fire," enkindling our intuitive wisdom. (*On the Chaldean Philosophy*, fr. 2) He is reminding us that the intuitive mind—understood as the original source of spiritual light, the spiritual sun, what he refers to as "Lord of intellectual fire"—is also the original source of heat, which melts and opens the heart, allowing its wings to sprout, and so, as Plotinus put it three centuries earlier, to "fly to our dear country." (I.6.8.16)

Bibliography

Primary Sources in Translation

Chaldean Oracles. Translated by Ruth Majercik. Leiden: Brill. 1989.

Damascius, *Problems and Solutions Concerning First Principles.* Translated by Sara Ahbel-Rappe Oxford University Press 2010.

Epictetus. *Discourses.* Book I. Translated with an introduction and commentary by Robert F. Dobbin. Oxford ; New York : Oxford University Press, 1998. Harmless, W. Desert Christians. An Introduction to the Literature of Early Monasticism.: Oxford University Press. 2004

Heraclitus : Greek text with a short commentary. Miroslav Marcovich. Sankt Augustin, Germany : Academia Verlag, 2001

Marcus Aurelius : *Meditations*, Books 1-6. Translated with an introduction and Commentary by Christopher Gill. Oxford University Press 2013.

Plato. Complete Works. Edited, with introduction and notes, by John M. Cooper ; Associate editor, D.S. Hutchinson. Hackett. 1997.

Plotinus with an English translation by A.H. Armstrong. Cambridge, MA: Harvard University Press. 1986

A few books that discuss the spiritual practices of Greco-Roman philosophy

Chaldaean oracles and theurgy. Mysticism, magic and Platonism in the later Roman Empire. Hans Lewy. Publications de l'Institut français d'archeologie orientale. Le Caire. 1956.

Epictetus : a Stoic and Socratic guide to life. A.A. Long. Oxford University Press. 2002.

Philosophy as a way of life : spiritual exercises from Socrates to Foucault. Pierre Hadot ; edited with an introduction by Arnold I. Davidson ; translated by Michael Chase. Oxford ; New York : Blackwell, 1995

Philosophy as a way of life: ancients and moderns : essays in honor of Pierre Hadot edited by Michael Chase, Stephen R. L. Clark, Michael McGhee. Hoboken: Wiley. 2013

Reading Neoplatonism: non-discursive thinking in the texts of Plotinus, Proclus, and Damascius. Sara Rappe. Cambridge. 2000.

53521765R00231

Made in the USA
Charleston, SC
12 March 2016